Breaking Glass Barefoot

HAZEL O'CONNOR

Breaking Glass Barefoot

HAZEL O'CONNOR

WYMER PUBLISHING
Bedford, England

First published in Great Britain in 2012
by Wymer Publishing
www.wymerpublishing.co.uk
Tel: 01234 326691
Wymer Publishing is a trading name of Wymer (UK) Ltd

This edition copyright © 2014 Hazel O'Connor / Wymer Publishing.

ISBN 978-1-908724-22-9 (paperback)
ISBN 978-1-908724-36-6 (eBook)

Edited by Ruth Kennedy.
Sub-editing and proof reading by Phil Syphe at Grammar Eyes.

The Author hereby asserts his rights to be identified
as the author of this work in accordance with sections
77 to 78 of the Copyright, Designs & Patents Act 1988.

All rights reserved. No part of this publication may be
reproduced or transmitted in any form or by any means,
electronic or mechanical, including photocopying, or any
information storage and retrieval system, without written
permission from the publisher.

This publication is sold subject to the condition that it shall not,
by way of trade or otherwise, be lent, re-sold, hired out or
otherwise circulated without the publishers prior consent in any
form of binding or cover other than that in which it is published
and without a similar condition including this condition
being imposed on the subsequent purchaser.

All photos except where otherwise credited are from the author's collection.
Every effort has been made to trace the copyright holders of the
photographs in this book but some were unreachable.
We would be grateful if the photographers concerned would contact us.

Typeset by Wymer UK.
Printed and bound in Great Britain by Clays Ltd.,
Bungay, Suffolk, England

A catalogue record for this book is available from the British Library.

Cover design by Wymer UK.
Front cover photo © Tim Jarvis.

CONTENTS

vii	Prologue

PART ONE: COVENTRY, FIFTIES' CHILD

2	Chapter One
14	Chapter Two
24	Chapter Three
38	Chapter Four
56	Chapter Five

PART TWO: BE CAREFUL WHAT YOU WISH FOR

77	Chapter Six
96	Chapter Seven
113	Chapter Eight
136	Chapter Nine

PART THREE: A NEW LIFE

159	Chapter Ten
169	Chapter Eleven
185	Chapter Twelve
199	Chapter Thirteen
207	Chapter Fourteen
221	Chapter Fifteen
232	Chapter Sixteen
240	Chapter Seventeen
242	Postscript
244	Acknowledgements

PROLOGUE
London, February 1979

Sitting in a waiting room of the United Artists Film Company, I wondered what the hell I was doing there. I looked down at my script. I didn't even like the writing much. I was reading for the part of a secretary, and my line was, 'Cigarette me,' which apparently meant, 'light my cigarette.' None of my mates spoke like that. It was getting uncomfortable. Then Toyah Wilcox walked in. She was already well known on the punk scene. We'd met before when I'd rehearsed at her place in South London. Great. So now I was up against Toyah. I figured I didn't stand a chance and the script was silly anyway. I'm a singer, not an actress, I thought. I wanted to drop the script and run.

My whole life I'd run away, got up and left if I didn't like something. At that pivotal moment in my life I asked myself why I was always leaving and never giving anything a chance? Then I had my epiphany. I always left people, places, and things before they could leave me; before they could reject me. I was afraid of failure, and for a few brief seconds in my life, I decided I wasn't afraid of rejection; I'd just try my hardest. I put the script down and I took out a book that had been given to me by a faith healer: *Bring Out The Magic In Your Mind*. I tried to visualise what I wanted from the audition. I closed my eyes and dreamed a dream. They would rewrite the script, changing the lead part to a girl's (it was originally about a boy); they would choose me to play the lead, they would ask me to write the soundtrack, and I'd get to choose my favourite record producer, Tony Visconti – David Bowie's producer – to make the record with me.

I was called into the audition room. There were about six or seven people there, including the producers, Davina Belling and Clive Parsons. I nodded hello to Brian Gibson, the director; Esta

and Beth Charkham from the casting agency, and read my 'Cigarette me' piece of script to them. Davina Belling said, 'Give Hazel the bass player's part to read.' I was being upgraded already. I felt very excited. After the reading they asked me if I belonged to Actors' Equity. 'Yes, I got that when I was a dancer in Tokyo and Beirut.' I blurted out.
'When was that?' someone asked.
'Oh, just before the civil war in 1973,' I replied.
'Have you travelled much?' I knew they were warming to me fast now. 'I ran away to Amsterdam when I was sixteen, travelled Europe, crossed the Sahara Desert from West Africa to the North, but I haven't been anywhere lately,' I said. They were all smiles and I knew something was changing, and I was so glad that I hadn't run away before I'd even tried. I left the audition a very happy girl, with the events of my past playing through my mind.

PART ONE
COVENTRY, FIFTIES' CHILD

CHAPTER ONE

'Let's all play Mums and Dads –
come on, where do babies come from, Mum?'
"Cover Plus", 1981

The Hendrys lived over the back alley from the Brindleys. My Mum – Joyce Brindley – was originally from Birmingham, but her Mum, Florence, and Dad, Cecil, moved to Coventry when she was six weeks old. Cecil Brindley was a co-op manager, who had dreamed of being a doctor, but never had the money to fulfil his dream. He cycled to work every day of his life, and was a hoarder of things, and quite a wearing, 'grind-you-down' sort of a person. His wife Florence, on the other hand, was full of joy, light, and song. She worked as a dinner lady at the same school that Mum went to. Mum's childhood was marred with ill-health in the shape of a lung disease. She had something similar to cystic fibrosis and she wasn't expected to live into adulthood. By her early teenage years the war had started, so most nights were spent in the bomb shelter in the back garden, as Coventry was a priority target due to its industry, and was blitzed to smithereens by Hitler's Luftwaffe. Sadly the beautiful and ancient cathedral was blasted out of existence.

Even with all the odds stacked against her, Mum continued towards adulthood. Perhaps out of sheer bloody-mindedness she prevailed against her disease and held it in abeyance. I think this characteristic was passed on to me, as was her sense of independence. By the age of eighteen, Mum had moved out of home, after landing a hotel receptionist job in the nearby town of Warwick. Maybe due to the health prognosis ('she'll not make old bones'), she decided to live what life she had to the full, and it was at this point that she and Dad first met. She was introduced to him by a school friend who was going out with him at the time. He was smitten at first sight. She already knew of the dark-haired handsome Irishman staying at the Hendrys', and eventually they ended up going out together. She loved to dance, and he was a superb dancer. He was also witty, charming, and very handsome; she was pretty, independent, and strong minded. Love blossomed. He had a secure job at the Rootes Group Car Factory, and they decided to marry on the 30th September 1950. They tied the knot in the 1,000-year-old Wyken Church. The ceremony took place in the Protestant church even though Dad was Catholic, which didn't go down well with the Irish in-laws. Mum was so appalled by the interfering ways of the local Catholic priest, and the insistence that any kids from their marriage must be brought up in the Catholic faith, that she rebelled saying, 'When our children are old enough they can decide for themselves whether they want to worship God the Catholic way or the Protestant way.'

With the help of Mum's parents they scraped together the deposit to buy their first home at 136, Wyken Avenue. Neil and I were born; Dad worked hard at the car factory; Mum was a model 1950s housewife. We'd go for Sunday family outings in Dad's car which would invariably end up at a country pub where he would enjoy a few pints. Mum, who wasn't a drinker, had a bitter lemon, and us kids drank lemonade and stuffed ourselves with crisps. At home there always seemed to be music present. Dad sang with the Wyken Working Men's Male Voice Choir. He could play tunes on his piano accordion by ear, and Mum was a brilliant hostess. There were always parties with music sessions and dancing at our house. Neil and I would hear them all coming in from the pub, and we'd sneak downstairs after bedtime hoping to join in. I'd waltz with Dad, standing on his feet, whirling around our living room. Wonderful sing-songs would happen as the choir members were all party people. Musicians would play jazzy songs, or sometimes we would listen to melancholy Irish tunes, with Dad singing "Danny Boy" or "Molly Malone", with everybody throwing harmonies in. Our uncles and aunties would invariably be slightly tipsy and I'd get lots of compliments about my pretty long white-blonde hair. Maybe they'd give us the odd sixpence to save in our money boxes – the parties were very lucrative for Neil and me. Halcyon Days.

Around the age of two, my eye had a severe cast in it. They called it a 'lazy eye' in those days, and I had to wear a pair of National Health glasses with a patch over the good eye to try to teach the lazy eye to work. I hated wearing those glasses. I always felt set apart by my crossed eyes. I also inherited the 'O'Connor feet' which were very crooked, and the doctor made me sleep with splints on to try to straighten them. I hated my ugly feet and always hid them from view.

I loved going out to play in the back alley, where we'd meet up with the Delo kids, a big family from two doors down. My first kiss came at the early age of four with David Delo: I was dressed as an Indian squaw, he dressed as a cowboy, and on his three-wheeler bicycle we galloped off into the sunset. One lad hit my brother one day, hurting him, and I was so angered by it that I jumped on him and kept hitting him in the face, shouting to Neil to go fetch Mum. I didn't like anyone hurting my brother.

Mum's health was bad when Neil started school, and because Mum had to take a rest in the afternoons, I was expected to rest too. I was too lively to lie down all afternoon and would get so bored. One day Paul – one of the Delo kids – came calling for me to come out to play. I was supposed to be napping. I sneaked downstairs and Mum heard the creaking staircase: 'Hazel, what are you doing?' she called. 'I'm just going out to play with Paul Delo, is that all right?' I said in a super soft voice. As I didn't hear the word 'No' I thought, 'Well then, I can go out to play, as Mum didn't say I couldn't.' So feeling I'd covered myself against being in trouble, I blithely skipped out the house barefoot and in my underskirt! Of course Mum hadn't heard me announce my 'going out to play plan', so when she woke up to find her little girl missing, she was frantic. She searched for me for over an hour. Meanwhile, Paul and I were having a great time in my pedal fire-engine oblivious to the worry I had caused. When she found me her eyes told me I was in big trouble: that was one of the only wallops she ever gave me.

The other was the day all of us kids played doctors and nurses in Jane Barr's garden. Jane went and told her Mum about us so her mother caught us with our pants down, and chucked us out, calling us filthy little creatures. I was so incensed by her shouting at us I said 'Let's carry on the game in my Dad's garage,' so as not to be beaten by that nasty woman. We were now enraged with a sense of injustice and started to really do the filthiest things we could think of, like pissing and shitting on the garage floor. Mum caught us, probably because Jane Barr's Mum reported us and – wallop. 'You just wait until your Dad gets home, you dirty girl!' This was my first major rebellion, even though my child mind, my conscience, my sense of right and wrong told me it wasn't correct social behaviour to crap on our garage floor. I remember feeling a huge sense of justice 'showing Jane Barr's Mum and all the other grown-ups what-for!' It was that silly woman who made us feel dirty in the first place. We had no notion of wrongdoing when we first took down our pants and played doctors and nurses inspecting our different genitalia. We were purely inquisitive.

    Lung problems seemed to be a theme running through my entire childhood. Mum often had terrible bouts of wheezing, phlegmy, breathless lungs. My brother had dreadful asthma attacks, which would leave him caravan-bound during our family holidays to Wales, and I succumbed, at the age of two, to pneumonia. I was taken to hospital and put on this big machine which seemed like a giant iron beast closing its jaws on me. I remember the fear and terror as that old-fashioned x-ray machine looked like it was going to eat me. I screamed and screamed. I recovered my health, had one more bout of lung problems in the form of whooping cough, where I coughed so badly my breath stopped. I used to dance around in circles, pointing to my mouth, trying to tell my parents I couldn't breathe. I thought I was going to die and my parents sat laughing at me, thinking I was doing a typical Hazel show-off dance routine; only when I turned blue did they realise it was serious.

Anyway I didn't die, but I grew up hating all lung disease, and I never had another bout like that.

    Illnesses and abnormalities do set us apart from our fellow human beings, and my worst was a small birthmark on the back of my leg, called a lateral verrucous nevus. It basically grew of its own accord, so every week Mum took me to the hospital to have it painted with some kind of serum. We would be in a treatment room with five or six other people, adults and children, most of them sporting horrific birthmarks, like a big red cyst coming out of a man's forehead, or a girl's whole face covered in a port wine strawberry mark. I felt like we were all circus freaks and these marks set us outside 'normal' society. Even though mine was hidden, I knew it was there, just like my crooked bones in my 'O'Connor feet' were there just hiding, waiting to be discovered and called strange, different, an outsider.

Mum became very sick with pre-TB virus, and the doctor said she must either go away to a sanatorium to rest, or rest at home for at least three months. I was four at the time, and with no one to look after me whilst Mum tried to get well, I was shipped off to school early, which I was really looking forward to because most of my playmates, being older, were now in school.

Mum left me at the Wyken Croft Infants School on my first day. She cried a little and so did I, but I was looking forward to the adventure. The teacher introduced me to the class and at break time some of the crueller kids surrounded me shouting, 'Hazel Paddy O'Connor, you're in the wrong school; we're English here. You should be at the Paddy Catholic school down the road. You don't belong, you don't belong, Paddy, Paddy!' I didn't really understand what they meant, but I did feel very alien and disappointed that I wasn't welcome. I never cried or got visibly upset, but I burnt inside. I had no notion of what English, Irish, Protestant or Catholic was – I was just a little girl. I toughened up very quickly and became a joker, so nobody could tell what I was feeling. It was then that I developed some very good coping mechanisms, a good sense of humour, and not showing hurt, which I probably inherited from my Mum.

The times that Neil and I looked forward to most were Mum and Dad going out and our Nan coming over to babysit. She'd bring sweets and she'd be such fun. The minute Mum and Dad were out of the house was the cue for our dog Judy to go crazy. She'd run round in circles, around the sofa which we all sat on, and jump up behind to nip Nan's hair, and we'd just be laughing hysterically. I loved Nan so much.

When did things change in our household? I'm not sure, really... I remember Mum and Dad were in a car accident. Uncle Jeff drove into a telegraph pole and Dad's throat was cut as he was launched through the windscreen. They couldn't give him an anaesthetic when they stitched him back together, because his alcohol levels were too high. I found Mum's white handbag behind the sofa the next day, covered in his blood. I couldn't get that bloody handbag out of my mind – I still see it now. Mum and Dad seemed to be arguing more and more regularly when they came in from the Working Men's Club. Mum didn't drink and Dad didn't need to drink much before he'd be drunk. Drink made him jealous and he'd get angry with Mum for dancing with anybody but him, but he'd be too busy buying his friends drinks at the bar. At times they didn't have enough money for food, but he'd spend it on his mates – acting the 'big man – sometimes dipping into the children's savings account for money. So Dad would be jealous and bolshie, and Mum would be fuming that he'd just spent the last of the housekeeping on drinks, and then the shouting would begin. I'd put my hands over my ears and sing songs to block out the sounds. I asked Neil if he heard it; he said he didn't.

Their arguments became violent and my new strategy was to feign sickness. 'Mummy, I've got tummy ache!' She'd fetch me downstairs and Dad would often say nasty things to me. I know he didn't mean to be so cruel, but the drink made him say stuff like, 'Ah, you're not my kid anyway.' He would just say this kind of thing to hurt Mum. Like, 'She's always siding with you.' Hence, 'Not my kid, she's yours.' Not understanding his cruelty I would start to sob and Mum would say, 'Now look what you've done, Pete.' Then he'd start to cry and take me into his arms and sob into my hair. I didn't like him like this; he wasn't my hero anymore.

One rainy Sunday afternoon when I was eight, Mum came in with her best grey suit on, and swollen red eyes. 'What's wrong, Mummy?' I asked. 'Listen, Hazel darling, be a good girl and look after your Daddy, I have to go,' she said. 'Go where, Mummy, where?' 'I'm leaving Daddy.'

I couldn't bear the thought of Mum not being there, she was so upset and didn't want to uproot me from my home. I just had to be with her. I thought it over for a brief second, and then said, 'I'm coming with you then.' Neil, my dear, sweet-natured brother, who had been out with mates all this time, came home in the middle of the drama and I collared him and said, 'Look; Mum's leaving Dad. I'm going to go with Mum. So what are you going to do?' His sense of fair play prevailed; not wanting to leave Dad alone, he said, 'I'd better stay with Dad then.'

Mum and I left. We went up the road and round the corner to Nan and Granddad's. I met up with Neil at school the next day and we discussed our family dilemma. Then a miracle took place: Mum and Dad together, hand in hand, smiling, met us at the school gates. 'We've made up,' they said. 'Are we going home then, Mum?' I asked. 'Yes love,' she said. We were overjoyed; all of us back together, secure again. The peace lasted for a few weeks and then everything I had ever known changed forever.

It was a Sunday morning. I saw Dad, unshaven, drinking milk straight from the bottle: something he'd never do if Mum was around. 'Where's Mum?' I asked. 'I don't know,' he said in a nasty tone. 'Go ask your Aunty Sally.' Aunty Sally was our next-door neighbour. I sensed something was happening. He walked out of the kitchen, and a few moments later Mum appeared at the back door. Through the window I saw the congealed blood around her nose and swollen lips, and her throat an eyes were bruised. I opened the door to her but she didn't want to come in. 'We're leaving again, aren't we?' I said. 'Yes,' she replied. 'I'll fetch Neil then, shall I?' This time Neil and our dog Judy came with us. We packed a few clothes and toys and that was the end of 'Happy Families'. I'll never forget our sad faces; Mum's puffy from bruises and sobbing. Dad's unshaven and glowering, with tears in his eyes. Neil's were stoic and brave. Mine, sad and disappointed.

We went to stay with Nan and Granddad again. They were obviously upset to see their daughter in such a state. And from that day on, a bitter enmity started from my Nan towards my Dad; she wanted to kill him for harming her child. We all slept in the spare bedroom; Neil and me in the big old double bed, Mum in the old sofa bed. Life became very gloomy from my eight-year-old perspective: Nan and Granddad's house smelt of mothballs, and everything was dark wood. They weren't used to having three extra people around. Granddad being a man of ritual, and Nan reacting to his moaning with eye-rolls, but his moaning would chip away at her. Nowhere to play, no proper garden, grumpy Granddad, sharing a bedroom with two wheezy people – Neil had asthma and Mum her usual lung problems. The dark old-fashioned house, Nan and Granddad angry with Dad, and Dad angry with Mum: knives were drawn. Neil kept his head down, read books, and quietly made the best of a bad cooped-up situation. I didn't seem able to please anyone and I wasn't very quiet, and the worst thing of all was that my Nan, whom I adored, now seemed to dislike me nearly as much as she disliked my Dad. It hurt so much – where had my lovely Nan gone? I became very fearful of upsetting her.

Everything I did was wrong in her eyes. I would always try to escape out of the house before our paths would cross. One day I tried to prove I could slice my own bread, make a sandwich, and get out onto the streets before she came home from work. As I cut, the bread kept crumbling, so I sliced again. It crumbled again and eventually I'd made a big hole in the bread. I started sobbing hysterically: 'Neil, help me, please help me, look what's happened to the bread; Nan will kill me.' My wonderful brother came to my rescue and carved all the crumbled bread away, leaving only a small piece of bread.

I ran off into the streets and alleyways: my only safe haven those days. My favourite game was to wander off into housing estates and purposely get lost to see if I could find my way out again. During those times, alone and lost, I was at my happiest. I would feel so free of constraint and worries, all I would have to think of was: 'Which way do I go?' This trait seems to have followed me throughout my life – when in doubt get lost and find myself again. It's a way of feeling in control of life's mayhem.

I visited Dad on my own every Sunday. Mum told me I mustn't lose my relationship with Dad just because they had split up, but to be honest it was very upsetting to see him. He would come to the door unshaven, smelly, and dishevelled. The house would be in a total mess. He'd take a swig of milk from the bottle. He'd ask how Neil was and how I was. Then he'd get angry about Mum leaving, how it was her friends' fault for the break-up, which would secretly annoy me, because I'd witnessed so much of his nastiness and violence. He always forgot that I was the witness. Then he'd put Nan and Granddad down, and I'd hate the feeling of confusion, of split loyalties. So I'd go into the garden shed and play with my beautiful wooden dolls' house, and all my other toys, which were now shoved in there.

The whole of the grown-up world seemed to be screwed up and there was nowhere to hide and no one to turn to except my brother Neil. Sometimes I'd be mean to him at night when he had wheezing asthma. I'd say, 'Stop wheezing, I can't get to sleep. If you don't stop, I'll sing really loud!' Struggling to breathe, he'd say, 'I can't help it, Haze,' so I would sing really loud. We also used to play a game called 'Name the Tune', where we'd bang out a tune on the headboard, and the other one had to guess what it was. So I suppose these were the first musical collaborations I had with my brother. Neil was always 'the musical one', though. Mum and Dad bought a piano for Neil to have lessons on. I was only 5 or 6 at the time, but it rankled that I wasn't allowed to play, unlike my brother!

Mum was working all hours God sent, trying to get enough money for a deposit on a home of our own, so she didn't realise how bad relations between me and Nan had become. Worse than being continuously shouted at was being compared unfavourably to my brother. In Nan's eyes he was the angel – I was the devil. Granddad wasn't as cruel to me as Nan, he just didn't like me around him; he'd be more inclined to Neil. He used to build bicycles in his back yard shed. I'd want to watch, but he'd always shoo me away, telling me this was men's work, not for girls, and that I should go and help Nan with the housework. So I'd just run off down the back alley. Then I'd lose myself in the housing estate streets.

One day it all came to a head. I'd done something that really pissed Nan off and to this day I don't know what it was. I asked Granddad years later but he couldn't remember. I think my very presence wound her up. Maybe I was a reminder of Dad, and maybe she was having a tough menopause. She was breathing fire. We met on the stairs; she at the top, me at the bottom: 'What is wrong with you, child? Why can't you be good like your brother? Why are you so bad? You're a bad, bad girl!' she shouted. I could hear Neil splashing away in the bathroom just behind her. I wished he was this side of the door to protect me. Her voice started rising to screech mode: 'Answer me! Why can't you be a good child like your brother? I'll tell you why; 'cause you're a bitch, you hear me? A bitch, and I won't suffer you under my roof for another night – do you understand? I want you out, bitch, out!' She pointed to the front door, screeching. She started to pass out. Granddad came pushing past me and caught her up in his arms, and took her into their bedroom. I was terrified; I thought she had died. I ran up stairs to their open bedroom door. He was administering smelling salts to her as she lay motionless on the bed. She started to come round, saw me, pointed, and shouted, 'Bitch, bitch! Get her out of my sight!' and passed out again. Granddad pushed me hurriedly into our bedroom, our dark, gloomy, bedroom and said, 'Stay there, don't move, wait until your Mum gets home.'

I sat for five or six hours meditating on her words: 'Bitch', 'bad girl', and I was to be thrown out – not to spend another night in her house. All I could think of was, where can I go? All my bridges were burned. I felt a great sense of injustice as I had, without question, left our family home to back Mum up, twice. Now no one wanted me and I had no home and nowhere to go. I had a picture of myself with my few belongings in a bag over my shoulder, outside, alone in the dark. I spent six hours alone in that room with those thoughts before Mum came home, and burst into that bloody dungeon. 'Did they tell you, Mum, I have to leave tonight, but I don't know where to go?' I sobbed. She swept me up into her loving arms and said, 'Anywhere you go I'm going too. Don't worry, we'll find somewhere to go. You are not alone, and I love you very much.' That speech saved a vestige of my sanity: my Mum saved me, my Nan hurt me, and Granddad just did the best he could.

We didn't leave that night, but Mum worked even harder to get us a home of our own. Nan and I tried to co-exist. We didn't have another major blow-up again. We kept out of each other's way. Maybe because our dog Judy then became very sick, and we both softened our edges, nursing the dog. Nan would hold poor old Judy next to her on the sofa, as the dog was shivering and suffering. But we couldn't get her better, and she died. We all sobbed for days over Judy. When I told Dad, he sobbed too, but somehow I blamed him for her death.

My Dad, who in my Nan's eyes was worse than the devil, had got himself into a financial hole that he couldn't get out of, and he didn't care anymore, with his wife and children gone. What was the point? So he sold up our family home, paid off his debts, and went to lodge at his new girlfriend's house. This was a definite end to childhood bliss: home gone, toys gone, and my beautiful dolls' house, all gone.

CHAPTER TWO

'What do you do when the cat gets your tongue?
No way to say it's all going wrong.'
"If Only", (*Breaking Glass*, 1980)

After our family break-up holidays were in short supply, but memories of holidays together stayed with me. All of us hopping into Dad's car and driving to Barmouth in North Wales, staying in Uncle Jeff's caravan, meeting up with Mum's friend Auntie Hilda, playing with her kids Steph, Leslie, and Bev, getting cut off by the tide and Dad coming to the rescue. Dad, Neil, and I climbing Snowdon. Travelling to Ireland with Nan and Granddad to meet our Irish grandparents, uncles, aunties, and cousins in Galway. Laughter, singsongs, and drives in the country. All those days were gone, and I quietly mourned them.

After a year at Nan and Granddad's, we moved across Coventry to our own place. It was a small, two-bedroomed garden flat. Mum slept on the sofa bed in the living room, so as Neil and I had our own rooms. We each had household chores to do, which left me with a strong dislike of ironing!

Alderman's Green was a great area to move to: there were fields everywhere, a canal and a boating lake called The Slough. But money was forever tight. Mum was an expert seamstress and often a pair of curtains might magically become a lovely dress for me or for her in seconds. She taught me this skill very early on. She also taught me to cut hair, and 'do' hairstyles, as she had now become a fully-fledged hairdresser and was managing a salon near town. Her apprentices and juniors were all 'mods' and they educated me in all manner of cool and groovy music, clothes and makeup. So, early in my life, it was clothes and fashion that attracted me, not music.

Neil and I were both growing up now, and beginning the trials of our teenage years. So much fun and adventure, but I would also find that my happy-go-lucky personality couldn't mask the past for ever. I was befriended by a trio of local girls a few years older than me – Judy, Linda, and Tina – and we became like the four musketeers. I had such fun with those girls. They were all gymnasts and dancers, and we'd borrow our friend's ancient windy-up record player so we could perform dance and gym shows in the fields. We went to Saturday morning dances for kids at the Locarno Ballroom in the centre of town, and my love of

Chapter Two

Tamla Motown soul music began here.

I started my secondary school, Foxford, which was for boys and girls – very unusual in those days – my three friends already attended and it was only a fifteen-minute walk away, and five minutes if I crossed the back fields through a herd of bullocks. Being lazy, the latter became my preferred route. My alarm would go off at 8.30a.m., my clothes would be laid down in order of what was to go on first, my cereal already in the bowl only waiting for the milk to be thrown over it. I would splash my face with water, brush my teeth, throw on my coat and schoolbag, and run out of the house by 8.40a.m. I'd be in school by 8.45a.m. Sometimes I'd have trouble with the bullocks in the field when they were feeling hormonal and frisky – their spring fever hormones made them braver and they'd charge at me. At first I was terrified and ran, until they surrounded me, but I soon realised all I needed to do was turn around and chase them and they'd scatter.

All through my first ten turbulent years I would draw pictures, mostly of people in different costumes and characters like Miss Happy, Miss Grumpy, etc., but at Foxford my artistic bent began to flourish, as did my love of History and English Literature. In Junior school I had come top of the class for maths but now I came bottom of the class for maths, and my grasp of languages wasn't much better. Funny that as a grownup I have a flair for languages, and speak French and German fairly well, as well as smatterings of Japanese, Arabic, Spanish, and Dutch. There's just no telling what any of us can do until we try.

Mum had a few good male friends, but no romance, and then she met Roy. He was a scaffold worker from the North of England. He had a swarthy complexion, black hair, and was very handsome – very similar in looks to Dad. He was very good fun to be with and he took time with us kids, played silly board games, and talked to us as people. He moved into our flat, sharing Neil's bedroom – I was so happy we were a family again. Roy was such a laugh; we all adored him. I pretended to myself that he was my new Dad.

I still saw my real Dad, but not so often anymore, and it always seemed to be me who made the effort, and my life was becoming so full now. I was coming to that age when my pals and I were becoming curious about boys. We always played out in the fields with a gang of boys and girls, but now we started egging on some boys who came from another area, insulting them, hurling abuse and clods of mud just to get them to chase us, and the game was on. At the Saturday morning dance clubs, Judy – being the most attractive – would always get the boys. They'd be the most interested in her, then Linda, then Tina, then me – the last in the pecking order. Judy's big sister Jane said one day that I would blossom and have the pick of the bunch. Ha! And pigs will fly, I thought.

At the age of thirteen I put on my first bra, a thirty triple A, and was very conscious of my pointy chest. I also recall a sixteen-year-old boy called Robert Shropshire, who seemed to spend all his time making my playtime a misery with such pranks as tying me down in the cow field, so the bullocks would come and walk on me, or shit on me, or by aiming his airgun at me and telling me to run. One day he collared me and pulled me into our underground den, where he pinned me down and kept trying to kiss me. And as I kept dodging him, all I could think of was my pointy chest, and I hoped his two front false teeth wouldn't fall on my face – he didn't kiss me, he didn't harm me. I ran home crying to Mum for the umpteenth time, as his bullying had been wearing me down over the months. She hushed me, saying, 'Hazel, I think he likes you, mark my words.' 'Why does he try to hurt me then?' I asked. 'Because we only hurt the ones we love,' she replied.

Out of the blue, Mum and Roy had a big argument. I didn't know what it was about, but I knew the vibe – the sort of atmosphere you could cut with a knife – and he left that day, just like that. Mum was very sad and distraught, so was I – it was like losing Dad all over again. I missed him. I loved him like a second Dad. We moved on as best we could. Mum had her own hairdressing shop now in an area of Coventry due for redevelopment. A fair few of her clients were local hookers. I was her Saturday shampoo girl, and I tell you, her hooker clients were often a lot cleaner than some of the 'normal' clients, and they paid better tips.

Chapter Two

Our Neil had his eye on a girl who was one of a set of twins. I showed her a nude photo of me and Neil in a paddling pool as toddlers, but as his willy was in full shot, he went ape-shit with me and we never saw that photo again.

Finally I had my first love affair. I was around fourteen, he was fifteen, and we went to the same school. We lasted about six months. I had my first sexual encounters with him, but when we tried the full monty, it hurt too much, and I though it wasn't what it was cracked up to be anyway. We parted under sad circumstances and I began a turbulent time in my life, probably brought on by hormones; first love, first sex, and general teenage confusion. It began with a double date. His best friend had just come back from South Africa and we had all gone out in his car. He was trying to screw this girl from my school on the back seat of his car and my boyfriend kept trying to get me to have full sex in the front. I didn't want to, especially with two strangers huffing and puffing in the back seat of the car. I got out of the car and ran across the quarry where we were parked. My boyfriend followed me. I thought he was sympathetic to me, but then he pushed his hard penis into my hand and wanted relief from me. I was horrified by the whole scenario and started to cry. He said, 'Ah, forget it,' and we all drove back to his pal's house.

There, waiting in the car outside the house, I started to feel anger and fury rising from the pit of my stomach. Where was my Dad? Where was Roy? Why did my sweetheart treat me like a cheap hooker in the quarry? Then I began a scream that just wouldn't stop – I screamed, and I screamed, and I screamed – the doctor came I was sedated, taken home, and I never saw my first love again, apart from an awkward 'hello' across the school corridors.

After my breakdown, Mum and I sat in our family doctor's office. He consulted his medical book and decided on a little green and white capsule called Librium. 'This should help if you get upset anytime; just take one if needed. I'd also like Hazel to come and see Miss Woolard, our social psychologist. She's here every week. I've made an appointment for next Wednesday at 4.30p.m.'

From then on for the next year Miss Woolard was my Wednesday date. I used to play a great game of cat-and-mouse with Miss Woolard. I was at that snotty teenage stage when I thought I knew it all. She was a nice enough lady, though, and we'd talk for hours. Well, I'd mostly talk while she nodded her head. I'd tell her about the break-up of Mum and Dad, the fights they'd had, the way Nan had treated me, how Roy had been a huge part of our family, and now was gone entirely. But I wouldn't tell her about my ex-boyfriend and the sex things. I was very sure I knew what was wrong, and it had a lot to do with my mistrust of the men in my life.

I always found Miss Woolard a tad ineffectual. The person who helped me move on from this impasse was my main schoolteacher, Miss Bates. If anyone saved me it was Miss Bates. Miss Bates looked like the archetypal storybook witch with her long nose and sticky-out chin, thin straggly hair, no tits, and her long thin body perched on little winkle-picker stilettos. It was Miss Bates who noticed I wasn't my usual chirpy self. Maybe the school had been notified of my mental health problems, I don't know. I do know I was slowly becoming more and more down. I couldn't hold back emotions, and sadness overtook me at every difficult juncture of my day. When I freaked out at home, Mum would suggest I took one of my tranquilisers, but they made me feel so dull. When I freaked out at school I would be overcome with dark sadness that I couldn't articulate, so I would turn and run out of the school gates, across my back fields, and lie sobbing in a hidey hole in the field.

One morning Miss Bates collared me after class and asked me to wait behind; she wanted a word. 'Yeah, yeah!' I thought belligerently, but when she began to talk, I was astonished. She proceeded to open up her past life to me. She had been abused, and her upbringing sounded a zillion times worse than mine, and she told me that she suffered no illusions about her ugly face and body – she knew herself, warts and all. 'Now look at yourself, Hazel; you're pretty, clever, a bright spark, and a very popular girl. I know you've had some family upsets and you're feeling down, but let me tell you how it is in the real world. At first your friends will rally round you and give you their sympathy when you cry, but if you're always crying your friends will get bored and move on. And sooner or later your audience of sympathetic friends will be gone and you will be alone. So Hazel, try to rejoice for the things you have, and don't waste your life crying for what you don't have. Do you understand?'

Feeling very shocked that she'd spoken to me like an equal, not a schoolgirl, I looked her full in the eyes and said, 'I understand and I will try to change this habit of sadness. Thank you for talking to me Miss Bates.'

From that day on I began to recover myself. I would check myself when I felt the surge of sadness and not indulge it, mostly spurred on by the chilling thought of being left out in the cold – alone, no friends – boring Hazel. So I dragged myself back from the edge of the abyss with the help of her words. My art teacher, Mr Clayton, was also very important to me; his teaching was turning my childish talent into a very serious ability. I was becoming a very competent artist and I loved to paint and do portraits. He felt I was bound for Art College. At the age of fifteen I felt I had fully recovered from the nervous breakdown, and I'd long since chucked the tranquillisers down the toilet. Life had changed drastically all around. Mum started dating a new man who lived up the road with his Mum. He was okay, but a bit stodgy compared to Roy. He asked her to marry him, bought a house for us all to live in, but at the last minute she decided not to. I was glad as he wasn't the right one for her.

As the Summer of Love hit Coventry in 1968, life was becoming very interesting. Neil started to play guitar, and was always a natural musician. I'd no interest in music apart from knowing that singing songs – as Neil played guitar – always soothed my soul. Singing made me feel warm and happy. Neil went on a holiday to America and brought back Frank Zappa, Jimi Hendrix, and Haight Ashbury psychedelic posters. Neil left school and became an apprentice draughtsman, grew his hair, and he and his pals smoked the odd joint and I forced them to let me try. I saw other young folk around the city of Coventry becoming hippy, hairy, smoking pot and dropping acid, and I wanted to be part of it. I loved the music, the clothes, and the free spirit that surrounded the scene. I was cutting my friends' hair like Julie Driscoll and making beautiful hippy mini-dresses with bare back and belly showing.

It was also at that time that I began to see more of the nastier side of some men. A married neighbour tried to make a romantic date with me whilst waiting for the bus and Mum said it was my fault for wearing skimpy clothes. It made me feel dirty that this guy had tried his luck, and my mistrust of men was underlined by the incident. Worse was to follow. A few months later, I was rushing to get to school after a dental appointment, and the door bell went. I opened our front door and there was Roy, Mum's ex-boyfriend, who'd left two years before. I was thrilled to see him. I invited him into the house and made a cup of tea for him. We sat chatting in the living room and he told me to sit closer. 'Don't you have a hug for old Roy?' he said. 'Of course, Roy. Where did you go? I missed you so much,' I said. 'What about a kiss for old Roy?' I went to kiss his cheek and he moved his face and forced his open mouth over my lips and tried to stick his tongue in my mouth. Shocked, I jumped backwards. 'You'd better leave,' I said. 'Please go – get the fuck out of our house!' I was screaming at him now. He ran out the door. I was so shocked. I'd loved him like a second Dad. He'd disappeared two and a half years before, and then he turns up out of the blue and tries to snog me, and God knows what else, totally abusing my trust. We never saw him again. Lucky for him because I told my Mum that night and she said she'd kill him if she got her hands on him. She was so angry with him I felt very upset, confused, and self-critical – as if it were my fault somehow. My trust in men was so eroded.

It was the wrong time to start going out with a new boyfriend. Jim was six years older than me. He was quite the man about town; a handsome, long-haired Scottish guy. I was now properly initiated into the world of sex, which I didn't enjoy much, but wanted the cuddle that went with it. I was nearly sixteen. Unfortunately I caught a nasty little bug from him called Chlamydia, and ended up at the VD clinic feeling mortified. He'd obviously been unfaithful. We saw each other off and on until fate overtook the situation and he had to leave England in a hurry – he had a bit of trouble with the law.

I did my GCE exams in eight subjects and went on summer holiday to Morocco with my friend and her older sister. I could hardly believe my luck. Mum reluctantly let me go, and then only because I would be with an adult; my friend's sister, who was in her early twenties and had often travelled to Morocco as part of her university degree in anthropology. The idea was to fly to Spain, take a boat to North Morocco, and the train down to Casablanca to stay with a Moroccan family who were good friends of hers. It would be my first ever holiday on my own.

CHAPTER THREE

'I remember the day in a grey misty way
As we boarded the boat for the Hook
I was sick of the sea that was becoming me to its end.
In the light of the dawn feeling ragged and worn
I pointed my thumb to the sky over and over
and over that road again
Runaway is there something you're trying to say?
Runaway please come home someday'
"Runaway", (*Cover Plus*, 1981)

All my life I've been returning to Morocco like a home from home since that first holiday, which is weird because some of my worst experiences took place there: maybe that's the reason because those experiences shaped the fabric of my being. Morocco was my first catalyst, the starting point in my life's map, the place from whence I began running away. At that time all I could think about was to keep moving. There was no plan or pattern to my travels. All I could do was keep on going, so that which was inside me wouldn't catch up with me. The funny thing was; it always did.

When we arrived straight off the boat from Spain, Morocco was a total culture shock, with the hidden women, the cheeky men, the clothes, the buildings, the smells, the colour, and the beautiful call to prayer from the Mosque tower. We'd travelled south from Tangier, through Fez – amazed at that beautiful ancient walled city – and Rabat, before finally arriving at our destination, our chaperone's friends' house in Casablanca. The only reason Mum had let her sixteen-year-old daughter go was because we were chaperoned and staying with a family. My pal and I got bored and asked permission to take the train to Marrakech for a few days. Amazingly, our chaperone let us go. Hurrah! Two sixteen-year-olds alone at last, no chaperone!

Marrakech was a marvel to our senses. It was so lively and the souk seemed to go all day and all night. The main square was filled with eating stalls and the smells of cooking and fires permeated the air and mixed with the scents of strange spices and herbs. Colourful clothes and shoes adorned every stall. We loved it. We found a room in a cheap hotel just off the main square and went out for our first meal and walkabout. God it was thrilling, we felt so grown-up. Sometimes the local lads would get on our nerves by always whistling, 'Hey, Miss; Miss you speak English? *Parlez-vous Français? Sprechen Sie Deutsch?* Come look here; come buy nice shirt, ajid, ajid.' They knew more languages than me, so you had to admire them, and we'd seen enough poverty on our travels to know how important one sale to us tourists could be: it could feed a family for a week. So we just giggled, walked, spent a little money on bits and bobs and giggled some more. When we curled up in our beds that night we felt so free.

We woke early to the sound of the call to prayer from the Mosque. We had another day of wandering around the souk and said hello to our neighbours across the courtyard in our hotel. The two young men said they were from Algeria, and one of them offered to show us the King's Palace Gardens the next day – obviously we said yes.

That night my friend came down with an itchy rash and felt unwell, so she decided not to go on our outing with our neighbour. Should I have gone alone? Probably not, but I thought it would be okay, him being our neighbour and all. I met up with him outside and he hailed a horse and carriage. 'What a lark!' I thought. We arrived at the Gardens. They were beautiful with many big pools of water, but not for swimming in though, as they were filled with piranhas! He spoke no English, I spoke no Arabic, but we both spoke a little French, and we seemed to get along fine. What happened next seemed to happen so fast, it took me by complete surprise. I was pushed from behind to the ground and I saw the glint of a knife at the side of my throat, at the same time my pants and jeans were being roughly pulled down – '*Ne bouges pas* – I kill you!' the voice of my escort screeched in my ear. He tore my clothes away and forced my legs apart from behind. I struggled to keep them together, but he was stronger. I was scared, and he held the knife. I'll hate myself forevermore because I gave in. He forced his penis into me and at that moment three things popped into my head: a curse on him and his dick, that it would shrivel up and drop off, and please don't let me get pregnant. Apart from the violence of him violating my body, the actual feeling of him inside me wasn't as bad as I thought it would be – I blocked my mind out.

He finished his attack very quickly, stood up, zipped up his jeans, waved his knife at me, and turned and walked away, leaving me facedown in the muck, pants round my ankles, sobbing my heart out. I felt so ashamed, so dirty. I wiped him off me as best I could with my shirt, I pulled up the clothes, and hobbled back to the Hotel, terrified I'd bump into the bastard.

I told my friend what had happened and I was quite hysterical and just wanted to leave that place immediately. So, we parted company: I took a lift with a group of Canadians in a VW driving to Spain. I think I was a bit deranged at this point, and all I wanted was to get out of Marrakech, now, immediately, and I'd got it into my head I would go and see my Scottish boyfriend who I knew was living in Ibiza. I said I would be at the Spanish airport to meet up with my friend and her sister in three weeks' time to fly home.

The Canadians were lovely people and one of them taught me how to throw a knife, and to use it as a weapon. I now had my own knife and would use it if anyone ever messed with me again. The Canadians and I parted company at Algeciras. They were going in another direction to me, so I decided to hitchhike to get to Alicante and get the ferry across to Ibiza, foolish girl that I was. I stayed safe for most of the journey, except for one lorry driver on the desolate road to Murcia. I'd fallen asleep in the passenger seat, having a lovely dream, when I suddenly heard, 'Pisst, pisst heh, senorita.' I opened my eyes to see the silly bugger steering with his left hand and masturbating with his right. I was disgusted. I gathered my thoughts for a split second, clutched my knife ready for if he lunged at me, then decided against it. I'd best jump out, as I figured it was my best bet 'cause if he came at me I would kill him, or die trying, and if I killed him, then what would I do?

The whole scenario zoomed through my head - I grabbed my belongings and jumped from the truck travelling at about forty miles an hour. I landed badly, hurting my ankle, as he pulled up a hundred yards ahead. If he'd got out of the truck and walked back he would have caught me as I couldn't walk. Luckily he didn't and eventually he drove on. Nothing else bad happened apart from some silly car-driver showing me his condom stash. I saw my boyfriend in Ibiza but to be honest, all feeling had left me since the rape, and after a few days we parted and I went to the Spanish Mainland to meet my friend and her sister. Her sister was hopping mad with me for taking off on my own, rightly so, of course.

I told no one of the ordeals of my sixteenth summer, and I tried to forget the whole episode; I buried it deep in my psyche. School began again in September, and once more I donned my school uniform and tried to act like nothing had changed in me – but it had. I couldn't concentrate at school; I felt it was all stupid and I didn't want to be there. It was like I'd been dragged into the grown up world and I couldn't be a silly schoolgirl anymore.

So when a friend told me I could get into a pre-degree art course at sixteen if I had an exceptional portfolio, I decided to give it a shot. Coventry Art College wouldn't take me at sixteen, as they'd only accept over eighteen-year-olds, but I was accepted at Leamington Spa College of Art and could do my A-level exams there as well as a two-year pre-degree course. I was so happy that I had succeeded in something all by myself. Mum and I scoured around looking for grants of money. The County Council gave me a travel grant, the Quaker Society gave me money for books and materials, and I had a weekend waitressing job.

I was sad to leave my fantastic teachers at Foxford, especially Mr Clayton, my art master and Miss Bates, my first life coach. And life as an art student wasn't all it was cracked up to be; probably my own fault, being younger by two years than the rest of my fellow students. I wasn't ready to call our teachers by their first name and be treated as an equal.

I enjoyed being in a new environment, though, and I loved the projects we were given, however the thirty-mile-a-day journey on two buses was beginning to grind me down. I found a great room five minutes from the college and one of the girls on my course, called Nora, had a room next door. Nora became my new best buddy. We had great times together, and the local lads would always be hanging around our place, as I guess we were an attractive proposition, so young and hip with a pad of our own. I worked and partied hard during this brief period of my life. Near Easter break Nora and I gazed up at a jet crossing the blue sky, and Nora said, 'I wish we could go somewhere exotic.' 'We could,' I said. 'Let's go hitchhiking to Ibiza for the Easter holidays, it wouldn't cost much.' I'd first gone to Ibiza with my Mum the year before, and hippy friends in Coventry had given me thirty tabs of LSD to sell so I'd have spending money! The next visit I'd gone to see Jim, after my rape. And now I wanted to return. So the plan was born. Mum said I could go. Nora lied to her parents, saying we were going on a college trip.

The trip went fine except for a few hiccups, the first was we fell in love with some American hippy biker boys, and stayed longer than we said we'd be. The second was I left my passport in a French truck, which we'd hitched a lift with (the truck driver posted it back to me later, bless him), and we had to go to the Embassy in Paris to get a provisional one to get home. The end result was that we were two weeks late back to college and we were in big trouble. I'd told Mum the truth about hitching and where we were going, and when we got delayed I let her know. Nora hadn't, and when her parents went to the college to find out why she wasn't back, the college obviously didn't know and they were furious.

We were summoned to the Head of the Faculty's office; Nora first, then me. I was blasted; treated like the ringleader of a rebellion. I'd obviously led Nora on, he said, even though she was two years older than me. I think I ended up getting blamed because Nora's parents had been so angry, and had blamed the college so the college blamed me. I was told if I didn't pull my socks up and get a change of attitude quickly, I'd be thrown out. I saw his lips move, heard the words, but didn't give a shit anymore. I didn't like Art College anymore; I had already made up my mind to leave and go to Amsterdam, because all the hippies in Ibiza had said Amsterdam was the place to be. Nora and I had already made a secret pact to run away to Amsterdam's hippy heaven. Years later I met an ex-student from my Art College in Los Angeles and she told me that the College showed my work to new students. Seemingly the College was proud of me once I became famous!

I prepared my escape. Mum and Nan arrived in the middle of my going away do, bringing me clean linen, and were more than surprised. Obviously I hadn't told her. I felt a total shit at this point because I loved my Mum and I knew that she'd be hurt, worried, and angry that I'd let her down. So I wrote a letter to Mum, on leaving, and one to Dad explaining why I felt I had to go. I took a bus to Harwich, and boarded the boat to the Hook of Holland.

Amsterdam was amazing, full of young travelling people, full of canals, full of trams, full of life. I went to a friend called Jan whom I'd met in Ibiza. He lived on a houseboat just off Prinsengracht. He said I could stay until I got settled. I eventually found a room in the squat known as *The Factory* in Koningsstraat, just off Nieuwmarkt. It was great; it was mine, my Hippy Heaven at last; my seven-foot by seven-foot home. I painted murals all over the walls and furnished it from the trash people left out for the likes of us squatters to take if we wanted it.

I needed a new job, and was very lucky to land work on an organic farm, which was a forty-minute cycle ride out of Amsterdam. I borrowed a bike at first, and then earned enough to buy a second-hand one. I loved working on the farm. Organic was a new concept then. My neighbour had a Hari Krishna priest visiting daily and the Hari priest started popping by and leaving delicious Indian sweets called burfi by my doorway. We chatted sometimes, and he told me to visit their temple on Sunday for a lovely meal, and to see what they got up to. I loved it, and became a regular Sunday visitor, enjoying the chanting, the dancing, and the food; the gorgeous food.

I may have ended up becoming a full-time devotee except that a very nasty meeting took place. One day that Hari priest came into my room and began preaching about Krishna, as he often did, but something was weird with him this time. He talked about Krishna's eternal consort Radharani, and how theirs was a spiritual, conjugal love. He started to rub his crotch and I tried to ignore him, thinking he's celibate, as he told me so. As quick as a flash he'd whipped his bottom half off and was waving his erect willy in my face. I was shocked and confused. I trusted him; he was my priest. With a swift deft hand he pushed my head onto his penis and wouldn't let go. Yes, I should have bitten it perhaps, but I didn't. I was a passive victim. He talked all sorts of Mumbo-jumbo about how his cousin did this to him back in America. He thrust and he ejaculated in my mouth, which was something I'd never encountered before. I retched the whole time and finally vomited. Afterwards he just gathered his clothes and left.

I hated those Hari Krishnas from then on and never went back to the temple, and spat if they passed me on the street.

I moved squats soon after the rape of my face to an attic room in the Tweede Laurierdwarsstraat; it was finally my dream come true. I started to do loads of paintings. I was now the artist in the attic. My job was going well at the organic farm until the potato picking season came in, which was back-breaking work, so I decided to try to sell some paintings instead. An American back-packer bought a nude painting and with the money I bought a hand-operated sewing machine.

So began my first bona fide business. I'd go to the flea market at closing time and pick up all the scraps of material thrown out, such as beautiful velvet curtains and bits of cotton from the end of a roll. I took them home, washed the material, then made some flared trousers, or a hippy dress or shirt and sold my wares on the Vondelpark free market. It was a real winner, and I now gave up the farming job, and funnily enough, I never painted again either – clothes design became my passion. My clients were the rich hippies and back-packers passing through Amsterdam that year. I loved Amsterdam but business was slowing up, as all the summertime hippies were going home, back to college, back to the USA. A group of South American friends and I decided it was time to travel to the south of France to earn some money picking grapes. We ended up in a big house in Paris, being looked after by French movie star Elizabeth Weiner – but I felt very much the outsider. I didn't speak French and I didn't feel in control of my own circumstances, so I ran away again. Back to Mum, back to Coventry.

I hitch-hiked back to Coventry, and climbed over the fence from the M6, the motorway they'd built over my back fields. When I knocked at Mum's door, a year had passed and I looked very weird with my long, henna-red hair enclosed in a bandana, my long Indian dress and fringed shawl. Mum took one look at me and said I could 'bugger off'. I know she didn't mean it. I'd hurt and frightened her so much when I'd run away, and my suddenly appearing on her doorstep looking like a weird stranger had shocked her. Mum went back in the house and left me standing at the front door. Neil came out to me. Eventually Mum simmered down, but there wasn't any spare room at her flat anymore. She had moved into my bedroom since I'd left and her boyfriend Geoff had now moved in. It's funny because I'd come back intent on being the perfect daughter and to try to make amends for the pains I'd caused her. Now I realised, with a heavy heart, there's no going back. I just hoped we could mend our relationship. I certainly didn't blame her for blanking me – I just wanted her to hold me and tell me she loved me. She thought it'd be best if I stayed at Nan and Granddad's. Life repeating itself, I thought, as I made my way to Nan and Granddad's house. Eventually Mum forgave me and on my eighteenth birthday she bought me an electric sewing machine, which I used to make clothes for the hippie shop which I'd started in Coventry, which was very successful for a few months, but soon I was restless again, and wanted to move on.

So I moved south to London. I arrived in Prince of Wales Crescent, Chalk Farm, thinking I'd arrived in Amsterdam again. It was full of squats, colourful hippies, musicians, artists and loads of street love-in events – I was in my element. I stayed above a health food shop, called Community Supplies, run by a very clever young fellow called John Law. I worked in the shop and got to know all the people in the area very quickly. The whole area was buzzing; it was a fantastic place to be. Through the shop, I met this small group of friends: Jim, Stace, Steph, and a New York chick, Barbara, who were going to Morocco, over the Sahara to the Congo, and on to East Africa. I asked if I could go with them. I also began having a very passionate affair with Stace, a tall, handsome, double-bass playing, funny, sexy man. This gang were such fun and so way out for anybody on the outside looking in. For instance we all generally lived naked in our apartment, and slept on a load of mattresses in the same room, however we weren't having sex with each other. Stace and I were a couple, and Jim and his New York girlfriend were together, and Steph was single (however I think she and Stace used to be an item). A musician called Magic Michael also lived with us but he wasn't coming to Africa. I met the next-door neighbour at this point who was the first short-haired guy I'd met for years. I thought he was a cop when I first opened the front door to him. His name was Adrian, he drove a Harley Davidson, and little did I know then, but he was to be the love of my life.

We did all kinds of activities to earn money for Africa. My main money-spinner was go-go dancing in pubs. By the time we were ready to depart I'd put away a great wodge of money – we had a coach and twenty paying passengers to take to Marrakech and an Army truck to take across the Sahara, filled with hand-operated sewing machines to barter with in Zaire. We decided we could live in the coach, and then sell it on departing Morocco. We waved goodbye to Magic Michael and our neighbour Adrian, thinking it would be years before we returned.

Eventually we arrived with our passengers in the Marrakech Souk. Our clothes were all holes, as the diesel had leaked and spat out of the coach engine all over anyone who sat in the front seats. We set up in a Marrakech camp site for a while and out came Stace's double bass, guitars, and Tim on his saxophone – a group of musician friends from Chalk Farm linked up with us and we had a blast. I was glad to leave Marrakech though because of my ghosts. We were moving on to a famous hippy beach near Agadir, called Taghazout.

When I first saw the hippy beach, I'd never seen the like of it before; young travellers camped in a mile long stretch of glorious beach. There was the Moroccan fishing village up on the high rocks and down on the flat were the hippy enclaves, a hundred yards from the ocean. Music, hash, and incense filled the air. There were two beach cafés which had become very well off from hippy patronisation. We set up camp here for the next two months. Of course things were routinely stolen by the Moroccan kids, but hey, we were camping for free, so it was like paying rent. We girls would go out to the hippy campers selling hash cookies; unfortunately we would eat one at the outset and become useless saleswomen – just giggling all over the place. We made friends with a French group next door to us and one of their group – a girl called Françoise – started to take an unhealthy interest in Stace, and literally moved in on us. I found her in our bed one night.

Stace said that nothing was going on and that she was a disturbed young girl, and he was merely being supportive. I started to become very upset and jealous, and arguments ensued. In tandem to this, Jim and his New York girl were arguing all the time. Eventually we had a big pow-wow, and it was decided we would all split up. Jim and Stace would take the Army truck and go on across the Sahara without us girls. The coach was sold to the beach café owner, and the proceeds were divided between Jim's lady, Steph and me.

Jim's girl went back to the U.S., and Steph and I bought a Citroen 2CV, and decided we'd still continue over the Sahara. This wasn't to be. I discovered I was pregnant. I was devastated. I'd always said if I got pregnant, I'd have the baby, and now here I was pregnant, boyfriend gone, and living on the beach in a car. I went to a French clinic where a lady doctor said she'd perform an abortion. I was ravaged with guilt beforehand and terrified on the day of the surgery, as I couldn't see my doctor in the operating room – only a big Arab guy – the anaesthetist, I presumed – but I panicked saying, 'Where's my lady doctor? I want a lady, not a guy doing this.'

That was the last I remember until I woke up in a recovery room with a terrible bellyache. The doctor saw me for five minutes, gave me ampoules of penicillin, and syringes to inject the antibiotics, and off I went back into my foggy, hippy world. We'd moved our camp inland a few miles, up into a beautiful valley, aptly named Paradise valley, next to a rushing river, and a Dutch friend of ours said he'd stay with us and do my injections for the next week. I was totally lost, in pain physically and emotionally, slumped under a tree losing a lot of blood. It was a terribly wretched thing to do and I knew it, and it changed me. I was filled with self-loathing and regret.

Within a few weeks I had a little more strength. I borrowed money and flew back to London, and I needed a good doctor as I was still bleeding and ill. I thought I would go back and continue on with Steph but I didn't. On my departure I heard the sad news that Françoise had set fire to herself in a field in Paradise Valley, and died.

I arrived back to my apartment in London and stayed there with Magic Michael. I saw a doctor and told my story day by day to Adrian, my next-door neighbour. He seemed so sane compared to the madness of all the journeys I'd been on. After a few weeks I felt stronger and went for a photo model job. The whole thing turned into a disaster, as the photographer talked me slowly out of my clothes and then jumped on me. My head exploded: 'No more, no more the victim,' I thought. I kicked up hard into his balls, then I grabbed my clothes, kicked him again for good measure to keep his distance and ran, partially clothed, down the street.

When I arrived back to the apartment I went to Adrian. I wanted tea and sympathy, I suppose. Adrian sat next to me at the piano. He could play by ear like my Dad and he doodled around his fave melody from Casablanca, 'You must remember this...' As he played he said, 'So what's up, Haze?' I recounted the horror of the evening: I wanted total sympathy, but I got something very different. 'Well Hazel, you sort of deserved it, you're a bit of a cock-tease.' I was shocked at what he was saying. 'You go round sticking your tits out, always living from one guy to another, an aimless hippy life, living off your charms. Why don't you throw away the hippy rags and learn a trade or do something useful with your life?' The more he talked, telling me how he viewed me, the more I saw there was a glimmer of truth to it. I hated hearing it but respected him so much for telling me how it was. I seemed to be forever moving on, going from hurt to hurt; always on the run from some unseen spectre. I was definitely aimless and since my rapes I'd had a lot of boyfriends.

I thought 'Yes, enough of this hippy life.' Adrian then looked me square in the eyes and said, 'I need to know if you're going or staying, Haze, because I want to go to bed and if you're going, I need to lock the door behind you but if you're staying, I can lock it now.' I was shocked. One minute he's telling me I'm living off men, next he's propositioning me. My jaw dropped for a second time. I'd not viewed Adrian in 'that way' at all. He was my friend whom I loved to talk to. Well, Mum had always said to me, 'The best love is one that dawns on you slowly and isn't to do with looks.' I liked Adrian so much, but I wasn't sure I fancied him, however, I was curious and his practical forthright no-nonsense invite to spend the night with him was intriguing. 'I'll stay then, I guess.' This man was like a father figure, and my best friend, and now he was to become the love of my life.

CHAPTER FOUR

'I think about you when I could be scrubbing floors or
plotting a bank robbery – do you think of me?
And sometimes when I'm feeling like a lost child –
I imagine you are close to me, your breath on me.'
"Thinking About You",
(*Beyond the Breaking Glass*, 2000)

The next day I moved in with him. This was to be the most inspirational and formative relationship of my life, and because of Adrian I ended up going on extraordinary travels and adventures, which expanded my understanding of the world both politically and culturally. I learned new languages, threw my hippy rags away, and grew as a direct result of knowing Adrian. This was a time of great emotional highs and huge lows – and hurts.

Adrian was great: I loved his energy. With him I never stopped learning things about life, love, art, movies, and books: about everything. He was – and still is – the most fascinating human being I've ever met. Life was always interesting and fun around Adrian; also he filled my emotional void that the loss of Dad, the loss of Roy, and the loss of respect for men that those incidents had created in me. Even though he was only six years older than me, he seemed wise beyond his years, and he felt like the Dad I had not had as well as a very sexy lover.

His house was full of antiques as he loved the things of the past. He loved the film *Casablanca* and its leading actor, Humphrey Bogart. Like me, he loved classic and antique cars which he collected as well as motorbikes. I fell head-over-heels in love with him. He was unique. I know he really liked me too, but he didn't want to be tied to anyone, and the more he said that to me, the more clingy I became. Then one day during an argument he said, 'Why don't you go earn your own living and stop living off me!' Wow, that had stung, and it was true. So I thought, 'Right, you bastard, I'll show you.'

So I answered an ad in *Stage* magazine for go-go dancers and showgirls to go to Tokyo, Japan, on Equity contracts. Although it was a French company based in Paris, I went to an audition in Covent Garden and met the choreographer, who was a woman of around sixty years old called Madame Luska. There were around twenty other girls, and we followed a few dance steps, and that was that. I got the job. Not that I'm a great dancer; I just could follow a tune and had an all right pair of legs and a curvy body. Within the month I was at London Airport leaving for Paris to rehearse. Adrian was seeing me off. I kept hoping he would say, 'Don't go, Haze, I love you, need you,' but he didn't. I started to cry then; I sobbed then I screamed, and he had to peel me off him and frogmarch me to the plane. It hurt like the day we left Dad and my first home.

I pined for Adrian every night in my little hotel room in Pigalle, Paris. I wrote a letter to him each night, and studied my *Learn French in Three Months* book, in between watching the line of ants crawling up to the sink in my room and listening to the prostitute up the hallway bringing back her eighth trick of the night. When I'd get lonely in my room, I'd walk the streets of Pigalle and get to know all the barkers, and often went into the burlesque shows for free. Rehearsals were hilarious: I was by far the worst dancer for remembering steps. I take a long time to learn anything, but once I do, I never forget. So eventually I caught up with the rest of the twelve dancers. Most of the girls were French; there were three English, a lovely girl called Dash, another Hazel, and myself.

I made friends with a musician at the local music shop called Marcel Dadi, he turned out to be a very famous guitarist in France, and he invited me to a big concert of his in Paris, just before we left for Tokyo. On the night of his concert he was very upset because he'd heard that some students living on a Kibbutz in a place called Ma'alot in Israel, had been killed by the PLO. He was Jewish and felt this tragedy very keenly.

After three weeks' rehearsals I was off, flying Russian Airlines to Tokyo. My arrival at Haneda Airport was a total culture shock: everything was written in strange writing, the roads were on two levels, and many people down on the streets below were wearing white surgical masks to protect themselves from the polluted air. We were taken to an area called Akasaka, the burlesque part of town, and we were to stay in the home of the theatre owner, Mrs Saito. Our rooms were only divided by paper walls, and I thought, I'm not going to last in this house of girls for long. She seemed nice enough presenting us with a box of sushi, but of course none of us knew that all this raw fish stuff was a wonderful delicacy from the Japanese point of view – the French girls were mostly snobby about things Japanese.

After getting over my jetlag, I trudged around our local streets. We were very close to a beautiful temple; one of the oldest in Tokyo. Big pots of incense were burning at the doorway, and shaven-headed monks sat with begging bowls. All the trees round about and the cracks in the walls were filled with small pieces of paper. Apparently the papers had people's fortune written on them, with which they would adorn the outside of the temple. I then went over to see the theatre where our 'Festival of Paris' cabaret show was to be held. It was mid-afternoon and there was a Japanese show on.

What I saw shocked me. The dancers would start off fully dressed in Kimono, doing traditional moves to traditional music. Then the music would change pace into something like Tom Jones's "Why, why, why Delilah?" and layer upon layer of kimono would be unravelled until they were naked, but you'd not be able to see the pubic hair, which would be covered by their beautifully long black tresses of now unravelled hair, but now came the dodgy part, to my mind. The music changed to a slow electronic red-light type of music, and these ladies would come to the front of the stage, squat down, and open and close their legs, and deftly hide full view of their vaginas by their hair falling between their legs. The men in the audience were only inches away from open-legged ladies and would now poke money at them. The girls would catch it with their privates. Oh God, I thought, our show was very tame compared to this porn.

It turned out to be true: our show was definitely not the roaring success the bosses thought it would be. It was just too tame, but I didn't care, as long as I was getting paid. I decided to try to learn Japanese, so I bought a motorbike a – Kawasaki 250 (Adrian had taught me to ride) – and now I decided to move out of the dancers house, because the French girls were driving me crazy. They didn't want to know about anything Japanese but I was loving it.

With the help of my new friend George – a university student doing stagehand work – I found an eleven and a half mat room (rooms were measured by the tatame mat), reasonably priced, just across the road from our theatre. I began giving English conversation lessons to George's student friends, who were very grateful, and besides paying they would bring beautiful gifts. Gift giving is a Japanese talent. They are great gift givers.

All this time I was missing Adrian, but I was having the best adventure of my life. I was earning good money, meeting new people, and seeing amazing things. The tone of Adrian's letters began to change from when I'd first left. They were brusque and matter-of-fact. Slowly they changed to, 'I miss you, Haze, when I should be scrubbing the floor or plotting a bank robbery.' This was a big move forward. In a later letter he said he was going to Africa to find our old pal Jim (of Jim and Stace), who seemingly had never reached East Africa and was somewhere in Ghana. His postcard from Africa was even hotter suggesting I come back to Africa with him when I finished my contract in Japan.

Meanwhile, the dance troupe moved to Kobe for the last month of our contract. I made a new friend called Keiko and her family welcomed me in. I thought how strange it was that these wonderful warm people had been at war with the Allies because it didn't seem possible.

It was time to go back to Europe as my contract had finished. As the plane took off, I wrote in my diary that I would be back to this lovely land – that was forty years ago and I'm still trying to get back there. I stopped off in Paris and Monsieur Bertin, my boss, said he felt I could have an acting career in France, and begged me to sign on for one more tour of duty with a troupe going to the *Crazy Horse* in Beirut, Lebanon, for four months. If I would just do that then he would bring me back to Paris and present me to film producers and directors and get an acting career going. Adrian, I knew, was now in Australia, and I thought I may as well carry on with the dancing lark, as he's not going to be home. So I signed a new contract. I had a week to relax in England, and then back to Paris, and on to the Lebanon.

I came home to Adrian's house; some friends were looking after it for him. There was a letter there saying he was going to Tokyo to see me. 'Too late,' I thought, and rang him in Australia. He wasn't in, so I left a message with his friends. The next morning a telegram arrived from him saying, 'Stay put, don't go anywhere, I'm coming home, flying in tomorrow – come on an African adventure with me.' The day he flew in, I had exactly twenty-four hours before I left for Paris. I met him at the airport where we hugged awkwardly. He blushed – I was shaking inside – we hardly spoke on the drive home.

When we arrived home we disappeared into our bedroom and stayed there until I left early next morning. He decided he would follow me to Paris and stay with me during my week's rehearsals. This was the peak of our romance. I was on cloud nine that he finally realised he loved me, and yet now I was going to Beirut and he back to Africa. We made a plan to meet up in Ghana in four months' time. We then flew our separate ways. It was wonderful to me that Adrian wanted me as much as I wanted him and the old adage 'absence makes the heart grow fonder' had obviously worked by my having gone to Japan. However, as I was already contracted for Beirut, I had to bite the bullet and honour the contract – I had no desire to go to the Lebanon, so now I felt like I was just waiting in limbo until I'd done my time.

Beirut felt more familiar to me than Tokyo, as I'd spent time in Morocco and was cognisant of the Arab culture. Phoenicia Street, where the *Crazy Horse* was, had the *Holiday Inn* at the bottom by the seaside and posh boutiques up the top end. It tickled me that in the midst of this bustling Arab culture there was a *Wimpy* bar opposite the *Holiday Inn*, which stayed open until 6a.m., to catch us cabaret girls coming out of work at 4a.m. The nightclub owner, Kareem, put pressure on all the dancers to have a drink with customers after the show finished. It's called consummation in the cabaret trade. Well I thought, 'No bloody way am I sitting with a drunken dickhead and encouraging them to drink more.' So I refused, which got me in deep trouble, but I asked Kareem to show me where it was written in my bona fide Equity contract that I had to drink with the punters. Kareem backed down, but forced me to sit in the 9' by 9' dressing room crammed with costumes, chairs, and make-up, from end of show time at 2a.m. until 4a.m. I read zillions of books during this period of my life, with my favourite authors being Herman Hesse and

Kurt Vonnegut Jnr; I read every one of their novels.

I did sit with a customer towards the end of my time in the *Crazy Horse*. The waiter came backstage and begged me, saying, 'Look, Hazel, he's a young guy – they're all young like you.' I went out and met the party, sullenly saying, 'Don't drink alcohol.' Walid, the youth next to me, said, 'I don't drink either. How old are you? I'm nineteen.' 'Same as me,' I replied, smiling. We became firm friends. He turned out to be one of the Princes of the Saudi Royal Family. We'd go for outings to discos after work, or just a drive in the hills. One day he took me to the Palace he was living in. As we came to the gates, he was hustled away by one of the guards, and I was driven home by a silent guard. I met Walid again years later. It seems they had intelligence on an attack that was about to happen, and all the royal family left that night.

Most of the other performers were great women, but there was one – the youngest and most beautiful – called Giliane, who really had it in for me. I think I was threatening her supremacy of being the youngest with the best legs and tits, as I was now the youngest, and I had a good bosom myself. On the odd occasion I would sit in the Cabaret with a regular, youngish man called Sam. He was a rich banker, and I once made the mistake of referring to him as an Arab. He really took the hump over this and pompously announced, 'I'm a Phoenician and a Christian, not an Arab.' We had a tacit friendship and he treated me to driving lessons for a pre-birthday gift. I eventually took my first driving test in Beirut.

My driving instructor was an Arab man called Mr Aberatif, and I ended up injuring him a few times because of our lack of common language. In Arabic to say 'No' you can nod your head, click your tongue and say, 'La!' So Mr Aberatif would be standing on the gravel track in front of me and my Willis Jeep, and I would signal, 'Shall I go forward?' he would nod, so I'd think, 'He means yes, come on,' but of course he was saying, 'La, la. No, no.' I ran over his foot once.

On the day of my driving test, I was a big attraction to the local Palestinian lads, from the refugee camp nearby. I suppose I looked so different with my long blonde hair and cabaret-girl style. They kept applauding when I got things right. Anyway I did get my first driving licence in Beirut, because of those lessons. I saw a part of Beirut that most of the Westerners wouldn't see, namely the utter sadness of a Palestinian camp: people living in shacks built from cans, plastic bottles, bits of corrugated iron and plastic bags, open sewers running through between shacks, and little kids with mucous running out of their dead-pan eyes, and flies all over them. I didn't realise they were living like unwelcome guests in many places in that region. They must have been living like this for the last twenty-six years, since becoming exiled from their homeland: an event they remember each year as 'Nakba Day' (the day of the Catastrophe).

A light went on in my brain, the penny dropped. 'No wonder these people are fighting a war; they have been forgotten about for nearly three decades. Being brought up in that environment and knowing nothing else but plastic bag housing is bound to make the younger generation angry. Like Dylan wrote: "Freedom's just another word for nothing left to lose." ' Beirut was my first real political experience and I'll take it with me forever.

My contract was coming to an end. Within the month I would be leaving Beirut and joining Adrian in West Africa. I had passed my time there taking singing lessons as well as driving. Most days I'd hop into my rubber dinghy and row out into the bay of Beirut. I was always surprised to see that the only beach in the city had rolls of barbed wire across it. I asked a cab driver why and he explained that it was there 'to stop the Israeli landing boats when they try to raid the Palestinian camps.'

The day before my twentieth birthday I was enjoying a singing lesson up in the old part of the city. I was at the top of a tallish building singing "Doh, ray, me," etc., when a siren started to whine, like in the old war films. I asked my teacher, 'What's that noise? It sounds like an air-raid siren.' 'It is,' he said. 'The Israelis are probably coming over.' I panicked. 'What do we do? Will they bomb us? Is there an air-raid shelter?' 'Yes, they'll bomb us; they do that sometimes, that's why we have the siren, but they'll go for the shipping and the Palestinian camps, as there's no targets up here. Don't worry. Sing "Doh, ray, me" again, please.'

That night all the cabaret girls were discussing the air-raid and where they were when it happened. Some of the girls had been on the beach south of the city by the airport when the air-raid siren had gone off. The beach emptied in seconds, but my friends were still paddling in the sea, and didn't know what was going on. The Israeli jets flew in a few seconds later, battering the airport.

The 16th of May was my birthday and I went out in my inflatable dinghy into the middle of the Bay of Beirut. I lay across the little boat, bikini top down, sunbathing. In the depth of my slumbers I heard a faraway buzzing getting closer. I looked to see if an insect was about: no insect. I looked further afield into the distant sky and saw a v-shape of aeroplanes coming in my direction. I read that the Israeli bombers had in their sights the airport, Palestinian camps, and the shipping in the bay. 'Bloody hell! I'd better make like the wind and get out of here pronto,' I thought. I pulled up my top and began rowing. All at once I was rowing so hard and fast that the sides of my boat were being pushed down and the front and back coming up in the air – up and down like a concertina. I got my boat to the concrete siding and pulled it out of the water, dumped it, and ran under a concrete bridge to get my clothes. Time seemed to slow down and my thoughts were very clear. I must get my clothes – can't get caught in an air-raid in my bikini – I must get my clothes.

The bombers passed overhead, and a few seconds later an enormous bang shook everything, especially the glass windows in the overhead bridge. Glass showered all around. I heard a second bang, worse than the first. The jets were supersonic; they'd drop a bomb, then break through the sound barrier. All around me crumbling masonry and glass were falling. Someone was running behind me with blood on his face, a kid was screaming, more stones were falling... Had time suddenly sped up? I guess my fight or flight instinct had kicked in. Forget the clothes – get away from all this falling concrete, I thought – and in seconds I was up the steps and on to the eerily still boulevard. Others stood around in swimwear, all traffic had stopped, and we all stared up cowering at every bang, as the sky became black with dust and smoke. I realised that if I was going to die, I'd rather die under a direct hit than be buried under tons of concrete. I realised that whoever was dropping bombs from above didn't give a shit if I was British, Irish, Arab, or from Timbuktu. Bombs don't care: it's all very impersonal. I can't remember when it was finished, nor when I collected my clothes and the boat. The rest of the day was a total blank, until I got to work and all the girls were discussing it. I felt a terrible tragedy was afoot. I had a very strong premonition, and I knew I'd better get out of Beirut as soon as possible.

The next day I tried to get across town to my driving lesson, but it was impossible. Thousands of people were out demonstrating against the authorities. It seemed that the Lebanese Muslim Arabs were joining forces with the outraged Palestinians, who had sustained the most horrendous losses, while old cannons were being dragged around. Much of the ordinance dropped on the camps had been cluster bombs; these explode about two feet off the ground and are filled with all kinds of nasty shrapnel. These bombs are anti-personnel bombs. I was outraged. I waited for the British papers to report this atrocity. Three days later I found an inch-long column in a couple of British papers, and that was that. It seemed Israel had bombed Beirut for two days in retaliation for an atrocity (the one which had so upset my Jewish musician friend, Marcel Dadi) that had happened in October of the previous year, when the PLO had come over the border from the Lebanon.

It was difficult to get flights out of Beirut as the runways at the airport had been bombed in the air attacks. A few weeks later I managed to get a flight back to London, as I had an airline pilot friend who I'd played darts with, and he swung a seat for me on his flight. A footnote to this story is that within two weeks of my departure, beautiful Beirut and the Lebanon were thrust into a horrendous Civil War in which thousands of innocents died. I found it so strange watching the news in safe old England, where they'd been talking about the battle of the *Holiday Inn*.

Almost immediately I flew off to Accra in Ghana to meet up with Adrian. My penance done, time served, I could now be with him. It was 1974. I'd put my long blonde hair in ringlets on the overnight flight so that I'd have my hair looking all lovely on arrival and my reunion with Adrian. I stepped off the plane and the humidity was so heavy, my lovely hairdo was plastered to my head by the time I got to the bottom of the steps of the plane. I was also sweating like a pig and soaked by the time I reached Adrian for our first sticky embrace.

Adrian and our old friend Jim met me at the airport and we went off to a hotel and caught up on each other's adventures. Adrian had found Jim, split up from Stace, living above a pub called the 'Rock of Ages', in a little village by the sea called Dixcove, where he had been very ill with malaria, but was being nursed by a big African mamma.

We stayed only one day in Accra and moved on to Takoradi to organise the shipping of some hardwoods (ebony being the main one) – one of Adrian's entrepreneurial ideas. We inherited a little monkey called Lady, but she hated being on a leash, and she would bite at every opportunity.

West Africa was so full of colour; the straight-backed women seemed to do most of the work (surprise, surprise), carrying water and bricks on their heads, whilst the men got drunk on a local brew called Guinness.

After a few days in Takoradi, we moved to Edubiase – a little village in the jungle –where Jim and Adrian had made friends with an eighteen carat gold character, who was an evangelical preacher called Simon Peter. He was so effusive on meeting me, that he nearly shook my hand off whilst simultaneously clapping me on the back saying: 'Welcome, Sister Hazel, welcome.' We stayed with Simon Peter and his family for a week to check out some land Adrian had bought off the local chief to build our house on. That week the heavens opened and the monsoon rainy season began: Oh my God it rained and it rained. Eventually we took our leave of Simon and the family, and began our overland drive back to England via Upper Volta (Burkina Faso), Niger, Algeria, Tunisia, Italy, France, and England.

Once out of Edubiase, we let Lady, the monkey, go – as Adrian untied her, she climbed up and bit him one last time for posterity. We crossed the border into Upper Volta and the jungle became more scrubland and the road was full of bicycles as we neared the capital city, Ouagadougou, where the main consumer goods were bicycles. We bought some supplies here and moved on towards the border and into Niger. It was around this time I began to get violent headaches every other day or so. I was so sick as we neared Niger's capital, also called Niger, that I didn't want to swim in the river Niger, and this would be the last big water we would see for many weeks, as we were entering the beginning of the Sahara Desert. I was so sick, I couldn't rouse myself.

At the first serious bit of desert we were told we would have to take a guide or join a convoy, as three Italians had been lost three months ago, and had recently reappeared dead under a sand dune. They had gone *off-piste* looking for water. When travelled, the desert route is marked by big white-painted oil-cans every hundred feet, and the traffic makes the roadway. There was no such thing as a tarmac road, as the sandstorms would just cover any proper road.

We joined a convoy with some Belgian people, but they were so slow, always stopping to have tea parties every few hours, and we got very impatient with them. So we roared off ahead of them at one junction and we were going miles too fast, and the *piste* suddenly became a sea of three foot deep gouged tracks, where the rain had come and trucks had churned-up deep ditches. Our Land Rover hit the gouges head-on and we bounced all over the place; everything fell off the top of the Land Rover and we nearly wrote-off our vehicle and our lives. Our possessions were scattered along a two-hundred yard line, but we were lucky, as it could have been our limbs. The Belgian holidaymakers came past saying how stupid we were. It was true!

In the Sahara Desert the most precious commodity is water. There is, believe it or not, a lot of water around, but it's down below the desert crust and Sahara maps tell you where the wells are. Some are crap to fill bottles and drink from, because they're magnesium water, and it doesn't taste good. But you can have fun at any well, nice tasting or not, because you fill containers and then throw the water on each other, from head to toe, and you get total relief from the searing desert temperatures – within minutes your clothes are bone dry again.

The other trick we learned was to wet a piece of thin cloth and tie it across your nose and mouth, and it cools the air you inhale for about three minutes, then it's dry as a bone, just like the clothes, but it was worth it. Sometimes we would come to an oasis and the red and grey gravelly terrain would suddenly have a circle of greenery. One clever oasis dweller had a big tank of water for travellers to hop into – at a price of course. It's funny how every shanty town, village, and gathering place across the Sahara also had a Coca-Cola shop with a fridge, obviously supplied by the Emperor Coca-Cola. In those days, I'm ashamed to say, I paid into the Coke empire, as I'd always be getting headaches and fevers as we crossed the desert, and would hassle Adrian for Coca-Cola when we saw the sign, because I knew it would be ice-cold. He'd get quite pissed off with me saying, 'You're a pain in the arse, Haze. One minute you're complaining of sick headaches, then you force us to buy cola, and suddenly you're well again.' It did seem like I was feigning sickness. I later found out I was already sick with malaria, hence sick one minute, then right as rain again.

When we came to bigger settlements we'd often be surrounded by Tuareg women with their braided henna red hair and blue tattooed lips and faces. Oh they looked so beautiful, so exotic. Jim would always be so entranced, asking them to marry him and stuff like that. They, of course, would like some money. Their men were usually off on a caravan across the other side of the Sahara and these people had so little, but they were always happy, clapping and singing. The peoples that we met above and below the Equator in the Sahara were truly magnificent. My favourite tribe from below the Equator was the Pearls, who were black-skinned and very tall, with beautiful facial features and long necks, made longer by the rings they wore around them, and always big decorations in the earlobes. The ladies didn't care about being topless because their breasts were functional for their babies. Above the Equator the Tuaregs were my favourite looking people.

One day we were invited into a Tuareg chief's tent, as he

desperately needed quinine, because the monsoon rains had come too high into the desert that year bringing the malaria mosquito to his tribe. He wore blue loose clothing and a bluish turban, which made his face shimmer kind of bluish as well. He was very handsome and we spent a few hours drinking mint tea with him. We gave him what quinine we had, and on departing, he asked us to give his friend a lift to the next village. As our Tuareg passenger clattered into the back of the Land Rover, his sword, which a Tuareg man always wore, got stuck in the doorway – we tried not to giggle. He travelled light, and apart from his sword and dagger, he carried all he needed in little leather pouches around his neck. On this necklace of assorted needs he carried his teapot – the nomad's second most important tool, after his sword. It was such a thrill to have him travel the day with us and make camp that night. We had no shared language except for signs and gesticulations. He made a wonderful tea, and said it protected against scorpions. We had a wonderful night under the vast desert sky, sipping tea and sharing stories.

As I said, water is the most sought-after commodity in the desert, so when we found drinkable water we'd long since stopped boiling it, and quite literally lapped it up. This was to be my downfall as I caught hookworm from the oasis water that would fall in from overhanging bushes, and I had an awful time of it. There's nothing worse than going to the loo and seeing hundreds of little squirmy wormy things moving around in your crap. One night I had the worms and the runs so I allotted to sleep a good distance from the Land Rover. Adrian came with me. We fell into a sound sleep, only to be awoken by the ground moving and rumbling. 'Adrian, what the hell is that noise? The ground is moving, I'm sure it is.' He just grabbed me up and said, 'Run, run!' The next second over the hill came the first of a convoy of heavy duty trucks, going at very high speeds, right over the place where we'd been laying. I never slept that far from our vehicle again!

The first town we hit towards the latter end of our desert journey was called Tamanrasset, in southern Algeria. It rose up amongst the rocks of the terrain, as sandy desert was nearly finished now, and we were crossing huge gravel plateaus. We stayed a few days and met a lovely old English gent called Peter. I think he'd stayed behind after the Second World War; he seemed to love North Africa. He was quite a colonial type of old boy, and he was thrilled to be speaking English again, but oh my God, he loved to get drunk. Tamanrasset was great because I finally saw a doctor and got my worms sorted out, and Peter was delightful company and knew all the local lingos and the dos and don'ts of the area. He talked about the Algerian War of Independence and told us always to be careful of unexploded mines on our final trek across Algiers.

The first green grass we saw was on our final descent from the plateau which had been fifty miles across. We'd snaked down on a fairly proper road, and saw that grassy field calling to us – we all agreed to set up camp there. We drove down and as I jumped out, I scratched myself on a piece of dislocated barbed-wire sticking out of the ground. I decided to stick very close to the Land Rover in case I tripped on barbed-wire in the dark. Being knackered, we all went to sleep fairly soon after making camp.

We were rudely awoken at dawn by a truckload of Algerian workmen shouting out, 'You fools! Get out of there, you silly fools! It's a minefield.' 'Oh shit!' we all thought. 'Best retrace our steps,' said the ever-practical Adrian. Jim led us out by foot. Adrian drove and I decided to sit next to him, and if he was about to get blown-up, well, so would I, 'cause I loved him, and that was that! My heart was in my mouth though. When we got out and realised the danger, our stupidity, our fear, all we could do was laugh from the shock of it all. The barbed-wire sticking up was there to mark the unexploded mines left since the Algerian War of Independence – our friend Peter had warned us!

Finally we were in Algiers. We went sight-seeing at the Roman Forum at Carthage, and quickly into Tunis to catch a boat to Italy then across Europe, and home, back to London!

At home, I cast my mind's eye over the previous eighteen months. I'd fallen in love with Adrian, and relished every adventure and travel I'd undertaken because of him. With him I was a changed woman, and not yet twenty-one.

I'd made some money as a dancer and now tried to use it to

better myself. I enrolled in a modelling school, and lent Adrian some money towards a workshop he was trying to get in London's posh area of Hampstead. Besides getting the odd modelling job, I started a course in gilding, as Adrian had won a contract to refurbish an old gypsy wagon that stood on the grounds of Kenwood House, Highgate in London. He said I could do the painting and gilding if I went to learn how – so I did! This was the first time I'd used my artistic bent since living in Amsterdam – and I relished it. My gilding teacher, Mr Sullivan, was fairly secretive with his knowledge, and only taught as much as the class needed to know, but as I actually had a major gilding job, Mr Sullivan would give me tips of the trade if I flirted a little.

I did one last cabaret dancing job in London's Piccadilly, at a place called Murray's, where I funnily enough met up with my friend Prince Al Walid Ben Saud again. I had not seen or heard from him since he'd been whisked off from the Palace gates in Beirut, which by 1975 was a raging battleground.

While I was working at Murray's, Adrian went back to Ghana, as our friend Simon Peter was in some legal trouble and needed our help. During Adrian's absence, which was only supposed to be a couple of weeks, I became very ill and our neighbour, a very kind guy, took care of me. Adrian delayed his return for an extra two weeks, and all I can say is that when he did finally get home, the butterflies I usually got when I saw him were absent. We plodded along together. I kept getting very ill, and eventually Adrian took me up to the casualty department at Hampstead Hospital, and left me there alone. I was in my nightdress, shaking like crazy with a dreadful thumping headache, and this had been coming on and off for three weeks by this time. The snotty hospital staff seemed to leave me until last – I think they assumed I was a junkie, cold turkeying. Anyway I sat shivering and shaking in severe pain for three or four hours. By the time I was brought to an examining cubicle, even the fluorescent light caused me extreme sick pain.

Eventually a doctor came in and I told him about the head pain and the throbbing under my left ribcage. I told him I'd been in Africa the year before. He came back with a group of doctors, who all felt under my left ribcage. 'Her spleen is enlarged to three times the size it should be – let's get some blood,' the doctor said. By this time I was getting very hot and drifting away, and the pain was leaving me.

'We think you have malaria – Did you say you were in Africa?' 'Yes, I told the Casualty receptionist that four hours ago,' I said. 'We'll test your blood, but I think we may not find the parasite in your blood now, as it's too late. We would have needed to test you a few hours ago, as once the fever begins, the bug runs back to your spleen, where it lays dormant. But it is cyclical, so I'd say you'll have another fever within forty-eight hours, and we'll pinpoint it then. We need you to stay in hospital.'

The next day I was weighed on the ward. I was shocked, as I'd gone from eight and a half stone to just below six stone, in three weeks. I felt fine though, so I phoned friends to bring books and my guitar in. I phoned Mum who said she'd come down to London. The next day I was sitting in the visitors room surrounded by friends playing guitar, having a laugh, when I started to feel those now familiar pains in my wrists and ankles – like a prelude to going down with flu – the dull pains got more throbbing, moving up my back, through my shoulders, knees, head, neck. Oh God, it's coming back, I thought. 'I think I'm about to get ill again, so please leave: I don't want anyone watching,' I said to my visitors.

I called the doctor as this, he'd explained, was the best time to get a blood sample. During the pain phase Mum arrived. I really didn't want her to witness me so sick, as by this time everything hurts – people talking, lights, touch, everything – and I was effing and blinding at the ladies in the beds next to mine because their voices were like chainsaws in my head. 'Mum, please go away – come back later please – it's not as bad as it looks.' She waited outside, feeling really worried, and after a few hours the fever came. Then I felt great; just very hot, but no pain. Then Mum sat holding my hand and the doctor came in, very excited... 'We found the malaria parasite, now we know how to treat you,' he said.

Adrian ended up in the Tropical Diseases Hospital with another kind of malaria some months later. He'd become really ill on the eve of my English driving test. Poor Adrian, he was swelling up like an overripe tomato, and I was selfishly worrying about my driving test the next day, and the fact that he was disturbing my sleep.

We didn't end with a big bang or an argument – we just didn't spend time together anymore, and I was no longer his adoring puppy dog. He'd helped me to grow so much, and it now seemed as if I'd outgrown him. When we finally called it a day, it was very painful for both of us. I found a new flat around the corner from him, and moved out, but we remain good friends to this very day.

CHAPTER FIVE

'Put on your face, put on your clothes,
going out dancing, gonna pose
Gonna wind our bodies round and round,
move to the rhythm of the fave rave sound.
These are the decadent days'
"Decadent Days" (*Sons & Lovers*, 1980)

I'd always imagined getting married to Adrian and having his children, and to be honest, that was all I ever wanted; to love a man, marry, and have kids. I certainly had no wish for fame. I didn't enjoy painting, it seemed to irritate me – I think that's because I'm quite obsessive, and once I'd start a piece of art I'd not put it down until it was finished, even if I missed a night's sleep. I designed clothes, but only for myself. I had a small collection of music that I loved, but I had no thoughts then about a career in music, unlike my brother, Neil. I was alone. I was twenty-one and I felt like my whole life was behind me. I had no idea what – or where – I was going next. I tried to imagine what made me most happy and I remembered singing my teenage blues away with Neil, and how totally happy I felt singing, so I thought I would try singing. I answered an advert in a music magazine for a three-girl group, managed by a husband-and-wife team, Mick and Jan O'Leary. Jan was also the lead singer. A lovely girl called Maggie – who I am still friends with now – and I were chosen to complete the trio.

We were called Lady Luck and specialized in three-part harmonies. Trying to be the Three Degrees, doing songs like, "Breaking up is Hard to Do" and "Angel of the Morning." Because I could sew, I made our two sets of costumes, which were identical all-in-one body suits with flared bottoms, one in blue satin, the other silver lamé.

Jan did the lead vocals, and Maggie and I the harmonies. Even though I'd sung harmonies with my dad as a child, I didn't really understand harmony singing very well and I couldn't stay in tune. At our first gig at the boozy Working Men's Club, I was threatened with being chucked out of the band because my tuning was so bad. Anyway, I soldiered on and tried to improve.

Within a few months, Mick O'Leary had got us a tour of the U.S. G.I. bases in Germany. The problem was we had no transport. I decided to lend Lady Luck the money to buy a van. During this time Mick, whose business card read, 'Mike Scott, Manager', presented Maggie and me with contracts, tying us to him and Jan for eternity. We found it very upsetting, and didn't see the need to sign a contract. Jan and Mick kept badgering us with their favourite catchphrase: 'Now, girls, just look at it this way: We all need to feel secure together, or it safeguards against one of us leaving the others in the lurch – or you need us, we get the gigs.' In my brain I was thinking, 'But I bought the van, made the clothes, which is commitment enough.' Anyway, we signed.

Before we did our German tour, we had a gig at the Galtymore Irish Club in Kilburn, London, and my mum, step-dad Geoff, Nan and Granddad, came down from Coventry to see us. They were thrilled to see us in our blue satin costumes singing and prancing around the stage, and I was thrilled that Nan had come, as she was due to go into hospital in a few weeks for an operation to sort her haemorrhoids out. As I was hugging and kissing my family after the gig, I gave my Nan an especially big hug to wish her well with her surgery, and as we embraced I had a very strong premonition. I get premonitions sometimes. I have had a few in my life, and when I hugged Nan, I felt that I would become very famous one day, I had a picture in my head of a massive amount of people and fans. In tandem with this, I knew my Nan would never get to see me sing again, or to see me become famous. My premonition was so sad and ominous, and I knew her haemorrhoids were something far more serious – I knew all this as we embraced.

In the weeks leading up to our departure for Germany we found three musicians: a drummer, bassist, and keyboard player, and prepared for the tour. It was so exciting on the departure day, driving to Dover, getting on the ferry to Ostend, and on to Germany. Our first gig was memorable only because we performed to a tent full of horny uniformed men and women, and I had a big tough woman in combats trying to get a kiss from me after!

On the second long journey of the German tour the van started to act strange, as did one of our band members, who I was initially attracted to and nearly did the 'wild thing' with him, until, on arousal, he started to get all crazy about his ex-girlfriend – how she'd left him for another and how he'd bought a shotgun and enough bullets for the ex, her new lover, and himself – after he'd shot the other two. I carefully extricated myself from his embrace, and kept my distance from then on. The poor fellow became more and more deranged as the tour progressed, and his nickname became 'I can't handle it'.

The van was breaking down daily, and towards the end of the tour some horny G.I. stole our lamé catsuits. I was mortified: a) because I kept imagining some big muscleman soldier trying to squeeze into our catsuits – Yuk! And b) because I had worked really hard making the bloody things. I had met some really nice soldiers on this tour, one poor lad was your basic home-grown hippy who'd been caught with a small amount of marijuana, and been given the choice of gaol or the military. There were a lot of those kinds of guys – poor bastards.

The last few days of the tour were terrible and the van just kept breaking down. Mick, our 'manager', didn't seem to have the wherewithal to sort anything out and some people were saying 'He couldn't put together a piss-up in a brewery.' We arrived back at about 3a.m. to the hotel we'd been staying at, where our rooms had been saved for us, and lo and behold, all of us except for me had strangers in our beds. The receptionist had gone for the night, and it was snowing outside, so we all slept together in one room. 'I can't handle it' started to sleep under the sink but decided he 'couldn't handle it.' Sleeping in the same room as all of us, he said 'I can't handle it' for the millionth time and went to sleep in the van. We found him with icicles sprouting from his beard the next morning.

On our drive back to England, Mick seemed to give up, and the drummer and I did all the driving home. On the boat nobody was talking to each other. Maggie and I didn't want to work with Jan and Mick ever again. 'I can't handle it' was in his own world, jabbering away about shooting his ex on arrival home. The drummer and bass player thought that Jan and Mick were dickheads, and I was heaving sighs of relief that it was over.

I arrived back to my flat in London where I'd left my new boyfriend and his four-year-old daughter to look after the place. I hadn't slept for forty-eight hours and had been driving non-stop. I opened the door expecting to just slide into bed to relax; to be home, and the place looked like a bomb had hit it. I was mightily pissed off with the boyfriend for not keeping my place clean and together, and was about to read him the riot act, when his little girl ran up to me hugging and kissing me. I melted quickly, but I knew I didn't want to be living with this man because we'd only just started our relationship before I'd left to go on tour. Partly because he was untidy, but mostly because he did cocaine and I started to get into it with him. Coke is such a self-centred and insidious drug. When you take it you feel great, you want to talk loads to the point of boring people, and you're full of the joys of spring and you want to stay up all night. When you run out of it, you become very greedy for the drug; moody, bad-tempered, and obsessively needing to find more.

I'd had enough of cocaine and the tour had helped me distance myself from it, and within the week of my return I ended the relationship. I dabbled for a while longer on the coke trail, but was cured for good and forever with the help of my friend's five-year-old daughter. A few of us coke friends had run out and had scoured London for more. We found a small amount and immediately started chopping lines, ready to start, when I had one of my psychic premonitions: My friend's five-year-old came into the room, but none of the addicted adults gave her a second glance. They were too busy anticipating the cocaine, but I noticed her, and knew what she'd do before she did it. She walked across the room to the table and blew all the cocaine away.

The adults erupted with anger at her and at that moment came my epiphany. She was obviously sick of having to share her parents' attention with a line of white powder, and I was sickened by the stream of abusive anger that was being dished out to her. I thought how disgusting we all were over the need to get high. Yuk! And that was that. Lucky really, 'cause I would never have got much else together in my life if I'd stayed in the cocaine zone.

Maggie of Lady Luck and I started another band. We called ourselves Orizaba. We did a photo shoot and a few gigs. Our final gig was in a club in Mayfair where some booking agents were coming to view us. I was very enthusiastic with my tambourine, slapping it against my thigh, which at times was exposed through the side slit in my homemade skirt. I thought I was the bees' knees. The next day Maggie phoned me to say the agents didn't like us, and thought I looked like a right old prostitute, as my thigh was full of bruises from the enthusiastic tambourine slapping. Maggie wanted to quit, so I said, 'Okay, but I'm going to carry on. I'm going to try to write my own songs.'

My Nan's operation had not gone as expected. They found cancer in her bowel. They decided to take the cancer and her bowel away and she was given a colostomy bag. Poor Nan, so much pain and indignity to go through, but we all thought it'll be okay now that they've cut the cancer away. I kept remembering the premonition I'd had earlier in the year at the Lady Luck gig and hoping she'd make it through. She recovered a few months after the operation and with Christmas coming we all thought, 'Phew, great! Nan is going to get better.' Then suddenly she seemed to worsen. The doctors told us the cancer had spread and she only had a few months left to live. We didn't tell her, because Mum and Granddad thought she would give up.
Christmas Day came and we all spent it together. St. Stephen's Day (Boxing Day) came and she went to bed very poorly, and didn't rise again. Her painkilling drugs were increased to the point where my Nan didn't seem to be present anymore. She was just a skin and bone, pain-ravaged, moaning old body. I remembered our closeness as a small child:
'What happens when we die, Nanny?' I'd ask as a little girl.
'I believe we go to a better place to be with God,' she'd answer.
'Nan, if you die before me, will you come back and tell me where you are and what it's like?'
'If I can, I will,' she had said.

Nan died on January 17th 1977. Mum phoned me in London to let me know she'd gone. It was too late to go home to Coventry that night. As I lay in my bed – tossing and turning, trying to get to sleep – I was terrified she would come and visit me as a ghost to tell me where she was. The dreadful thing was that I didn't want to see her cancer-dead self coming to me like a vision – I couldn't have handled it. Her cancer-dead self didn't come to haunt me and the next day I went to see her body. 'Where are you

Nan?' I said, as I looked down at that empty shell that once was my Nan. I kissed her cold hard forehead and left.

The day of Nan's funeral was dark and pouring with rain. I couldn't control my sobbing in the church service. Then we all got into the cars and went to the other side of Coventry to the Crematorium. At the Crematorium we were asked to wait, as there'd been a problem with the oven and there would be a twenty minute delay. I sat blubbering away in my grief. I could hear my Granddad talking in the back of the car about 'what a wonderful wife she was.' I didn't want to be cooped-up with anybody else's grief. Then something strange and gentle happened. I felt an urging to stop crying and look at the sky. 'Look over there,' the urging said. I wasn't interested initially; I wanted to wallow in my tears. 'Look over there,' I was re-urged. This time I looked across the dark sad sky and saw that a thin strip of bright sunlight – thin like a window blind – had just let an inch of the morning light through at the bottom. We went into the Crematorium Chapel, and halfway through I witnessed the whole room light up with sunshine that had been hitherto hidden. I fancied I saw her sitting in the beam of light which now crossed her coffin. Then the coffin went into the oven. When we came out of the chapel, the rain was gone, the sun shining, and a big, bold rainbow stood right over us. 'Thank you, Nan,' I thought. 'No hauntings, no ghosts, just a simple thing I can relate to. Darkness, rain, sun pushing through, and a rainbow has formed.' I was left with a message of hope. I tried to share this with Mum but she was too grief-stricken.

A week later I'd gone to Coventry to inter Nan's ashes in the churchyard, and as usual it was dark and rainy. It was terribly sad and gloomy all over again. Later that day while I was on the bus going back to the train station, I decided to get off at the cemetery alone. As I neared Nan's newly dug patch, I noticed the rain had ceased. I looked up to the sky thinking, 'I wonder?' and lo and behold, there was the rainbow again. 'Hello, Nan.' I always say 'Hello' when I see rainbows.

Our drummer, Malc, had showed me a few chords on the piano, and I started from there. I was shocked to find it so easy:

all it was, was eight chords; it couldn't be more complicated than that. There was really no hidden mystery. I was so shocked because I realised that I could write songs. I wasn't musically trained, and my dyslexia means that I see things in pictures, so when Malc showed me the chords on the piano, I could make sense of the shape of it. Five white notes and three black ones in between.

The first song I wrote was a sad, forlorn love song which never saw the light of day. Then something in the news moved me most passionately. A bomb had gone off in Berkley Square, London, and one poor man had taken his sandwiches there to have his lunch-break – then the bomb went off and that was the end of him. I thought of the irony of life, that there's me wishing someone would fall in love with me, and at the same moment there's that guy eating his sarnies, and boom, it's over. So I began a song which went:

'You drink your coffee,
 I sip my tea and we're sitting here playing so cool,
thinking what will be, will be.
 It's getting kinda late now,
 I wonder if you'll stay now, stay now, stay now, stay now.
 Or will you just politely say goodnight?'

This song was to become my most famous song in years to come, but back then in 1977, I shelved it.

I got together with different musicians doing a duet of pop songs in pubs with a Scottish friend called Alex, learning to play electric guitar on my new Gibson with some other pals, and all the time writing bits of songs. My brother Neil gave me lessons in the song-writing department. His band The Flys had just hit the jackpot. They'd produced their own single and sold it at gigs, and moved loads of them. Consequently EMI signed them to a huge record deal – we were so proud of them. It was all very exciting. They went on tour supporting the Buzzcocks. I went to see them and began my love of the New Wave. I started going out to all the punk and New Wave gigs. The Sex Pistols, Clash, Siouxsie and the

Banshees, the Ramones – there was so much to see and do. Suddenly music wasn't about beautiful people in designer clothes, it was about raw energy and I loved it.

I remember seeing a handsome fellow one night at a club, and he gave me a badge saying 'The Boomtown Rats', then he walked away. My pal said, 'That's Bob Geldof, the singer from the Boomtown Rats.' I thought he was very tasty. So when I saw they were doing a gig at the Rainbow Theatre in London's Finsbury Park, I hatched a plot to get to meet him; I wrote a letter saying how much I admired him, reminded him he'd given me the badge, and that I was now returning the badge – hoping to swop it for a backstage pass.

I hoped we could meet up before we both became too famous. What a daft, pretentious fan letter I wrote. Then I became very creative and dressed the letter up to look like a telegram. I drove to the backstage door of the Rainbow, put on my motorbike helmet (to look like a telegram delivery person) and declared, 'Telegram for Mr Geldof. Shall I take it to him?' 'No,' said the doorman. 'Just leave it with me.' That night I went to the gig – but surprise, surprise – there was no backstage pass. Funnily enough, I did manage to get backstage after the gig and spent the evening chatting to the band's publicist, B.P. Fallon, and a couple of years later I became very good mates with Bob and Paula Yates. I still bump into Bob from time to time, and quite recently he sent a message via a friend of ours to say he'd been going through some old papers and had found my fan letter!

Whilst at a gig at the Marquee, I was befriended by a very handsome fellow in a black leather jacket. We started dating; he was a drummer in a band which Chrissie Hynde was also briefly in. At that time I got to Andy Czezowski and his wife, Sue: both were inspirational people. Andy was the guy who started the Roxy, which was the most famous Punk Club in London. Adrian's neighbours had opened a recording studio next door to where we'd shared a home, and I would sometimes be around when people like the then unknown Adam and the Ants were there and I would listen in on their session.

In St. James Street in Covent Garden there was a building

housing a P.R. company, run by Alan Edwards, publicist extraordinaire of the New Wave scene, with such luminous clients as Blondie and The Stranglers. The Damned's manager had an office there, as did Andy Czezowski, and in the basement was a rehearsal room where some of the greats of Punk and New Wave rehearsed, including, Adam and the Ants, Chrissie Hynde, Shane MacGowen and his band The Nipple Erectors. I remember Chrissie Hynde being kind, by patiently showing me bar chords on my electric guitar, making me think how lucky I was to be in the middle of all the action. I went to the 100 Club one night to see a band called Sham 69. When they started the whole room erupted. Everybody was jumping and dancing – including me – and being small, I was on a stool and as I jumped around. As the stool fell from under me, I grabbed on to something next to me, which turned out to be a very embarrassed young man's bollocks – he was bright red and so was I. 'Sorry,' I said, then carried on dancing, 'cause that's how it was; raw, fun, and energetic!

Meanwhile my brother Neil and all The Flys had moved to London to record their debut album for EMI In their spare time they helped me to record a three song demo tape, of which I was very proud.

Things had been fine in my love life, then one sad day it was all wrecked in one foul swoop. We were at the Music Machine in Camden; we'd gone to see Siouxsie and the Banshees, which was fantastic. Then out of the blue my boyfriend got involved with another guy over somebody throwing a beer can. It didn't quite become a fight, but my boyfriend grabbed my hand and said, 'Come on, we're leaving.' I followed after him hoping he was okay – he seemed very angry. We walked up the street, him storming off ahead, me trying to catch him up. 'Are you okay?' I asked him. 'Course I'm not fucking okay, you silly bitch! I should have killed that guy!' he shouted. 'Hey, there's no need to take it out on me!' I said. Without anymore ado he turned on me with empty black eyes and punched me full in the face, then walked off saying: 'Fuck off you stupid bitch! It's all your fault.'

I was stunned, I hated him so much at that moment, and because of what I'd seen happen to my mum I'd promised myself never to stay with a woman beater. I was sad. 'It's over with him,' I thought. We'd been so loving and now he'd left me cold. He came back about five minutes later saying how sorry he was, crying. 'It'll never happen again. Please don't leave me.' So I foolishly gave him a second chance. It was almost as if I was sabotaging myself by hanging onto this man when I should have been forging ahead with my own music.

I had made friends around this time with Mick Jones of The Clash, and Glen Matlock, the original bass player of Sex Pistols, and author of such great songs as "Pretty Vacant". Although they were just friends, my boyfriend would get all wound up about my 'Art School Pop Star Friends'. I had met Glen as my brother's band were touring with The Rich Kids, which was Glen's new band since leaving The Sex Pistols. The lead singer was ex-Slik guitarist Midge Ure, who didn't really fit into the New Wave image, as Slik had been a very teeny-bop band, and Midge had also played with Thin Lizzy.

It was through Glen Matlock that I realised the importance of the song. He played a version of "Pretty Vacant" one night, and it was wonderful. It was really inspiring to hear a song that can be played in many different ways and it's just the fashion which decides really. That night, Glen played it in a more poppy way, because of course, Midge was lead singer in The Rich Kids, and it best suited his style.

My boyfriend's behaviour towards me became progressively more violent: anything from emptying a plate of spaghetti on my head, slashing my car tyres, and smashing stuff up in my house. I was forever phoning his manager Andy Czezowski after each outrage, as I'd always be worried about him doing worse to me – or indeed to himself. I banned him from coming to my house. Eventually I finished it with him, after he handed me an appointment card for the Venereal Disease Clinic. He'd contracted gonorrhoea and tried to blame it on me – implying that I'd been unfaithful.

I was breathing sighs of relief to be free of him, and hadn't seen hide nor hair of him for a few weeks, when suddenly he jumped into my car as I waited at traffic lights and demanded I drive him home. When we passed close to my house he demanded I bring him to my place, but I told him, 'No way, you always smash my flat up.' So he jumped out of my car and sprinted towards my front door. I followed him, trying to cajole him back into my car. At this point I should have left him, but I was scared he would just stay waiting at my door or smash my window to get in. I got out of the car and said, 'Come on, I'll give you a ride home.' 'I want to go to your place. I want to stay here,' he replied. 'Well you can't,' I said, rather too sharply, knowing how easily provoked his temper was.

His eyes darkened as they always did before a violent episode and he said, 'If I was one of your art school pop star friends you'd let me.' I ran, knowing he'd punch me any moment: the art school pop star line was always his warm-up line for violence. I'd nearly run to my friends Al and Annette's studio when he caught me. 'Leave me alone!' I screamed. Without further ado he punched me in the face and began dragging me back to my place.

Just as we neared my front door, I heard, 'Oi, you little coward! I saw you hit her from my flat – Are you all right, love?' the voice said to me. 'Yes, I'm fine thank you,' I said, fearing more trouble. The next second this bloke punched my ex squarely on the jaw. 'Do not punch women. Do you understand, you skinny little worm?' He then walked away. My ex was stunned, holding his jaw, then he ran at the guy from behind. 'You want some more?' said the guy. 'No, no,' said my ex, cowardly backing off. As soon as the guy was out of sight, my ex hurled the brick he had in his hand into my local newsagents window. I ran for my car and he managed to jump in with me. I wanted him gone, and my nose was sore and bleeding. He was spitting teeth and moaning about how his good looks could have been ruined, but he was very shocked to taste his own medicine.

A mile up the road, he jumped out of my car and disappeared into the night. This time I didn't pursue him, or go home. I went to my brother and The Flys band house and stayed the night. When I got home the next afternoon, I couldn't get into my front door as the lock was jammed with a broken-off key, because he'd obviously tried to break in. I went to my friends Al and Annette's studio around the corner. Annette opened the door saying, 'Thank God you're all right. Your boyfriend came to us late last night and told us about that guy from the flats attacking you both.' 'He's such a liar.' Annette said he'd spent the night at the studio with them and suggested I talk to him. Though I was scared of him, I did. He was so contrite by asking all kinds of forgiveness, saying he knew we were over, and would I meet him at his place for tea at 6p.m. that day, just to make sure we were both okay? I agreed, just to be done with him for good.

I got to his place at 6p.m. and said, 'I've got to be somewhere by 7.30, so I'll have a quick cup of tea, then I'll be off.' He started making tea and talked softly to me: 'I'm so sorry that I've been out of control with you sometimes. It's just that I get confused and upset sometimes, then I'm not sure what I'm doing. Do you remember I told you I'd been in gaol when I was sixteen?' I said, 'Yes.' He continued: 'Well, the reason was that I was driving my best friend and my girlfriend. It was my friend's car, but he'd drunk too much, and insisted I drive even though I was drunk and too young to drive. We had a terrible accident and they were both killed: She was decapitated; her head rolled along the road.' I listened intently and felt so sorry for him. What an awful memory to carry with him through life. 'I must go soon,' I said a little later. 'Please have another cup of tea; please stay a little longer,' he begged. So I did. He retold the story again and started to get emotional. I tried to gently leave again. This time he sprang to the door and locked it, taking the key out and pocketing it. Then he ran to a pill bottle and emptied it into his mouth, saying he was going to kill himself. He told the car crash story again. I made sympathetic noises and asked for the key so I could leave. He grabbed a razor blade, saying he was going to fix my face, so that nobody would look at me again, and then he would slash his wrists. Inside I was getting so angry, but I was trying not to let him see this as he seemed to feed off my fear and anger.

He then came towards me saying he wanted sex. I said 'No.' 'You'd let your art school, pop star friends.' I said, 'Don't be ridiculous. Just let me go home.' He jumped on top of me, he hit me, he tried to prise my legs apart and eventually he managed to do so. He had his sex and I lay motionless. After he'd finished, he started crying. 'I'm so sorry, Hazel. You made me do it though.' I asked weakly, 'Please let me go home.' It was 5.50a.m. and I'd been subjected to his madness and imprisonment for nearly twelve hours. 'I'll let you go if I can come and sleep at your house,' he said. 'All right,' I said, just wanting to get free from his locked flat. 'But you'll have to sleep in the spare room. There's no way you can sleep with me; not after what's just happened.' He agreed and unlocked the door. We didn't talk much on the way to my house. I just wanted to escape from him and started formulating a plan. As soon as he'd gone to sleep I would run round to Al and Annette's. Their place was a recording studio, as well as their home, so I was hoping there would be an all-night recording session in progress.

At my house he began undressing. His top came off, and as he unzipped his jeans he said, 'I want to sleep in your bed with you.' 'No, I told you that's not an option; you promised you wouldn't start.' With his jeans now at his ankles, he said, 'If I was one of your pop star art school friends you'd let me...' The minute I heard his cue line I ran like the wind, hoping he'd be stuck with his jeans around his ankles. No such luck. As I ran round the corner I saw him hot on my trail, dressed only in underpants and socks. I hammered at Al and Annette's door. Al opened it just as the ex caught up with me. 'Help me, Al!' I said. The ex grabbed my hand, and tried to pull me back with him – Al grabbed the other hand. The ex started hurling abuse at Al. 'Get the fuck off her or I'll smash your skull in! Fuck off and leave us alone!' I looked at Al and said, 'It's all right, Al. I'll go back with him, but please will you come over to my house in five minutes to make sure everything's okay?' I went back with the maniac in his stockinged feet and underpants. Al and Annette came over within five minutes. We made hot chocolate for all of us – the ex had an extra addition to his. Annette brought me a strong sleeping pill, which I crushed and added it to the maniac's hot chocolate. Al and Annette left. The ex fell asleep. I left and went to stay with Al and Annette the minute he fell asleep.

I never came close enough to get into harm's way with that

guy again. And he did me one good turn by putting me in touch with Andy Czezowski, who was to make such a difference in my life. Ironically, it was also through my ex-boyfriend that I met one of my best friends, Vickie. I'd begun sharing my flat with ex-Vibrators bass player, Gary Tibbs. He'd talked about his ex-girlfriend Vickie who he'd just parted from. I met a few of Gary's amours who later became famous. Jennie Matthias (AKA Jenny McKeown and Jenny Bellestar) of the Belle Stars, and a lovely girl who worked at Decca, called Siobhan Fahey, who eventually became one of Bananarama; but Gary was still obsessed with his ex, Vickie. One day he stormed in saying that my ex was now going out with his ex. He came home hours later scratched, torn, and bloodied. He'd gone to Vickie's, caught my ex there, and started a fight. My ex was shouting, 'Not my face, man!' and Gary and Vickie ended up fighting. Vickie ran out to her car with my ex. They drove off with Gary on the roof, bashing at her windscreen. She braked – he was propelled off. He came back to my place in a rage.

I decided to go to my ex's place and warn Vickie that she's getting involved with a violent girl-basher. I'd never met her before, and had only heard about her from Gary. When we met we instantly liked each other. We became firm friends from that moment on, and are still as close as sisters, and I'm her daughter's godmother. She and my ex didn't last long – luckily for her.

From then on I decided that there would be no more man trouble. I would make my next moves as properly as possible. This meant getting a manager first, then a record deal. I also decided to print a bright pink poster and stickers with a picture of me, saying, 'Where is Montana Wildhack?' which was a very obscure reference to a character out of Kurt Vonnegut's *Slaughterhouse-Five*. I had already been slapping these posters and stickers all over London and the Tube stations. (The original posters and stickers were used in *Breaking Glass*.) The thinking behind the posters and stickers was this: Whenever I travelled on the underground, I'd seen this great-looking guy, in a great-looking poster, with just his name on it – Johnny Cougar – and I was always looking at him wondering, what do you do? Are you a model? Are you an advert? An advert for what? Even though I didn't know what it was all about, I knew his name, and I knew his face. 'The power of publicity,' I thought. My poster was a poor imitation of this, I admit, but it was a good effort.

My search for a manager brought me to a guy called Dave Wernham, who managed a band called The Tourists. The Tourists had an old acquaintance from my Adrian days playing guitar with them – a guy called Dave Stewart. Dave used to run a second-hand record stall in the Swiss Cottage Market. I really liked Dave Wernham and we got on very well, but he was busy enough with the Tourists, so he said, 'Go and see Dai Davies at Albion. They've got more money than me.' So I did.

Albion consisted of a management company that took care of the Stranglers, Ian Gomm and 999. They also had a record label and a publishing company. I met Dai Davies, Derek Savage, and the guy who ran their publishing, John Telfor. When I told them about my posters they all laughed, and seemed to like me. They had a good pedigree, having The Stranglers. Then John Telfor played me a song called "Is She Really Going Out With Him?" by a new singer/songwriter on their publishing roster, by the name of Joe Jackson. John really wanted to do a publishing deal with me. Dai Davies and Derek Savage suggested we make a single and see how it goes. They were certainly enthused by my songs, my energy, and my cheek; and at that time they held nearly all the major London venues – and they wanted me. This wasn't exactly what I wanted because I felt I needed the guidance of a manager first. But nobody was begging me to let them manage me, so I thought, 'I really like John Telfor and I would feel safe with him.'

Derek and Dai wanted me to sign both a publishing (i.e. songwriting) and record deal. I took the contracts they offered me to Ian Adam, my brother's lawyer. The publishing deal worked out at £40 per week on a five-year commitment. The record deal was for one single with a possible extension, and for signing this contract, I was offered £1. Ian said I could sign the single deal, as it was not a huge time-binding contract, but he had a lot of changes to make on the publishing.

Thus I began my relationship with Albion. They wanted to

record "Ee-I-Addio" for the single, and a song called "Billy" for the B-side. They were the first songs I had written but I wouldn't have chosen either because I didn't think they were my best. But they insisted. I thought: 'Well, they're paying the record bill, and they probably know better than me, being management, records and publishing.'

My first proper recording session had Rusty Egan on drums, Glen Matlock on bass, Steve New on guitar, and Clive Langer producing. It was okay, but nobody doing the session liked the songs anymore than I did, so the result wasn't spectacular. I didn't choose the songs, Albion chose. Albion just put it on the shelf, telling me to go write some 'hit singles' – a phrase I have heard a million times since, whenever a record company or publisher can't figure out what to do with an artiste. I told them, 'I have plenty of songs, just give me some gigs and I'll prove it!' I put a band together comprising a couple of lads from The Boys and Gary Tibbs. We played at the Rock Garden in Covent Garden and the Nashville, both in London, both controlled by Albion.

A budding young music journalist from Belfast called Dave McCullough spotted me, liked me, and wrote about me, saying I was a cross between Barbara Windsor and Debbie Harry. Suddenly Albion wanted to make an album, and tie me to a long-term contract - funny that; as soon as favourable publicity comes your way everybody and his brother wants to own you.

By this time I had no money and was becoming very depressed. A fellow called Dave, who worked for Albion, was going to see a wonderful faith healer and he asked if I wanted to meet her. Anything was worth a try, I thought. The healer was a wonderful lady, very down to earth. She put her hands by my belly, and said, 'You have troubles with your periods; you must take vitamin B6 – and you're depressed. I'd like you to read this book.' I'd expected a lot more hocus-pocus, but that was it; B6 and read a book. The book was called *Bring Out The Magic In Your Mind*, by Al Koran.

I read it from cover to cover and then I read it again. I didn't like the way it was written much, as it was in the style of those American quick-fix books. But the content shone through to me, especially the chapter on visualisation. The concept being that we are all transmitters and receivers, and if we transmit our message or our needs, then the message will be picked up and acted on by another receiver somewhere. The fundamental part of this process is total belief, total faith, imaging that you have actually received what you are asking for before it has physically arrived. So I began the process. I imagined something life-changing and wonderful was just around the corner, coming to me very soon. I let my imagination run riot, and I felt on the verge of something very special.

    I couldn't pay my rent and I heard that the telephonist from my record company was going on holiday for two weeks. 'Could I take her job over while she's away?' I asked. They kindly let me. The first morning on the phones was hectic because I'd never done a receptionist job before, and putting the phone-calls through to the right offices was a nightmare. Lunchtime came and everybody left the building. The calls came few and far between. I sat eating my sandwiches when the phone rang. 'Hello! Albion Records, can I help you?' 'Yes, I'd like to speak to the boss, please,' said the female voice on the end of the phone. 'I'm sorry, he's out on his lunch break.' 'Can I speak to someone else in charge then please?' she said. 'Well, actually, I'm the only one here. Can I help, or take a message?' I said. 'My name is Beth Charkham, from Charkham's casting agency. We're trying to contact a singer on your label called Hazel O'Connor.' Well, I nearly fell off my chair. 'I'm Hazel O'Connor,' I spluttered, trying not to sound as shocked as I felt. 'Oh no,' said Beth, 'the Hazel O'Connor we're looking for is a singer.' 'Yes,' I said, 'yes, that's me, I'm a singer, and I'm answering the phones as well!' 'Well, Hazel, we've had your name passed on to us, and we're wondering would you like to come to our office tomorrow, and meet us? We're casting parts for a new punk musical film. The Director Brian Gibson will be here and he'd like to see you.' 'Oh my God,' I thought. 'The exciting thing just around the corner that I've been visualizing has arrived!' I got even more excited and the butterflies in my belly were going crazy.

    When I went to meet Brian Gibson at Charkham's casting

company the next morning, I was chaperoned by Dai Davies, who kind of invited himself along and I let him. Brian and I got along very well. When lunchtime arrived, he invited Dai and myself to eat with him. At the restaurant Brian and Dai did most of the talking, with Brian asking zillions of questions about New Wave bands and gigs, and about The Stranglers, another act of Dai's, and his partner Derek Savage. I hardly spoke and felt like a spare prick at a wedding. Then two days later I was invited to audition for United Artists.

So there I was at an audition which was to change my life. I was resolved to become an actress, singer, and soundtrack composer, and as I left the audition, it was becoming a distinct possibility.

****

PART TWO
BE CAREFUL WHAT YOU WISH FOR

CHAPTER SIX

'Wot can I do up here in the zoo, I've been here much
longer than I remember, remember.
Wot can I say, will there be a day when we can all leave
this place forever, forever
At the zoo you, you, wot do you do
At the zoo you, you we perform for you
At the zoo you, you wot do you care
You just stand there and stare.'
"The Zoo" (*Sons & Lovers*, 1980)

Chapter Six

Brian Gibson was the first person who seemed to really believe in my artistic abilities. We had great empathy with each other. But he also used to say that I'd probably end up a recluse like Julie Christie, living alone up a mountain with a bunch of dogs. Of course, I do now live up a mountain in Ireland, without a partner with my three dogs as my only companions. This isn't at all the way I envisaged my life going and perhaps when I used the *Bring Out The Magic In Your Mind* book I should have had a longer-term plan. Nonetheless, once the ball started rolling, I was so burnt out I never had time to spare, or space to dream up a better life plan; and of course, that old adage, 'be careful what you wish for: it may just happen', has often come back to haunt me. Maybe I didn't wish for the right things; the things that would make me happy. But all said and done, singing has always made me happy: it's just the business of singing, as in the music biz, that has definitely not brought much happiness.

It was now two months since the film audition. The producers had stayed in touch for a while, asking to hear my songs, but slowly I felt they had forgotten me. I had been recording an album for Albion Records with Vic Maile (producer of Dr Feelgood) at a snail's pace – Vic was a great producer, but every time I wanted to play my own keyboard parts, seeing as I'd written the song on keys, and the feel of the song came from the way I played, Vic would say patronisingly, 'Now, now little Hazel, you can go and make the tea, and we'll get a proper musician to play the keyboard parts.'– Grrrr! I did further gigs with a different set of musicians, and had a tiny altercation with the bass player, who felt that he had co-written a song because of the bass line he'd added.

When we all went into the Albion offices one fateful March afternoon in 1979, to collect £5 each, Dai and Derek said: 'What's the point in holding a band together, who are going to try to claim they wrote your songs?' So it disbanded. I went into their office for a meeting with Dai and Derek. The office had one long table with a window facing the visitor – me in this instance – and Dai and Derek sat either end, so that my head was ping-ponging between the two, or facing the sun flooding in the through the window, blinding me like some old brainwashing technique.

Derek Savage put a contract on the table in front of me. 'We think it's about time you signed the long-term record deal, Hazel.' 'I'm not supposed to sign it yet. My lawyer Ian Adam told me there are still some clauses he's not happy with.' 'Oh come on, Hazel,' said Derek, 'you can trust us. We've been pouring money into your album on spec, just on trust. The film company haven't contacted you, and no one else is showing any interest.' 'Yeah,' said Dai, 'and anything your lawyer doesn't like we can change tomorrow. Haven't we shown you that you can trust us? Let's get the signature done.'

Oh God, I *so* wanted to trust them. Wouldn't it be a wonderful world if we could trust each other, with no need for lawyers, and no need for wars? It sounds like a John Lennon lyric from "Imagine"! I tried to stay firm: 'No. My lawyer said no, I must wait.' They said, 'We've already shown good faith and spent a lot of money on you.' They were playing the guilt-trip card, and I felt myself softening. 'Look, Hazel,' said Dai most reasonably, 'you can trust us, and let's face it, who else would you trust? Not the band. They're already trying to get money out of you for your song.' My defences were crumbling. 'And when the time is right, we'll get you the right band, the right tours, and the right producers,' said Derek.

I thought, 'I just want a safe haven,' and I crumbled. 'I can definitely change anything tomorrow if my lawyer isn't happy?' I asked. 'Of course you can, Hazel,' they said in unison. I signed, and I started to feel weepy. A little voice inside me was saying, 'Don't do it, don't be so stupid,' but another voice was saying, 'Lay down your load and trust them.'

After signing a five-year record contract with no up-front money, they pushed a five-year publishing deal in front of me saying, 'You might as well sign this one as well. Your lawyer doesn't have any problem with this one, does he?' Tears filled my eyes – Why was I giving in so easily? Well, one reason, I suppose is that I had been receiving £40 a week from this writer's contract, and I had no money from anywhere else to live on. So I signed.

They then pushed a management contract in front of me, but this time I drew the line. 'No, I'll find a separate manager, thank you,' I said, snivelling at my own foolishness. It's sad that I didn't sign that management contract, because if I had done, I could have walked away from all of their bloody contracts. Because the law takes the view that it's illegal to own every money-making avenue of an artiste, it's known as conflict of interest.

I left the Albion office feeling raped. My lawyer went ballistic and immediately wrote to them saying the contracts were not valid, because I didn't have my lawyer's final approval. They, of course, changed nothing the next day because they didn't have to, and I believe, in retrospect, that they needed to get me tied to their company quickly, because, lo and behold, a few days later the film company phoned me at home, saying they were now considering me for the lead role, and there was only one other contender.

The contender, I later found out, was a wonderful singer/songwriter called Linda Lovich. In fact the only thing against her was that she was already famous. I think perhaps Albion already knew that I was now being considered for the lead role, as all communications went through their offices, and if I was totally linked to them they could make a lot of money out of the possible fame and record sales that might come as a spin-off from me becoming a film star. As I said, I was still a contender at this point, and before they could make their mind up, they wanted to see a gig. This was a huge problem, as Albion had talked me into disbanding my musicians a few days prior to this. Then the bass player, Andy, who'd been hassling for some song writing money, phoned me and said, 'Listen, Hazel, I hear you've got the chance to play lead in this film so we'll help you. We'll do the gig, don't worry.' And I bless that guy every day for his selflessness. We did the gig supporting the Ruts. The audience looked and acted fantastic. The band was great, and when I came off stage Brian Gibson, the director, and the producers, Davina Belling and Clive Parsons were very excited. They said I had the part and the script would be delivered the next day.

The script arrived and I felt it wasn't up to scratch, in terms of being life-like or streetwise. The song lyrics in the script didn't seem to have much cop either. I found a page with some lyrics which were supposed to represent a song with swear words which couldn't get radio airplay. I thought, 'I'm sure I could do better,' and I began the first song for *Breaking Glass*, "Big Brother":

'They tear out your heart throw it neatly in the cart
'Cause that's what they do with the scum like me and you
And you feel as if you died whilst you're standing on the line
And you wonder all the time why can't you cry
'Cause the people in control don't care for you, dear,
You're just a robot with a job to do
And when your use's exhausted they'll be rid of you as soon as look at you
Go to the back of the queue
B-B-Big Brother's got no heart
When I get my chance I'm going the kick him in the ah, ah, ah, ah, arse.'

In tandem I wrote a song called "Blackman" and took the two songs into Brian, Davina and Clive, as they'd been talking about getting some top, well-known songwriters like Elvis Costello to write the film score. I was just chancing my arm. I'd only written four songs before *Breaking Glass*. I blagged all the way through, because I really wanted it. I wanted to write all the songs, and to make the kind of album I really wanted to make, not the thing I'd been slowly recording for Albion.

They liked the songs and Davina said, 'Perhaps we should let Hazel write all the songs.' So I just kept writing and showing them. 'If you wrote the songs, who would be your choice of record producer?' Davina asked. 'There's only one,' I said. 'Tony Visconti, David Bowie's producer.' 'Well let's get him in for a meeting, 'was the response.

I couldn't believe it. Suddenly my life was changing so drastically, and my opinions were being listened to and noted.

This is what I'd visualised those few months back at the audition. Brian Gibson also wanted to re-write the script. The original script was about a boy singer trying to 'make it' during the punk era; it followed his relationship with his band, his manager, and his fame. Now it was to be about a girl singer, and I was that girl. So Brian and I began a very creative working relationship, where I'd phone him with some new song lyrics. He would write a scene around the themes of that song, like "Monsters in Disguise", which was written expressly and absolutely about Margaret Thatcher's Britain after I saw a news-clip of her trying to bring back the death penalty into English Law. I worried they would use this Law to deal with the political problems in Northern Ireland, or with the escalating violence of the miners strikes. Britain in the late 70s was a smouldering fire of discontent, and I was so happy to have the opportunity to write about it in all the *Breaking Glass* songs.

Within days I was sitting outside Davina and Clive's office in Notting Hill Gate, waiting to go in and meet my idol Tony Visconti, one of the kings of record production. I was going to show them a song I had written a year before called "Will You". I had played the tune on the piano at home and recorded the melody on cassette. I was now about to sing it live against my home-made backing track. They called me in to join the meeting. This was the first time I'd set eyes on Tony Visconti. He was in his early thirties, handsome, dark-haired, black-clothed. He was the legendary record producer from New York who produced David Bowie, T. Rex, and Phil Lynott, and married to the 60s Eurovision singer Mary Hopkins.

I said, 'I've written a new song; a sort of love song. Shall I put my cassette player on and sing it?' I began: 'You drink your coffee, I sip my tea,' etc., etc. I felt the thrill of energy go round the room. Even though my homemade piano track was crap full of mistakes, my song got top approval. Tony Visconti later told me that during the meeting, when he heard my other songs, he felt I was like a million other New Wave songwriters of that time, but when I sang that song, he was hooked and knew he could produce a unique album with me. The vision was complete. I was starring in the film, a new script was coming, I was writing all the songs, performing them, and had world famous producer Tony Visconti at the helm of that album.

We demoed three songs, one of them being "Will You", at Tony's Goodearth Studio in Soho, London. Then I had to do a photo shoot: the idea was a before and after set of photos. There was a makeup artist who did my face – a bit too much for my taste – and I was put into clothes I don't think I'd have bought. Anyway, I played along. Towards the end I was told to now do the makeup my own way, and put my own clothes back on for the last photo – Hazel the rough diamond. The funny thing is that the photo that everyone chose to use for publicity was the one with my own clothes and makeup!

At this point, unbeknownst to me, the film nearly didn't happen as United Artists – the financers – withdrew from the project because they were thirty million over budget with a Michael Cimino film called *Heaven's Gate*, starring Kris Kristofferson. Luckily, Clive and Davina went to Cannes Film Festival and met up with a young Egyptian man called Dodi Fayed who wanted to invest in a good movie project. His company Allied Stars financed the movie – the first of many. His next movie, *Chariots of Fire*, went on to land quite a number of Oscars. Allied Stars would also finance the soundtrack album. I ceased working on the album for Albion Records and started full-time preparations for the film.

It was quite a busy schedule as I had songs to write, dance training every morning, and I had to go clothes shopping. I preferred second-hand clothes and remodelling them, so wardrobe designer Monica Howe and I went searching the second-hand emporiums of London. I was asked to come to the leading man auditions and to read scenes with them to see who 'clicked'. Brian Gibson had asked me to watch *Quadrophenia* to see what I thought about Phil Daniels, as we would be meeting Phil quite soon. His performance was great in *Quadrophenia*, and sure enough he was coming to 'read a scene with me'. Phil came in wearing his mod suit (inherited from his last movie) and a cheeky grin. The scene we were doing was where his character (the manager) shows his artist girlfriend Kate (my character) a new flat he's purchased. The line was 'Voila! A new flat!' When he came to this bit he says 'Viola!' (as in big violin) 'A new flat!' I just fell about laughing. He was great, whether by design or not, I knew we'd have the chemistry.

I needed a manager to make sure I made no more contract/career boo-boos. I really liked a young P.R. called Alan Edwards, who I'd known from James Street, Covent Garden. His offices were now below Albion's in Oxford Street. I asked him if he would manage me. He said he'd give it a whirl and we began one of the best creative relationships I have had in this business.

I was told I would have to get my weight down to eight stone. I would normally be around nine stone but the film puts a stone on a person. I had to attend improvisation sessions with Phil Daniels and Peter Hugo Daley. Brian Gibson would log all the things we said and then convert this into the new script. He would always be asking me about my life and situations I'd been in, in the music biz. He'd ask about Dai and Derek at Albion, and he definitely modelled Phil Daniels's manager character on my own manager, Alan Edwards. The story that developed was that of a struggling singer who meets her manager whilst she's putting up her own posters, and how he helps her to make it, in spite of a couple of unsavoury agents, modelled on Dai and Derek, and how fame is ruinous to her mental health and she cracks up.

Mornings were dance training, afternoons acting sessions. I went to Brighton for a week to write the soundtrack. Before the filming began the soundtrack had to be recorded. Making the album with Tony was the most exciting time. "Will You" was recorded double length, and the session sax player Wesley McGoogan played a choice of six sax solos, which Tony Visconti mixed into one fine composite solo. The only song I hadn't written was the big scene of the film. I had the tune written but the lyric eluded me until the night before it had to be sung and recorded. I went to my bible for inspiration. Yes, I thought. The arrogance of man shown like God's seven days of creation in Genesis, and "Eighth Day", my first hit, was born.

Filming started in Production Village, Cricklewood (*forget*

Hollywood!) in autumn 1979. The acting talent in it was phenomenal: Phil Daniels, Mark Wingate (now of *The Bill* TV drama), Jonathan Pryce, Jim Broadbent, Jon Finch (who'd played *Macbeth* in the Polanski film of that title), and my old flatmate Gary Tibbs, who ended up playing the bass player in the film. A title for the movie came up during one of mine and Brian Gibson's 'think tank' get-togethers. I said that it seemed like my character Kate was bottled up and needed to smash the glass to get out: smashing glass, breaking the bottle... *Breaking Glass*... 'Yes!' we shouted in unison. Thus the *Breaking Glass* film and soundtrack was born.

Every morning was a struggle for me – it was like being in a factory. Up at 6a.m.. 6.30: out to the film studio, Samuelsons Production Village in Cricklewood London. 7: makeup, 7.30: hair, 8: wardrobe, 8.30: rehearsal, 9: start filming. Most lunch hours were taken up with publicity interviews, and I suppose because I was unknown, had written all the songs, and was a non-actor playing the leading lady, I was big news and everyone wanted to talk to me and photograph me. And my stories about being a runaway cabaret dancer in Beirut or crossing the Sahara were most welcome.

Davina, our producer, watched me like a hawk when afternoon tea and sticky buns came out – I was still on my diet. She'd appear from nowhere saying, 'Should you be eating that, Hazel?' 'No!' I'd say, and put the cream cake back pronto. Dodi Fayed would come in every day to see how things were progressing and was most courteous to us all. Brian Gibson had put together a fantastically talented crew, including people like cameraman Kelvin Pike, famous for his *Star Wars* camera work, and Monica Howe, fresh from the *Midnight Express* film. Pat Hay was responsible for my *pierrot* makeup, and Sara Monzani for my thatched blonde bobbed hair. All the actors and technicians helped and encouraged me to do my best. It was a huge learning curve for me, though. For three months I had no life at all outside the movie.

Brian Gibson had warned Phil Daniels and me not to become romantically involved, as this was a common occurrence between leading characters in acting jobs and Brian felt it might dissipate the buzz between us. During rehearsals before filming began Phil and I were left alone by our dear director in his house – I think he was leaving us alone on purpose to see if we'd get frisky! Anyway, we did get a little smoochy and then we remembered what Brian had said, so we refrained from further action. Phil taught me so much about acting. I consider myself a very lucky novice to have got to act opposite such a talent.

I learned quickly, though, by watching all those great actors work. Brian was always there to help me. He was an actor's director. He would talk you through the part and listen to what you had to say about it. Because he also wrote a lot around us doing our improvisation beforehand, it was very important to him that emotions were real and true. As he had just finished doing a big piece with Colin Welland and Helen Mirren, he brought me out to lunch to meet her. He wanted me to discuss my role with her, because she is a very giving woman. I thought she was great; really wonderful.

Brian would also make me practise something from *Uncle Vanya*, or *The Seagull* to find certain emotions. Anna's speech out of *The Seagull* was a particular favourite. I had been afraid of doing any scenes that had me crying, as I found it hard to 'find the emotion,' but once I was shown how to do it, like the other actors, I got really excited if there was a really meaty scene to be played that day. My acting coach gave me an exercise where I pretended to tell her I'd just run a person over with my car and I couldn't find an emotion, so she changed it and said, pretend now that you ran a dog over, and I found the emotion immediately. The other thing Brian Gibson had me do was to sit in front of a mirror and try to feel attractive, with a picture of Marilyn Monroe next to me – it took a long time, as I've never felt pretty – but Brian was always there to coach me through any problems

The worst problem for me was getting up in the morning and then straight into hair and makeup, then cast and crew would have a breakfast break. Usually the lighting guys ('sparks', as they'd be called) would have the scene lit and ready to go at 8.30a.m. Sometimes the simplest thing in filming can take hours and something I thought would be tough is whizzed through. I smoked cigarettes then, and I realised that in film-making, actors sit around waiting most of the time, so I'd smoke zillions of cigarettes. This is when I realised that with four months of this work I'd really be hurting my lungs just smoking out of boredom, so I endeavoured to give it up.

I learned new words like 'eye lines', which meant where a person looks when they are doing their 'close-up'. A close-up is when only your face is in shot, and in film – less is always more – the camera picks up so much that it's very easy to overdo it and look like a 'ham' (a ham is when an actor overdoes it and it doesn't look real). Anyway, I was learning as I went along and, thanks to all my co-workers, I got through it. Brian was always there to help me. He was what actors call 'an actors' director'. The working day would be broken for an hour's lunch, but I was nearly always doing a press interview with my lunch – we'd work until 5.30p.m., and sometimes, if Brian could get the go-ahead from Clive, Davina and Dodi, we'd go into overtime; maybe not getting home until midnight.

There is a union rule called the twelve-hour rule that says if an actor has gone into overtime he or she can't be called in again for twelve hours, so one can rest. Brian and I had our only argument ever over this point. He wanted me to waive the twelve hour rule, which would mean that I would be back to work in six hours, with no time to unwind or to have a proper sleep. I said no and he called me a bitch, but I didn't come in – I needed my sleep.

I did get very ill during filming and as I was needed every day, I had no time to get better. I came into work and couldn't keep my head upright. I just wanted to lay down, which was not possible on a film schedule, as it costs big money to let a leading lady go home for a few days. The film doctor was called in. He'd seen many knackered starlets in his life. He told me he cared for Judy Garland and Marilyn Monroe when they were filming in Britain. He gave me an injection of vitamins in my bum, and those 'vitamins' got my heart pumping so fast that my body felt like an animated rag doll. Luckily we were filming the 'big brother' sequence so my jagged movements worked. I was then given a weekend to recuperate.

Towards the end of filming, Tony Visconti asked if I'd like to meet David Bowie as he'd be recording at Tony's studio in a few days time. Would I ever? David Bowie was a big influence for me.

On the night of the 'meet', I'd left a pile of tried-on and discarded outfits on my bedroom floor. Finally, decision made, I took the bus to Soho. I stood at the Studio entrance trying to calm myself. I was just too excited. I was 'buzzed' in, and as I made my way downstairs into the basement studio, Tony beckoned me into the control room. There was the thin white duke singing "Ground control to Major Tom" on the other side of the glass – What a buzz!

Tony introduced us in his office, which was a place full of David Bowie and Thin Lizzy Platinum and Gold Discs. I felt so silly and little. Then David said, 'Tony tells me you're making a music film.' 'Yes,' I said shyly. 'What are they calling it?' he asked. '*Breaking Glass*,' I said. 'They must have named it after my song "Breaking Glass"?' he asked. 'No,' I said. 'I could write some songs for you for the film maybe,' he said. 'No thank you, David. They're already written and recorded, but thank you.' He turned round and smiled: 'I hear you cut Tony's hair. Could you give me a haircut?' he asked sweetly. How could I refuse the chance to cut my hero's hair? I didn't have my cutting scissors with me, so I made do with the office shears, and there were no clean towels to put around his shoulders, so a dirty tea-towel sufficed. God it was scary – What if I made a terrible slip-up? His assistant Corinne was watching my every move. Anyway, I finally finished, swooshed the fallen hair away with the dirty tea-towel, and as Phil Daniels would say, '*Viola*! A new hairdo, Mr. Bowie.'

The next day at work we were filming with a lot of extras, who all looked like they would be Bowie fans, and I felt so lucky. Most of *Breaking Glass* was shot chronologically, so by the time the 'Eighth Day' scene was being done, I did feel like a robot girl. The costume for that scene was made from a nude plaster cast of my body, to make a mould for the plastic see-through armour I wore. It looked brilliant with the special FX material laced through it. There was one *major* defect, however: no way to go to

Left: Great Grandad Kettle who died young after being run over by a dray horse.

Right: Nan and Grandad's wedding, 24th September 1924. *(Weale)*

Mum and Dad's wedding.

Mum and Nan.

Mum as a youngster with Nan and Grandad.

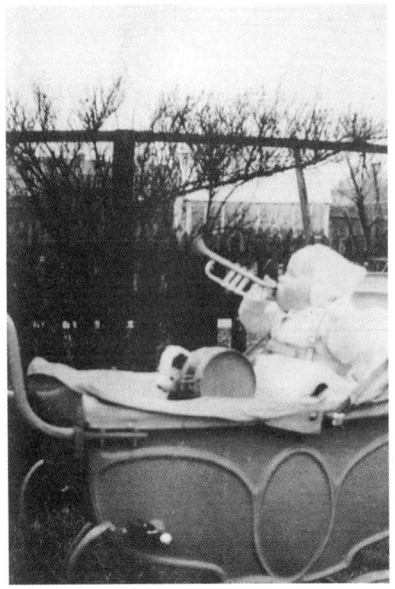

Above: 3 years old - a natural blonde, with Neil.
Left: Blowing my own trumpet.

Right: Aged 9, wearing a dress made from curtains.

At the fairground with Mum and Neil. I am 5 and Dad is behind the camera.
We are still happy together then.

Happy families.
Dad, Mum Neil, me and Nan standing in front of Dad's car on a day out.

At the seaside in Wales.
Mum, Neil, me, Nan and Grandad.

Above: Young teenagers, with our cousin Sarah.

Left: Aged 11 with Mum and Neil.

Above: With Neil, Geoff and his son Pete in our hippy days. Wearing another curtain dress.

Left: 19 years old in Kyoto, Japan.

English lesson students in Tokyo circa 1974.

Modelling, 19-20 years old.

Modelling, 19-20 years old.

Cabaret girls in Tokyo. I'm bottom right with my friend Dash top right. She was the first one of us to get a Japanese boyfriend and start speaking the lingo. Magali top left was the last girl to try to learn Japanese. We'd been there five months before she tried!

The satin jumpsuits that I made for Lady Luck. Not out of curtains this time!

Adrian. My first love. I would have gone to the ends of the earth with him. We're still dear friends today.

Above: In the tiny changing room at the Crazy Horse, Beirut, brushing my hair, chatting to Françoise, our dance captain.

Left: Lebanese driving licence - My first driving licence.

Below: Sitting in one of Adrian's classic cars in 1975.

"Eighth Day" iconic picture in my robot suit. *(Courtesy of Mohamed Al-Fayed)*

Who is Montana Wildhack? Self-made poster used in the opening sequence of *Breaking Glass*.

WHO IS?
MONTANA WILDHACK

Scene from *Breaking Glass*. *(Courtesy of Mohamed Al-Fayed)*

Birthday party at Cannes Film Festival. *(Alan Davidson / The Picture Library)*

With Phil Daniels, our first portrait together. *(Unknown)*

With Davina Belling, Clive Parsons and Laurence Myers. *(Unknown)*

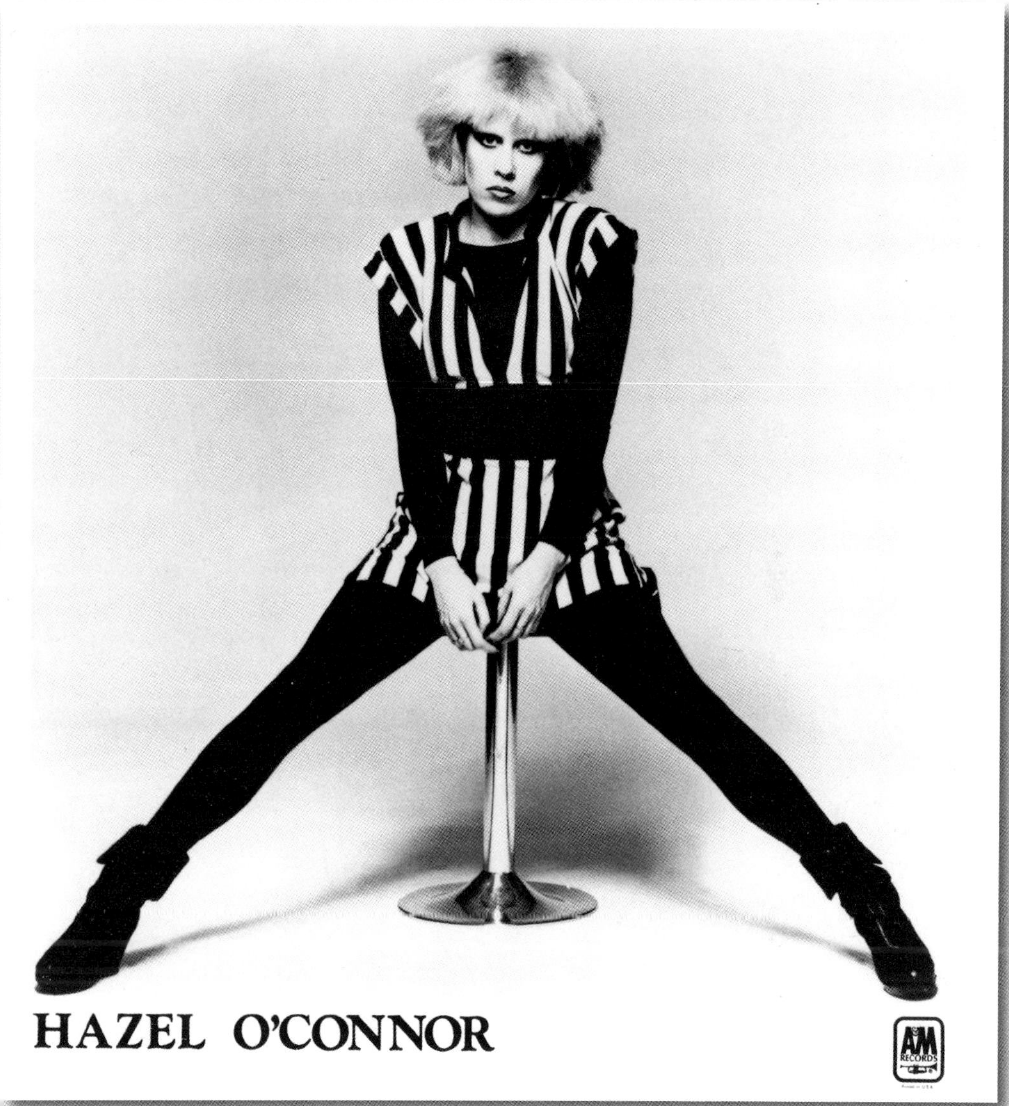
HAZEL O'CONNOR
A&M RECORDS

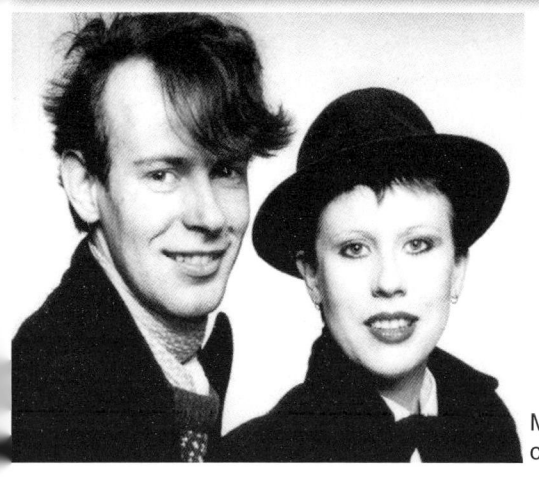

Being impaled. *(Brian Aris)*

My first publicity shot with my brother, a far cry from our toddler photos. *(Unknown)*

Above: Dad and his wife Doreen at the *Breaking Glass* premiere. *(Unknown)*

Right: Holding my Best Film Actress 1980 Variety Club of Great Britain award with Ronnie Corbett and Ronnie Barker. *(Unknown)*

Above: First press shot of Megahype. L to R: Neil O'Connor, Ed Case, myself, Wesley McGoogan, Wild Oscar and Andy Quinta (nicknamed "Roots" after Kunta Kinte the hero of the TV drama Roots.) *(Unknown)*

Above: Having a laugh after a gig with Simon Le Bon 1980.

Below: With Joan Collins and actor Neil Dickson who starred in the *Biggles* movie. I had done a performance for Joan's *Kerland Foundation*, which is for head injury, brain damaged people. She started this charity after her own daughter sustained brain damage from a head injury.
(Barry Langford)

Meeting one of my actor heroes, Jack Nicholson, at the after party of the London premiere of *The Postman Always Rings Twice* in 1981.
(Alan Davidson / The Picture Library)

Midge and I having a cuddle at my place. We took the pictures on self delay on the lovely camera Midge had given me as a gift.

With Jon Finch. *(Richard Young / Rex Features)*

My red period, wearing Paula Yates's petticoat.

With Chris Thompson, publicity shot for the Greenpeace single "Push & Shove".

Hazel O'Connor and Chris Thompson

Promotional shot from *Jangles* with Jesse Birdsall. *(Unknown)*

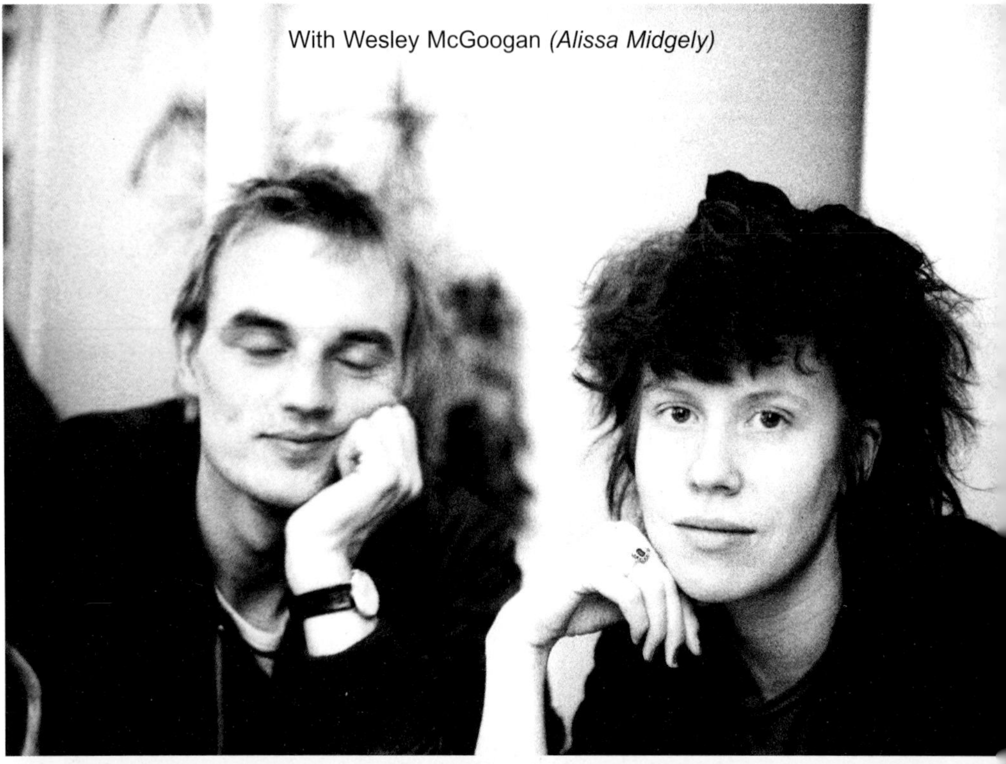

With Wesley McGoogan *(Alissa Midgely)*

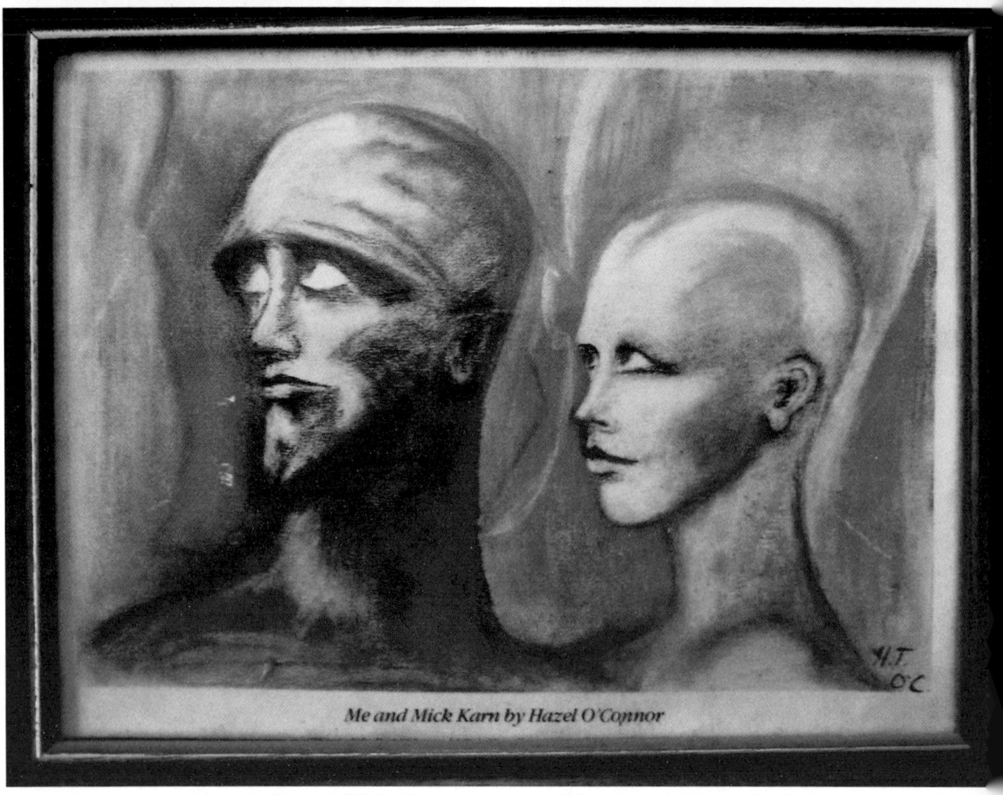
H.T. O'C
Me and Mick Karn by Hazel O'Connor

My painting of Mick Karn and myself for the *Mencap* charity.

the toilet. I was taped into that costume at 7a.m., and by 7p.m. I'd not gone to the toilet once. I was bursting, so Monica from wardrobe took a razor blade and slit a small strategic opening in the crotch of my bodysuit and unpeeled the tape and pulled the armour a few inches apart. I ran to the toilet, trying to hold the few inches of plastic and material out of the way of my twelve-hour build-up of pee; the equivalent of Niagara Falls proportions. Once started, I couldn't stop. Niagara was gushing all over my beautiful white robot bodysuit – I felt like a child caught wetting the bed. When I returned to Monica, the suit was covered in yellow splashes. I was cleaned up as best as could be done and returned to the stage and the five hundred extras for the crescendo scene of the entire film.

When the filming came to an end, Alan Edwards, my new manager, wanted to make sure I was seen as a live musician first and foremost. So a band was put together featuring Wesley McGoogan and Bob Carter who had already both played on the *Breaking Glass* album. I did some support gigs with The Stranglers, some small gigs on my own, and a support with Iggy Pop. A few weeks before my stint with Iggy Pop, I bumped into David Bowie again, literally. I'd been invited to a private showing of *Breaking Glass* in Soho. As usual I was five minutes late and it was total darkness that I stepped into. I took a few steps into the screening room and stumbled full-length across someone's lap. 'Sorry, sorry,' I whispered. I looked up into the face of David Bowie.

After the screening we all went to the pub and David said he would come to one of the Iggy Pop gigs. When the first night supporting Iggy came round, I was elated. Supporting a 'Rock Legend' and another one coming to 'catch' my gig; it didn't go very well at all the first night. No show David Bowie, and Iggy's heavily devoted audience seemed to really hate me. At the end of the night I thought if they hate me tomorrow as much as tonight, I should give up singing and maybe try the acting lark. The next night, with thoughts of giving up, I asked the band how they felt about playing "Will You". I'd never performed this song live before, and decided to play it at least once for a real audience before I gave up. The audience hated me the same as before, David Bowie still hadn't turned up, and amid the audience's booing and hissing I said, 'Okay lads, let's do a slow song,' and "Will You" commenced.

This was a defining moment of my life – I had an epiphany. That long sax solo began and I scurried to the back of the stage, where I noticed David Bowie in the wings. He winked at me. I waved back and turned to a very different audience mood. The song got a standing ovation with all the hecklers who'd hated me a moment before. They were now shouting, 'We love you!' Here's what I realised in that very moment: There is a sensitive part to every human being and you can touch people with a true sentiment. An audience demands truth, and from that day on, "Will You" always has a permanent place in my gigs. I aspired to truthful songs, truthful performance.

I'd been going out with the actor, Jon Finch, since filming ended. As he was a classical actor and I was punkette, we made an odd pairing, I suppose. Jon had something of an enigma about him, which I found attractive. He'd taken me to Ireland to his friends the Hennesseys in Ballybunion for New Year's Eve. Jon was quite a drinker and loved to be in the pub, but he was also a diabetic and the two didn't mix very well.

The first time I'd stayed over at his place he'd mumbled, 'If anything strange happens, just lob some of that in my mouth,' pointing to a packet of glucose lozenges. He then promptly passed out in his bed from a heavy session. So there we were on our first night in Ballybunion; he's had quite a lot to drink, and we were fast asleep. At 4a.m. I was rudely awakened by the bed violently shaking. I looked over at Jon to see his eyes wide open, his teeth gritted, and his body was rigid in spasms. I was terrified. I called Mrs. Hennessy and we decided to call an ambulance. In the meantime I gave him a glucose lozenge, which is easier said than done when somebody's jaw is locked in spasm.

Within minutes he stopped shaking and slowly seemed to be coming awake. The first words he uttered were: 'What the fuck's going on? Why are you all here?' The ambulance was sent away and he went back to sleep. I couldn't sleep after that. I'd never witnessed somebody having a fit at such close quarters before. Apparently he'd had a hyperglycaemic attack. I was to become used to these attacks, as they became a common occurrence during our time together. There was the time he collapsed facedown on his plate of food in a London restaurant, and as he was already drunk when I met him there, I didn't know if he'd gone into a hyperglycaemic attack or if he was just pissed! It turned out he was unconscious and needed hospital treatment. As soon as the doctors had seen him, he was back in the pub drinking within the hour.

I think the straw that broke this donkey's back was when Jon said he'd come over to stay at my house for a rare change. We'd had a non-pub evening and gone to sleep in my split-level bedroom. I was rudely awakened with the ominous shaking bed syndrome. I put the light on and forced glucose into his rigid mouth. It didn't stop. Even worse, he started making terrible gurgling noises, and was shaking even more violently. I thought, Oh, God, he's swallowed his tongue. So, without thinking, I put my hand in his mouth to pull his tongue back. Suddenly his teeth clamped shut on my finger and kept biting down hard. The pain was excruciating. His seizure had him rigid and shaking all at the same time. Blood bubbled out of his mouth and I didn't know if it was his or mine.

I screamed in pain: 'Jon, Jon, let go, stop!' Of course he didn't respond. His eyes were open and staring wildly yet he couldn't see me. It now hurt so much I thought I was going to pass out. I tried to prise his rigid mouth open and tried pulling my finger out, but still he bit down harder. I knew it wasn't his fault but at that moment I hated him. I pulled, I prised, and at last managed to almost wriggle my throbbing finger out. I put a spoon handle between his teeth and pulled one final time. Out came my finger – he'd bitten through to the bone. Within seconds it had swollen three times its proper size and of course it was very bloody. Jon was still shaking away. As I climbed down the ladder from my bedroom I was sobbing hysterically, holding my big fat bloody finger up in the air. I managed to call an ambulance for Jon, leaving blood spattered on walls, doors, and light switches.

Chapter Six

The ambulance arrived within minutes and in my shocked hysterical way I tried to explain what had happened. The ambulance men climbed up to the split-level to find Jon just coming back to himself.
'Are you all right, mate?' one of them asked.
'Who the fuck are you?' Jon snapped. 'What the fuck do you want?'
'It's all right, Jon,' I said. 'You've had a bad seizure. These are the ambulance men. They've got to take you to hospital.'
'I'm not going to the bloody hospital,' he said. 'Tell them to fuck off.'

The ambulance men took his pulse and Jon kept telling them to 'Fuck off! I'm not going to hospital.' So they climbed down the ladder saying, 'Sorry, Miss, there's nothing we can do if he refuses to come with us.' The man speaking looked at my swollen, bloodied finger, and said, 'You look like you need treatment on that finger.' 'I'll be fine,' I said, and saw them out.

I'd become good pals with The Stranglers' lead singer Hugh Cornwell around this time, but stayed faithful to Jon, that is, until the 17th March: St. Patrick's Day. The scenario began when the film studios phoned to tell me *Breaking Glass* snippets were to be shown in the 1980 Royal Film Premiere of *Kramer Vs Kramer*, on the 17th March. They wanted me to do TV interviews on the night with Judith Chalmers, and to be presented to the Queen. I wanted to meet the Queen to make my Mum proud, but didn't feel I could and retain my integrity. It felt all a bit patronising in the sense that my public image was rebellious and garish. So if I were to meet the Queen it would sanitize me, and I didn't want sanitization, and a curtsey later it would be said, 'That Hazel O'Connor isn't really scary,' and show pictures of an anarchist buying into the world elitism by birth. 'No thanks, I'm very sorry,' I said, 'but I don't feel it's politically correct for me to meet the Queen.' So it was agreed that I was to go to the Premiere, do my interview for the telly, and watch the film.

Two weeks prior to this I'd hopped on my first ever flight alone to the U.S. – to New York actually – to spend a few days with Jon, who was already out in the States doing publicity for the BBC

Shakespeare series *Richard III*, along with Tim Piggott-Smith. I took the JFK express into the heart of Manhattan and got off at 42nd Street to walk the few blocks to the Algonquin Hotel. The first thing I saw as I came out from the station was a knife fight on the street. Well, I made it fairly sharpish to the Hotel and into Jon's arms. The Algonquin was a very beautiful and very historic Hotel, where Virginia Woolf and all those racy artists of the 20s and 30s met up in the famous Green Room. However it was not as romantic as it could have been because, as I said, Jon liked to drink and our first night was spent in the bar of the Algonquin with Tim Piggott-Smith and Jon's ex-girlfriend, *Saturday Night Live* comedienne Carol Kane. I was jetlagged so I cried off early and went to bed.

The next day Jon was busy, so I went walking the streets of Manhattan. I ended up in Spanish Harlem, passing endless spiritualists, tarot card readers, and magic shops. I decided to go into one for a palm-reading. She told me a lot of stuff which could apply to anyone, but then she told me of the dark-haired man that I loved, who wasn't reciprocating, and how she'd give me a charm to make him want me, which I had to put under our bed for three nights, and then burn it by throwing the ashes to the four winds. I thought, What the hell, I'll give it a whirl. I paid my $20 and went back to meet Jon. The funny thing is that months later, after we'd finished, I went to visit him in Corfu whilst he was filming with Anthony Hopkins – and he got down on his knees and said, 'For God's sake I love you – marry me.' Again I thought, be careful what you wish for.

Anyway, America with Jon was one boozy night after another and very boring to a non-drinker. The next day we went to Coconut Grove, Palm Beach Florida. The Hotel suite was gorgeous, the sun was shining, there was a lovely swimming pool and all Jon wanted to do was drink in the hotel room. I wanted to go adventuring, swimming, and walking. Eventually, we went to Sea World to see the dolphins, and that was that. I spent most of the time on my own, swimming in the pool. We flew home together on the 16th of March. The plan was to go to our separate homes, where I had eight phone interviews to do, then meet up to go to the premiere in the early evening, then on to the Hilton Hotel for St Patrick's Day celebrations, and then finally home for sleep.

The Premiere was fun except for one of the newspapers calling me 'that awful punk thing' that 'arrived on the arm of classical actor Jon Finch'. The cheek of them – Jon came on my ticket, not the other way round. Anyway, I was starting to get used to the tabloid press, as I was anything from 'Punk Princess' to 'That Thing'. As my fame grew, though, their attentions really ground me down. Naked pictures of myself would turn up on the front of *The Star* from my modelling days, sold by someone who wanted to make money. Mum would then ring me, upset: 'I didn't know that had happened!'

After the premiere, Jon and I slipped away to the Hilton, but I really felt knackered and I left for home around 1a.m. After the *Kramer vs. Kramer* premiere, I stopped going out with Jon because his drinking was too much for me. For a little while I went out with Hugh Cornwell from the Stranglers, but Hugh had been busted for drugs and a week after we began our romance he was sent to prison for two months – the judge was making an example of him. Whilst Hugh was in prison, the Stranglers had a big London gig to do at the Rainbow Theatre, and no lead singer, so they invited other singers and musicians to do a few songs each. I did "Grip" and "Hanging Around", with a very young Robert Smith of The Cure playing guitar. I also sang the backing vocals with Toyah Wilcox for Ian Dury. As I stood on that stage I remembered that Boomtown Rats gig from a few years before, and now here I was, famous and singing at the Rainbow.

My life was moving very fast now and Clive, Davina, Brian Gibson, and I were to go to the Cannes Film Festival, where *Breaking Glass* was to be shown in public for the first time. I'd changed my hairstyle into a white plaited dreadlock style, as I'd become very bored with the *Breaking Glass* look. When Davina saw my changed hair at Heathrow Airport, she said, 'Oh Hazel, you should have left your hairstyle the same as in the film!' I was quite taken aback and said, 'This hairstyle will get us even more publicity.' Of course I didn't know anything about PR but I had a feeling that it's better to seen as a unique individual, rather than a clone from a movie. Luckily or unluckily, depending on how you viewed it, I was correct, as the paparazzi followed me, the weird white-faced, black-eyed, mop-head everywhere I went. I was the punk Bo Derek with my braids. I walked along the seafront with sixty photographers snapping away. When I reached the Carlton Hotel where all the big film business takes place, I heard one jostling photographer say, 'Who is she anyway?' That's how Cannes is – take photos and ask questions later.

On the night our film was showed, I sat with Brian in the circle, terrified in case it was hated. As the film finished and the credits rolled, the audience began to applaud. The applause grew as they shouted, 'Bravo!' and stood up. A spotlight shone down on us. Brian stood up to take a bow whilst trying to pull me up out of the seat to also take that first bow. I wanted to get up but couldn't because I'd undone the zip on my tight trousers, so as he stood he pulled me up also and my trousers got stuck on the velvety pile of my chair. As I rose up my trousers fell – and that's the way I took my first standing ovation!

CHAPTER SEVEN

'In the beginning was a world
Man said let there be more light
Electric scenes, amazing beams, neon brights
To light our boring nights
He said behold what have I done?
Made a better world for everyone
Nobody laughs, nobody cries
World without end forever, amen
"Eighth Day" (*Breaking Glass*, 1980)

Looking back, perhaps I should have had more of a game plan, or an understanding of the world I was getting into, but I didn't. I didn't think any further than getting ahead and improving as a singer and a songwriter and maybe I should have done. I loved it all in one way, but I was a bit like a child with too many goodies to choose from. Too many people to talk to, for too long, too little time to dream, too many people who all wanted a piece of me.

After making *Breaking Glass*, my life was now moving and changing so fast it was hard to keep up. During the summer months I was asked to go to New York and then Los Angeles to meet Paramount Film executives, Don Simpson, Michael Eisner (now head of Disney), and Jeff Katzenberg. I was to do PR in New York and then drive across America with Alan Edwards, all paid for by Paramount, to get ideas for future films that I could star in for Paramount. They wanted to sign me up for more films and a writing deal. I didn't want to go at first, as I was knackered, but I'm so glad I got the opportunity to see so much of the American landscape.

Firstly, I had lots of interviews to do in New York, and my hotel room was bigger than my flat in London. Then we travelled west from New York through Amish country in New England. I'd heard about the Amish community from a friend and thought it would be interesting to see them, talk to them, and thought that they'd be good material for a film. The Amish are a Christian group of churches who have their origins in Europe and who emigrated to Pennsylvania in the 18th century to escape religious persecution. They don't have electricity or cars, and they wear only homespun clothing. We did meet a couple of young Amish men on a small road off the beaten track whilst we changed a flat tyre. Clip, clop, clip, clop came their pony and trap; they looked like they just came off the *Mayflower*. They stopped to help us, and we chatted for a while. Something set in the Amish community would be a good film idea, I thought, and noted it down for the Paramount film guys who we'd be meeting in Los Angeles at the end of our odyssey. Strange that a couple of years later Don Simpson made a film with Harrison Ford, called *Witness*, set in the Amish Community.

I think the most amazing scenery for me was the salt flats in Utah, and indeed Salt Lake City, looming up like a city in the middle of a sci-fi landscape. The dried-up salt lakes looked like ice lakes. We stayed for a couple of days in a mountain resort called Steamboat Springs Colorado, and scoured the area's 'ghost towns' of which there are many, due to the Gold Rush in the 1870s. I read of a great local character called Baby Doe Tabor, and wanted to do a movie about her life. We went through Carson City, Reno, and eventually came to San Francisco – obviously checking out the old hippie quarters and Chinatown – then we hit the Pacific Coast Highway on our final drive down to Los Angeles and Hollywood.

Paramount had booked me a room at the Chateau Marmont in the heart of Hollywood. The Chateau boasted zillions of film stars as having stayed there. Jack Nicholson and Warren Beatty used to party from there; Marilyn Monroe, Judy Garland, John Belushi; the list goes on and on, reaching back to the beginnings of Hollywood right up to the present. I went into Paramount films to have lunch and deliver the three film ideas I'd put together. I handed my synopsis to Don Simpson and Jeff Katzenberg.

My visit to Paramount was great fun. I'd never imagined I'd be wined and dined by the top guys in a big Hollywood film lot like Paramount. I was shown all over the sound stages, and given the run-down on Paramount's history and stars. For instance I was shown the car park, which had apparently doubled as the Red Sea, which Charlton Heston, as Moses, had parted in the *Ten Commandments* movie, made in Hollywood's Golden Era. Alan Edwards and I had a long meeting with Davina Belling, our *Breaking Glass* producer, who lived most of the time in L.A. Alan was wearing running shorts. We'd both bought a pair in New York. As he slung his leg over the side of his chair, I happened to glance his way and saw his willy hanging out the side of his shorts. I tried to give him a sign discreetly, but he thought I was messing about, so he told me to 'stop messing.' Then he looked – God, he went so red, and I couldn't help laughing. Alan and I were great mates and our travels had been such fun.

Whilst staying in Hollywood I did photo sessions at A & M records, where I heard it through the grapevine that they wanted to sign me for my next album. Unfortunately, they had to do this deal, not with me or my manager, but with Albion records because Albion had me signed to their long-term record contracts the previous year, for the world, and they reaped the financial rewards now – not me. I heard Albion took $250,000 advance for giving the next Hazel O'Connor record to A & M America and they didn't share a penny of it!

I did lots of press and radio whilst in Hollywood and caught the obligatory cold one catches because Hollywood lives in constant air-conditioning systems, which I had never experienced before. It's boiling hot outside, so you put skimpy clothing on, then you get into a very chilly air-conditioned car to take you to an equally freezing office or radio show, so a novice – like myself – gets hot, cold, hot, cold, hot, cold. In the end I got the flu and just wished they'd switch the air-conditioning off, but oh no, that would make a star's face paint run – God forbid!

I got back to London and "Eighth Day" had been released as the second *Breaking Glass* single. (The first had been "Writing on the Wall" – a 'market tester' released in May.) It looked like it was going to be a hit. The film was set to open, and I was doing lots of publicity up and down the country. I remember walking behind Oxford Street in London, when a van went by and I heard my voice blaring away from the radio – it was the most exciting moment of my entire career; I got the biggest rush at that moment – my song on the radio; me walking by hearing it on a sunny gorgeous day.

I drove up north to do more movie publicity and bought the music papers. I knew "Eighth Day" had gone into the pop charts the week before at number twenty-six, but this week the *Breaking Glass* album was released, so I was interested to see if it had charted. 'Oh my God,' I said, dropping the paper. "Eighth Day" is number five and so is the album!'

The English premiere of *Breaking Glass* was a much more exciting prospect, as all my family and friends, and all my road crew were there. My crew were a group of guys called The

Chapter Seven

Finchley Boys. They also worked with the Stranglers and Toyah Wilcox. They had a big interest in army vehicles and paraphernalia, and so they arranged to bring me to the film premiere in London's Shaftsbury Avenue in a convoy of army vehicles. The only fly in the ointment that day was my dad, who came to my house prior to the premiere with his second wife, Doreen. My mum also came. When the press photographer wanted a picture of Mum, Dad, and myself, he got stroppy and wouldn't do it unless Doreen was in it, and basically my own Mum was pushed out of the picture – which really upset me and Mum.

My first taste of the real craziness of my new life was when I did a Saturday morning cult show, *Tiswas*, which was filmed in Birmingham. When I had finished I went to Mum's in Coventry for lunch. We popped out to the local shopping precinct and into the supermarket. As we walked through the supermarket I became aware of people nudging each other as we passed by and my name was being whispered. I just wanted to get home quickly as people were beginning to follow us. We finished in the supermarket and proceeded to walk through the shopping precinct. We'd gathered quite a crowd by this time, following us at a distance – nobody had been brave enough to waylay us yet... Suddenly the first person broke forward and caught my eye. They asked for an autograph, which opened the floodgates, and I became enveloped by twenty or thirty people. I stood signing away for the next forty-five minutes, every so often catching a glimpse of Mum.

Initially she looked so happy and proud of me, but time was moving on and our lunch was getting overdone in the oven back at her house. More and more people clustered around me, including some old ladies who were pushing paper into my face saying, 'You might as well do one for Darren,' or, 'I don't know who you are, but sign this anyway.' An hour had now elapsed and Mum was looking worried and pissed off. 'Her dinner is going to get ruined,' I heard Mum say. The people around me paid no attention to her. They just kept pushing pens and paper in my face, and shoving me.

I made a break for it and we ran into Woolworths. The

manager locked the doors of the shop against the fifty or sixty people chasing us. He told us that over the last hour he'd sold out all the *Breaking Glass* albums, so it was the least he could do to try and help us get away. He let Mum out the back way to fetch her car. She drove round to the side door, I ran out and jumped into her three wheeler Reliant car. The crowd ran, trying to catch up with us, looking slightly disappointed that the getaway car was not a limo, but a sort of 'toytown' car! Mum was so proud of me though, and so was my grumpy Granddad. I wished Nan were still alive to see what had happened to me. But all the attention and travel was getting me down a bit. I think a person isn't so much changed by fame, as the people around a famous person change their behaviour, and slowly but surely the famous person is treated like an object – not a human being. For instance, if I went to visit Dad, he'd always be asking me to autograph photos for his pub mates rather than asking me, 'How are you doing?'

Because "Eighth Day" had shot into the charts, I was asked to appear on BBC's *Top of the Pops*, which was so exciting for me, having been brought up on TV pop culture. A & M Records had sent a tasty Rolls Royce Limo to take me to the TV studios. I wasn't as impressed as I should have been because I felt a bit silly arriving in such an ostentatious car. The filming of *Top of the Pops* wasn't as much fun as I thought it would be. All my teenage life I'd imagined dancing to the bands on *Top of the Pops*, but when I got there it seemed quite false. The audience would be herded to each different stage and told when to clap, to dance – literally when to take a piss.

I left the show quite disappointed and climbed back into the ostentatious Limo. As the Limo neared the main gate of the BBC, there were loads of people waiting for autographs. I felt very embarrassed in this big voluminous car with only me as passenger; it really didn't feel right, and at this point I decided to dip down in the back so no one could see me. But of course the whole crowd swarmed around this beautiful car, and everyone saw me cowering in the back. 'Hazel, Hazel, can you sign this?' Loads of photo-flashes went off. 'Hazel, Hazel, smile.' 'Hey, Hazel O'Connor, I love you!' They started banging hands on the windows. I signed as many autographs as I could before the Limo pulled away.

"Eighth Day" was expected to go to number one the next week, but it was not to be, because a single sung by a girl called Kelly Marie – "Feels Like I'm in Love" – pipped us at the post. We were whipped by a plastic disco track, and had it not been that, it would have been Sheena Easton's "9 to 5".

Almost immediately after this I embarked on my first proper UK tour. My manager had talked about the possibility of a new band from Birmingham opening for me on the tour: they were called Duran Duran. They were happy to pay a 'buy on' (which is a fee to get on a big tour, as it gives huge exposure to new artists), and I liked their music.

My brother had now joined my band Megahype as The Flys had split-up, and it was such a thrill to play music and tour with 'our Neil'. So we began the tour. Every night I'd nip out into the Concert Hall to catch a song from my support band Duran Duran. The favourite song amongst myself and my band was "Planet Earth". Duran Duran were a Birmingham band managed by the Berrow Brothers, a smart pair, who also had The Rum Runner club in Birmingham, which was the Midlands version of Steve Strange's Club for Heroes in London. The New Romantic fashion era had begun and the Duran Duran lads wore a fair amount of frilly shirts, which didn't always go down so well with my punk audience.

Duran Duran had a great attitude. They were undaunted by the punk jibes. They had so little money in their tour budget, that they travelled in a camper van (I could have sworn it was an old Bedford, but twenty years later, when chatting to John Taylor in L.A. about our beginnings, he swore it was a Winnebago!) Each night they'd get one room in the hotel that my band and crew stayed at, and then pull straws to see who got the room. We'd all hang out together at the hotel after our gig, and dear Simon Le Bon would be asking me about the self-hypnosis I'd been doing, and would that help if one was afraid of losing one's voice? He was so intense and committed – all the Duran lads were – and we had so many brilliant times on that first tour.

I came a cropper in the second week when my foot went down a little crack on the stage in Brighton. As a result of that accident I busted my ankle ligaments, but I still had two more weeks to tour, so I ended up seeing assorted doctors and casualty departments up and down England. The hospital wanted to put my foot in plaster, but I wouldn't let them – How could I do my gig properly? I ended up looking like Long John Silver, going on stage with some old wooden crutches, hopping about and coming off with dreadful bruises under my arms from the impact of my hopping movements on stage. By the end of the tour my other ankle ligaments were also busted and the pain from the injury was just awful.

Our last gig was at the Dominion Theatre in London. It had gone very well for Duran Duran. They'd got themselves a brilliant record deal with EMI, and went on to bigger and better things. Duran Duran and my band Megahype did a David Bowie song together at the end of the Concert. Afterwards we hugged and went our separate ways. I was very proud of those guys as they started to become a household name and the frills were swapped for Anthony Price suits.

After the break for the *Breaking Glass* soundtrack, it was nearly time for me to go back to Albion Records, and I really didn't want to. My fame had come as a result of the film and it's producers, the money that they had spent on publicity people, and through A & M Records' hard work of selling me into the shops. All publicity had been paid for by the film people or A & M. Albion had not participated in any costs and yet because they'd sneakily managed to get me to sign those contracts of eighteen months before, they had all future rights to me, my songs, and performances for another five years.

I wanted to leave them as I thought they didn't have a leg to stand on if they tried to sue me. My manager took me to his lawyer, and they both took the view that it was more prudent to re-negotiate. It was a massive mistake. I should have walked away from their unfair, unearned contracts, but I listened to management and legal advice which basically amounted to: 'You are at the top of the ladder now, but if you ruffle anything, you could be put out of the music business in legal wrangles and your career could be cut very short – Don't rock the boat.' We re-negotiated and Albion agreed not to ever release the recordings I'd done with Vic Maile prior to recording *Breaking Glass*. But I was to pay their costs of £40,000. They agreed an advance of £20,000 for my recording rights, and the new contract was marginally better than the 1979 version. However, there was no clear amount or commitment to tour support or marketing money. I'd already spent all my wages from filming – which came to around £8,500 – on paying my band continuous wages. It's ironic that at the height of my fame I was 'church mouse' poor.

Now the contract was sorted, Dai and Derek wanted a new album as soon as possible. I wanted Tony Visconti to produce. He told me he wouldn't produce an album with Albion at the helm. He had no faith in them basically, so I was presented with the guy who engineered/produced The Police. He was a nice enough guy called Nigel Gray. His work with The Police was impressive. We set about recording my second album *Sons & Lovers* at the end of 1980.

In the meantime, I was often asked to different countries for the publicity and opening of the film. Rome was gorgeous and my pal Liz came with me, as an assistant. All the way on the flight over, I kept worrying whether the film publicity people in Rome had two rooms booked, as I'm useless sharing a room with anyone (unless of course it's my boyfriend – but even then, I liked my space). As we were being collected from Rome Airport in the limo, Liz suddenly chirped up, 'There are separate rooms, I hope?' 'Yes, yes of course, you will see,' said the PR rep.

The hotel rooms were the biggest, most beautiful, and best I've ever stayed in. Firstly we entered a room – the size of a medium dance-floor, or church hall – with tapestries and medieval paintings and panels. There were about five different sitting areas in this vast space, and two doors off either end of the sitting room, each leading into a bedroom, dressing-room and bathroom. Liz was gob-smacked. So was I, and we laughed at ourselves for worrying about sharing, when in fact we were staying in a veritable palace, all expenses paid – Yippee!

The funniest thing about seeing *Breaking Glass* in so many different countries was hearing my speaking voice dubbed by German, French, or whatever. It is so strange seeing and hearing yourself with another voice. Most of the film publicity was over by November 1980. There had been three singles released so far – the highest being "Eighth Day" at number five in the charts – and the album was still in the high end of the charts.

The chart success was all due to the film promotion and the wonderful job A & M Records did, but I was only to be with A & M for the duration of the film publicity, and it was now over. I really hated the idea of going back to Albion. Derek Green, the head of A & M UK had tried to sign me directly, giving Albion big cash incentives; but Albion categorically refused – they knew they could make huge amounts of dosh, and put their label on the map by using my name, fame, and success as the carrot – i.e. if say, Victor Records Japan wanted Hazel O'Connor, they'd have to take the entire Albion label acts or there would be no Hazel O'Connor. They did this worldwide and made a huge amount of money which they never shared with me, or my career; they bought property, cars and boats – lucky them! I was so disappointed that they wouldn't let me go.

The first single with Albion came out and didn't get high chart action and I wondered if Albion were 'able' for the job at hand. Other things made me insecure about Albion's abilities. For instance, John Telfer, the guy who headed-up the publishing division (and my faith in him was the reason I signed to Albion Publishing) left to manage Joe Jackson's career, and he was able to extricate Joe's publishing away from Dai and Derek. The Stranglers, who were published and had put records through Albion, walked away from Dai and Derek also. It made me think there's no smoke without fire.

For my next single I quietly went to Tony Visconti and asked if I could re-record "Decadent Days" in his Good Earth Studio, with his engineer Keith Fordyce, so that I could at least get the Tony Visconti Good Earth Studio's sound. The song had grown so much since recording it with Nigel Gray. I've often found my songs grow more after playing them 'live' for a while. Tony said

'Yes,' and then I asked Derek and Dai. I felt very strongly about "Decadent Days" as a potential hit. Luckily they went for it. Megahype re-recorded "Decadent Days", even though there'd already been advance sales of the album with the old version on. As we recorded, Tony Visconti kept popping in (as I'd hoped he would) and got more and more interested, until he said he'd mix it. I was thrilled with the result and my hunch paid off. The single shot to the British Top Ten.

One of the best new friends I made during this period was a blonde bombshell called Paula Yates. I wasn't keen on meeting her because she – according to what I'd read in the newspapers – had ensnared Bob Geldof and was now living with him, but I had to do an interview with her for *Record Mirror*. Well, that girl was such fun to hang out with. We clicked immediately and before I knew it I was spending most Sunday afternoons at Bob and Paula's in Clapham. Firstly I would play a game of Boggle with Bob, which he always won because he's so brainy. Then Paula and I would go upstairs for tea, biscuits, and gossip. Most of the gossip was hers and always had to do with the latest sexy pop star she'd interviewed. My own love-life had become non-existent by the New Year 1981 as a direct result of the demands on my time for touring, publicity, recording, etc., etc. To be honest I was so focused at that time, I didn't miss having a boyfriend.

On the eve of St. Valentine's Day I had a very racy Technicolor dream, and my leading man was a guy I had met through my brother's band The Flys supporting the Rich Kids, way before I was famous. The guy was the Rich Kids' singer. He now sang with Ultravox. Midge Ure (the ex glam teeny-bopper). I'd always liked Midge and we both liked old cars, but I never fancied him. Then I have this mad dream with him in it. The next morning I was thinking, 'Mmm, must get to say hello to Midge again,' when the phone rang: it was Paula Yates: 'Hi, Hazel. Was wondering what you are up to tonight?' she said. 'Nothing, why? Have you got something in mind?' I replied, always happy to chat aimlessly or purposefully with Ms. Paula. She was such a delight, such a laugh, and such a gossip! 'Well, I've got an extra ticket for the Valentine's Ball at the Rainbow Theatre with Ultravox topping the bill – Do you wanna come?' 'Absolutely!'

A night out with Paula was always fascinating. She had such a witty mind. She was great fun as long as one took the back seat when in male company because she was the Goddess of Flirt. The Valentine's Ball outing was fab. Ultravox were riding high with their new hit "Vienna" and Paula and I had a laugh with the band backstage after the gig. Midge and I discussed classic old cars again and I thought, Mmmm, he ain't bad at all...

Perhaps I was drawn to Midge because we were both famous, both caught up in the same unreal world. We both loved classic cars, and I'd given him a lift home once before, when Neil had been supporting him. We'd had a chat in his little bedsit, and I thought, Oh, bless him in his bedsit, down from Scotland in Maida Vale. Since we'd met, Ultravox had suddenly become famous with "Vienna". Midge had definitely re-rigged himself for "Vienna" with his Clark Gable 40s vibe. He loved all of that. I had a taste for it, too, because of Adrian and his Humphrey Bogart image. Midge was Clark Gable and for a while I wanted to be his Carole Lombard.

I didn't see Midge again for a couple of months as I had to prepare for my first American Tour. I was opening for XTC and "Decadent Days" (the new version) had been released in the UK and was getting loads of radio airplay. Suddenly it shot to number ten and we did our second *Top of the Pops*. I'd decided to wear my black bikini top and mini skirt, as I felt these clothes represented the song, but to add spice I put a wig, glasses, and an old overcoat on. (I had taken to wearing the wig and glasses if I wanted to go out and not be recognised.) The DJ Dave Lee Travis introduced me. I stood next to him, disguised, waving and mouthing, 'Hello Mum,' as I'd often seen people do on that programme. I then started walking towards the band – stripping off wig, glasses and coat – and jumped up to do the song in my black bra and mini. In 1981 I think I was the first to ever do this, though of course twenty years later it's *de rigeur*. The press slated me by showing a picture and accusing me of having love handles. I had to agree, they were right, I did seem to have love handles and I was mortified, my vanity was shaken.

The following Saturday I was at London's Camden Market buying some Body Shop stuff (in those days there were only a few places to buy Body Shop), when I was accosted by five teenage girls. 'Are you Hazel O'Connor?' one of them asked. 'Yes,' I replied. 'You were brilliant last week on *Top of the Pops*,' they said. 'Thank you,' I said. 'We're all at boarding school and we were watching it. You wearing your bra was great, but then our headmistress came in and switched the TV off.'

Fantastic, I thought, the headmistress switched me off. I was glad that 'straight society' didn't like me or 'get it', because I wanted to be a working-class rebel. I still felt stupid and ugly about my love handles though.

The following week Megahype and I left to begin our US tour with XTC. I found it hard going as we travelled every night after coming off stage, for five or six hours in the back of the band bus, and were usually arriving at the hotel at our next destination around 5.30a.m. I've never enjoyed long journeys by road at the best of times, but these were really gruelling and I'd get dizzy from the never-ending motion of the bus. We were getting great reactions and reviews wherever we went though, and loads of fun with XTC. I would often have breakfast with Andy Partridge of XTC. One morning the XTC lads seemed very down. It turned out that their record company, Virgin America, had gone bust and they were left without any record company support mid-tour, poor sods!

The New York review said I was reminiscent of a latter-day Lotte Lenya. I didn't know who she was, so I did my research and found out she was part of the Kurt Weil and Bertolt Brecht gang, and pieces like "The Seven Deadly Sins" were written for her, so I was very flattered.

Philadelphia was a wonderful night, except for the bloody groupies. God, the groupies backstage in the USA are very pushy, and I would always get annoyed if they came too close to my brother because he was now married. Although most of the band were not philanderers, one of the guys was, and he seemed to need sex every night. One night we saw him romancing a lady downstairs in the hotel, so we decided to empty his room of furniture on to the balcony, even his double bed. When he arrived at his room we all ran next door and listened. 'Come on darling,' we all heard him say as he opened the door to his now empty room. 'Oh bloody hell, you bastards!' he shouted as he entered the room. We all scattered, laughing hysterically. Of course we put his furniture back when he cooled down, but this episode didn't curb his ardour for the ladies one bit.

Our drive to Chicago was long and arduous. I got into my bed about 6a.m. Half an hour later, I was rudely awoken by a telephone call from London. It was Dai and Derek excitedly telling me we had *Top of the Pops* again, and I should come back to London to do this performance. 'I can't just drop this US tour,' I said. 'I'll never get another gig in this country if I cancel, talk sense, guys! What about making a pop video, send a film crew over here, and use a collage of photos and film clips?' I suggested. Thinking to myself how silly of them not to have a video done already, in case this situation arose. Even with all the money they had accrued by this time from licensing Hazel O'Connor worldwide, they didn't want to meet the costs of making a video in America, even though a video would have probably pushed the single up into the top five. Instead the same performance which I'd done two weeks before (the black bra vibe) was repeated and the single stayed at number ten.

On arrival back to England I was told that I had been nominated for two BAFTA Awards: one for best newcomer actress, the other for best film soundtrack. When I arrived at the awards ceremony, the first person I saw was Sting. I'd known him since before we all were famous back in the days of demos and knocking on doors. Sting walked up and gave me a friendly kiss saying, 'I liked your film, Hazel. I was on the panel of voters for the best soundtrack category, and you got my vote, but to be honest, I don't think many of the others 'got it'.' So I wasn't surprised when John Williams was announced as the winner. To be honest, I was just thrilled to be included in such salubrious company as Queen for their *Flash Gordon* soundtrack and John Williams for *Star Wars*. I was also nominated as best newcomer actress by the *Evening Standard* Film Awards. I was then nominated as best female singer in the Rock and Pop Awards, and also asked to perform. I was given to believe that I'd probably won it, but again prizes for Hazel were not to be: Sheena Easton got that one. I suppose it was nice to be gaining recognition within the film and music business, but I was forever struggling against the acting community saying, 'Yes, yes, lovely acting darling, but of course you're a singer really, aren't you?' and the music community saying, 'Well of course she isn't really a singer, she's one of those actresses trying to be a singer.'

I couldn't win either way. In those days nobody wanted to give me credit for being the first woman in history to star in a mainstream film and write the soundtrack music. I didn't credit myself either. In fact if I read good reviews, I couldn't quite believe them, and bad reviews or bitchy write-ups I always believed and they really hurt me. My skin wasn't thick enough in those days. I decided it was best to read neither good nor bad, and the only time I heard about something written about me was when Mum would read something hurtful and would ring me in tears, or pissed off about something the press had said I'd said, even if I didn't say it! The damage to my family had started and that's the price of fame.

One such example is my so-called 'two thousand lovers'. A tabloid journalist, with his dirty collar, nabbed me one day. 'How many boyfriends have you got, Hazel?' he asked. I said, 'Loads. I really like them. I have thousands of boyfriends, if that's what you mean; if you mean lovers, that's another thing.' 'Two thousand?' 'If you mean boyfriends, not lovers, yes.' Next thing I knew, it went into the paper: 'Sexual barracuda had two thousand lovers.' I hated that.

Finally I was nominated, and was told I'd won an award from the prestigious Variety Club of Great Britain. I asked a mate of mine, Skids' singer Richard Jobson, to escort me to the do. He called for me around 11a.m. on the day of the awards ceremony looking the worse for wear after an all-night drinking session. Then the press photographer who was covering all the winners for the tabloids turned up. The photographer said he'd just come from John Hurt's house up the road, as he'd won best actor category for his portrayal of John Merrick in *The Elephant Man*. He added: 'I wished I'd known you and John lived so near to each other, it would have been nice to get the two winners together.' 'Oh no,' I said, 'I'm only a newcomer winner.' 'No you're not,' he replied. 'You won best film actress in 1980.' I was shocked, I had no idea. I immediately got on the phone to Mum to tell her.

On arrival at the Savoy I was introduced to Rowan Atkinson, who I absolutely adored. I wanted to say something smart and witty to this icon of comedy, but as he shook my hand all I could say was, 'Oh, Mr Atkinson, I... I love you.' He gave me an embarrassed Mr Bean look and walked off. I've never been good in celebrity company because I'm quite shy, unless I've become mates first like with Richard Jobson; he's such a nice guy, and a hoot to hang out with, so I was happy enough to slink back to our table after my social gaffe of the day.

Terry Wogan presented my award, and I guess I did some little speech, but I can't remember. At the end of the ceremony I did loads of press photographs with other winners. My favourite photograph of the day was with more comic heroes of mine – Ronnie Corbett and Ronnie Barker – and this was the picture that hit the paper that night. Richard and I hopped on the number 29 bus to go back to my place at the finish. We'd gone a couple of stops, when I suddenly realised that I'd left my award on the dinner table back at the Hotel. 'What a fool I am!' I shrieked. 'The first prize I've ever won in my life and I forget to take it with me. I've gotta go back, Richard.' We hopped off the bus again and ran back to the Savoy.

Because of my colourful pre-fame past, my manager was able to a deal for a Hazel O'Connor biography; this was written by a fantastic journalist called Judith Simons. Judith was famous for having been the first journalist to go on the road with The Beatles in the 60s. It's said that "Hey Jude" was written about her. So in tandem with the book being written, there was also talk of writing a script for a TV programme for me to star in. I was introduced to a writer/comedian called Chris Cooper. He'd written lots of stuff for *The Muppets* TV show. I got along very well with Chris and he invited me to a place called *The Comic Strip* in

Soho where he did stand-up comedy every week.

The Comic Strip was a small dark box holding about fifty people and a small stage. The first act was okay but a bit too dry for me, but the second act had me rolling around and crying with laughter. It was two guys who called themselves 20th Century Coyote. Their real names were Rik Mayall and Ade Edmondson. They both wore matching maroon suits, and during their act also called themselves The Dangerous Brothers, and did a song called "I'm Evil". The Evil song was hilarious, with such silly daft lines like, 'I pick my nose and I wipe it on the wall', 'I don't answer when my Mum calls', and loads of other lines like that (as in not particularly evil things), culminating in a chorus of "Cos I'm evil, I'm really evil". All done to a twelve bar blues thing – and they were handsome young devils. The other act I really liked was another duo, this time two girls called French and Saunders. I was totally in awe of their talents. After the show I went backstage to say hi to Chris, and to tell these amazingly funny people how great I thought they were. Dawn French was a schoolteacher and she asked me if I'd do her a favour. Seemingly she had a very clever eleven-year-old student, who was quite troubled and didn't do her schoolwork. The only thing she was passionate about was Hazel O'Connor. 'She's kept a scrapbook on you, written down all your TV and radio interviews, word for word – Hazel, would you mind looking at it?' asked Dawn. 'I've got a better idea: Why don't we all meet up at the Hampstead Tea Rooms? I can look at her book beforehand, then give it back in person, and we can all have tea together.'

Dawn got the book to me and it was truly amazing. This girl had written down every word I'd ever uttered publicly, and every photo ever published. So we met up a few weeks later and I think the girl was thrilled. I hope so – I hope I made a positive difference in her life. One of the upsides of fame, I think.

CHAPTER EIGHT

'Animals cry at night a fearful tiger is a terrible sight
He remembers how he used to be free, like me.
And we don't laugh any more
Sit here wondering what we ever laughed for
Looking at the ever closed door
What more what more?
At the zoo you, you what do you do?
At the zoo you, you we perform for you
At the zoo you, you what do you care?
You just stand there and stare'
"The Zoo" (*Sons & Lovers*, 1980)

Chapter Eight

I was now immensely famous, which manifested itself by curtailing all my previous pre-fame freedoms. I couldn't just go out to the shops anymore without being excitedly mobbed by school kids. I didn't have a private life, all was on show, and the irony of fame is that any crack in one's character or emotional security just gets bigger and bigger. If I'd had the impression that I'd deserved more out of life, if I'd grown up with that, it would have stood me in better stead, but I hadn't. I always had the impression of myself that I didn't deserve anything anyway and so I would always come back to what I had been. My fame felt like an albatross – nobody really wanted *me*, they just wanted to be around my fame.

Then I bumped into David Bowie around this time and said how weird it felt when fans seemed to talk at me, not with me. He put me on the right track. He said, 'You see, Hazel, you have to understand that your fans think they already know you, because they've seen you on TV, read your interviews and so on, therefore you must redress that balance immediately by asking them a few questions and then the exchange is more equal; like what's your name? Where do you live? What do you do?' I've always followed his advice since. To have a relationship with someone in the public eye can be very hurtful, as the newspapers will usually make one partner look good and the other seem like a shit; like when I went out with Jon Finch – he was 'that wonderful classic actor', I was 'that Punk thing'. Your family and friends will sometimes unwittingly treat you like a trophy, and you start to wonder who knows the real me? Who really cares how I tick?

It was time to record a new album. I had proved my point that Tony Visconti was the right producer for me with the success of "Decadent Days". I now asked Dai and Derek again to get Tony to do my next album, if he would. Tony said he'd do it only if he got an advance of his royalties. He wanted £25,000 – he didn't trust them to account to him in the future – most astute of him, as they never did account to him later on.

Albion Records had now made loads of money on my back, so they could easily afford to pay Tony. They wouldn't though, and they told my manager Alan that if I wanted Tony Visconti so much, then I should be made responsible for paying his £25,000 advance. What they offered was this: They would loan me Tony's £25,000 initially but I must pay it back to them from my publishing royalties, and until it was paid off all my publishing (which was just starting to come in from *Breaking Glass*) would be paid directly into their record company. This is called cross-collateralizing, which has since been outlawed in the music industry.

We began recording *Cover Plus* with Tony. At the same time as this I was invited to Bob and Paula's for dinner. Midge Ure was coming, as was journalist Magenta, and musician Tony James (Generation X and Sigue Sigue Sputnik). Unfortunately, on the same day of the dinner party, the London daily paper had run a tiny piece about me having the 'hots' for Midge Ure. I was so embarrassed and wondered where it had come from. It may have been Paula saying something, somewhere in jest, but the upshot was that I was definitely not going to the dinner party now that piece had come out.

I phoned my Mum, feeling quite upset about it all, mostly because I really had been looking forward to seeing Midge again. Mum asked me what I wanted to do. 'Well, I wanted to go to the dinner party, but I can't now it's all ruined 'cos I know what a private person Midge is, and it makes me look like a silly plonker,' I said. 'And when have you ever worried about what people think, Hazel? I suggest you go and make like it's just another piece of silly rot the newspapers write. Go, and be brave, like I know my daughter is. You can never tell what might happen,' she replied. So I went.

I arrived before anybody. Paula was busy cooking. In those days she wasn't a great chef, but she really tried to be to please Bob. She'd run out of flour to thicken the savoury cream sauce to go over the fish dish, so she used a packet of sweet crumble mix. My God it tasted terrible! Anyway, as she's faffing around in the kitchen, Midge arrives. The minute our eyes met I put on a brave face and said, 'Hello, Midge, I'm sorry about that daft piece in the paper today. I want you to know it was nothing to do with me.

Chapter Eight

You know how the newspapers can be...'

'No problem,' he said, and we put it aside and had great conversations all evening.

At the end of the evening Midge gave me a lift home. I invited him in and I put *The Texas Chainsaw Massacre* on the video - God knows why! Anyway, Midge politely sat through the movie, we chatted a bit and then he politely said goodnight, giving me a friendly peck on the lips. I was very happy with the way the whole evening had gone. As he left I was feeling brave, so I invited him to come to *The Comic Strip* the following Friday.

Life was getting very interesting. A & M Records had released "Will You" as my next single and it was rushing up the pop charts. Megahype and I did our third *Top of the Pops*. Funnily enough, Ultravox were in the top ten as well, with their single "All Stood Still". The album *Cover Plus* which we were recording with Tony Visconti was going very well, and just before I left for my *Comic Strip* date with Midge that Friday, I sang the vocal "Do What You Gotta Do", and I had one of those feelings of portent like when Nan got cancer.

Midge and I started a relationship, but quietly. It was to be private and secret, as Midge didn't think it good for business if his girl fans saw him as taken: it might harm record sales. I respected his views, even though the secrecy was sometimes very hurtful. One time we spent a lovely weekend together in my favourite spot in Sussex, Bailiffscourt Hotel, and then on the Monday after we went to a *Guinness Book of Records* pop hits launch separately. If I was standing too close to him and a photographer was lurking, he'd jump away from me. Another time, after a hot night of passion together, I went to see Ultravox at an outdoor gig in London; Clapham, I think. I danced and watched from in front of the press enclosure and the dreaded music press wrote: 'Hazel O'Connor was dancing and squirming at the front, pushing people out of the way to get a better look'. Midge never defended me in the press. When asked about me he'd say: 'We're just good friends.'

I went on tour in Ireland and had quite a shock, as I'd been used to show time being at 9p.m. in the rest of Europe, but show time in Ireland was sometimes 1a.m.! I had a young guy driving me around from the Irish agents, called Louis Walsh, who was excellent company. Louis played me loads of Marianne Faithfull music as we travelled the highways and byways of Ireland and he always had great yarns to tell. He was very kind to me in those early days, even stopping on the road in the dead of night for me to nurse a cat that had been run over earlier, and it was dying. We became firm friends.

I found out my Dublin gig was to be twenty miles out of town at the Warrenstown Agriculture College, as it had been decided that as a punk singer, I wasn't allowed to play in Dublin City. I'd blown my top at Alan Edwards back in London when I'd arrived in Ireland because of Dublin and the schedule being so different to what I was used to, and I felt he should have known all the facts before sending me off to tour, so I demanded that he come over to join us. Poor Alan had a terrible journey through Ireland to meet me: a big storm blew up, and a tree went down in front of his car. He still recalls the tale nowadays whenever he comes to Ireland.

We played Galway City, where all Dad's side of the family hail from. It was such a buzz to see our Auntie Annie and all our cousins calling down to us from the balcony as we changed our clothes behind a little curtain 'backstage'. I'd booked a function room in a hotel for after the show so I could get together properly with the family. There were a lot of aunts, uncles, second, third, and fourth cousins there, who I'd never met before!

The Irish experience of 1981 culminated in performing second on the bill at the Slane Castle Festival. Top of the bill, and arriving by helicopter, were Thin Lizzy, then me, U2, and Megahype. The fans at that first Slane Castle gig were very 'revved' up, and I was being mobbed everywhere I went backstage. We had a caravan to change in, and fans were forever climbing in through the windows. Bouncers were cracking skulls with big sticks right, left, and centre. I went to watch U2 for a while before my show. I was having a great time, jigging around in the shadows at the back of the stage, until Bono noticed me and ran towards me, grabbed my hand and pulled me on stage with him to sing the song that he and the 60,000 pop fans were singing together. My mind went blank. I couldn't remember the song, and tried my best to wing it, mouthing words I didn't know.

When Megahype and I took to the stage, there was a roar from the crowd and we performed one of the most memorable gigs of my rock career. It was a huge success. After the gig, Lord Henry Mountcharles and his wife invited us all to the castle for food and drink, where I chatted happily with Phil Lynott (who was a good pal of Midge's) and his mum, Philomena.

The next day I was going camping round Ireland with a pal called Liz. Liz had been running my Fan Club for me, and the whole trip was to say thank you. The Sunday papers had all run a front page picture of me from Slane the night before, and as we came to our first camping spot, I realised it wasn't going to be as easy as I thought to have a quiet camping holiday in Ireland.

First stop was Ballybunion and it had been raining, so we decided a couple of hotel rooms might be best for our first night. We walked along the seafront towards the seaweed baths, and a black-haired punky-looking girl came out of the house opposite. She saw me and began screaming like I was a flesh-eating Zombie or something, then she darted back into her house. Word seemed to go round the town quickly, and everywhere I walked, people were looking and mumbling. That night when we were having dinner in the hotel, around thirty people walked into the dining-room with pens and paper looking for me! I couldn't face anymore people. I just crawled under the table, hoping they'd walk past, but no, they spotted me, and silently waited round the table until I climbed out again. I signed the autographs, the people dispersed, and we decided to move on to Galway to see my folks the next day.

Accommodation was hard to find, but my Auntie Anne found a room for us in a small hotel she worked at. My Auntie Della had invited us to dinner the next day, and I'd become quite sick with bronchitis; I needed to sleep and get well. The next morning at 7.30a.m. there's a banging at my door: 'Hazel, Hazel, let me in! It's your Auntie Anne.' 'Leave me to sleep, please. I'll see you later,' I called, trying to stay asleep. 'Hazel, Hazel, I need to talk to you now, it's urgent.' I opened the door coughing and wheezing, and Auntie Anne followed me to my bed and said, 'Hazel, promise you'll come to dinner at my house tonight.' I was incredulous: 'You woke me up to ask me that?' I asked. 'Yes, come to my house tonight, all right?'

I got dressed after she'd gone and decided I'd go nowhere to dinner in Galway. I'd go home to London. I needed some peace and quiet. I got the next plane home and scrapped my ideas of a leisurely camping holiday and looking for a house to buy in Ireland. It would be another nine years before I finally moved to Ireland.

My song "Will You" had been a huge success and as a result, permission was asked to use the sax solo part on a Ronson shaver advert. This started to get Wesley McGoogan going as he'd played on the *Breaking Glass* recording sessions, and I'd asked him to play in my band. So after nearly two years of working with me, he began asking for a share of my song writing royalties for "Will You". I didn't like this much as song writing is divided into two parts – fifty per cent for the lyrics and fifty per cent for the melody – and as I'd written both a long time before I'd ever met Wesley, I didn't think it fair. Another source of annoyance was that Alan had become Wesley's manager and publisher, as well as managing me, which meant I felt he couldn't give me unbiased advice on this issue, as this would be a conflict of interest. I told them both I conceded that the sax solo had helped the song and therefore I could give him a portion of the music-writers share, something like twenty per cent. He wanted fifty per cent, so the discussion was dropped for the time being.

The new album *Cover Plus* was due out, and the first single was "Hanging Around". A video was shot this time to prepare for Top of the Pops. The week "Hanging Around" came out, The Jam and a few other gods of the Pop Charts had released singles that had zoomed up the top ten, so a lot of other chart positions were affected. "Hanging Around" had gone in at number forty-three, and because the *Top of the Pops* producer assumed my single would go into the top forty the following week, they filmed Megahype and me at the end of the show, saying as long as the

Chapter Eight

single moves up, they would play it. Well if I ran a record company, I would try my hardest to make sure that single moved up, as having a *Top of the Pops* appearance already filmed is money in the bank, because the exposure is so massive. The single didn't move the following week, so *Top of the Pops* didn't show the song. The next single was "Cover Plus" and, believe it or not, the same set of circumstances presented themselves again. In went the single at forty-one, so *Top of the Pops* filmed us again in advance to play the following week, assuming the single moved up, but it didn't, it moved down.

The album came out and we began the last of my big rock tours in the UK with no added help of a 'hit' single. The tour was arduous, and I was fed-up with Albion Records. I felt they'd dismantled all the good work that A & M Records, Allied Stars, and I had put together. My last gig was at Hammersmith Odeon (now the Apollo). I'd invited Adrian to come to the show and the after-show party. There was a lot of love in the audience that night and I felt it, but I also felt a splitting apart of myself; it was as if I'd stepped out of my body and stood aside looking at my posturing Hazel O'Connor rock star self, and I hated her, I criticized her, and I didn't feel responsible for her. The love of the audience felt very painful.

My after-party was sad. I never got time to hang out with any of my true friends, as everybody else wanted my attention. Everyone treated me like something to be passed around, and if you don't feel like you're much of trophy anyway, it's even worse. That's what fame does, it makes all of the fissures in your makeup split open, and it seems like they can be seen by everyone. All my weakness and self-loathing came flooding back. Midge fits very nicely into that time: maybe it was all just an illusion, because he and I were famous. I'd bought into it all. I was so pleased to see Adrian at the party and he was fascinated by my trappings of fame. I went home that night and cried bitterly.

I seemed to weep a lot and I couldn't sleep, and I was always worried. I had a week's turnaround and then I was starting a German tour. The day before I was due to leave I couldn't stop sobbing, Midge said I should refuse to go to Germany until I'd seen a doctor. I went to the doctor and he said I was suffering from depression and should have some time off. Of course I couldn't do that, so he told me to get at least three hours a day to myself to go and do whatever I pleased, and not to do any interviews or photo sessions; literally three hours a day to see where I was! When the doctor asked me what my life was like these days, I said that for the past eighteen months it had been: get up in the morning, do an interview, fly to another country, go to sound check, the gig, go to the hotel, sleep (if possible), and on the next morning get up, do interviews, photo sessions, travel, sound check, gig, go to another hotel... The most exciting thing in my life at this time was if the hotel had tea and coffee-making facilities in the room, so I wouldn't have to ask anyone for a cup of tea. I'd had such freedom and now I had none. The payoff: I didn't have a life.

The German tour started with a bang, as there was no way I'd be allowed to just do my concerts. The German record company, Ariola, had paid Albion Records a lot of money for the privilege of having me on their label, and they had a ton of interviews, TV, and photo sessions that had to be done. They'd paid for their pound of flesh. I threw shapes every so often, stamped my foot, tried saying no, but nobody heard.

After Germany we arrived in Paris. The record company's (Virgin France) publicity lady collected us at the airport and she just went on and on about all the interviews she had set up ready for me to do. For the first time in my life I found myself falling asleep in the middle of this P.R. woman lecturing me on doing all the interviews she'd set up. I just kept nodding off standing, sitting, or driving. It was a sweet relief when she shouted at me. I referred her to Alan: 'Talk to my manager,' I said, and promptly nodded off again.

We arrived at the hotel and reception wouldn't give me my key. They gave it to the bellboy who took me up in the lift. He had a smirk all over his face saying, *'Quelle surprise.'* (What a surprise). My mind was racing. Maybe they'd called a press conference in my hotel room – maybe there were photographers waiting to lurch at me – I was quite paranoid by this time, and kept asking the bellboy to give me my key. At the door to my room, the smirking bellboy inserted the key, and turned it. As the door opened all I could see was the flash of a camera. I screamed and ran off down the service stairs. I ran out into the street still screaming and crying that they'd set me up. Suddenly I heard a familiar Scottish voice behind me, saying, 'Hazel, Hazel, hang on! It was only me taking your photo!'

It was Midge. I'd always been going on at him about keeping our romance going, saying that doing the jobs we were doing, we should try to visit each another on tour, so we don't forget each other. This was Midge's attempt at a romantic surprise, and he wanted to document that moment with a photograph (as he was a keen photographer). 'I thought you were the paparazzi hiding in my room,' I wailed. I couldn't stop my hysterical sobbing for ages. Midge and I had a wonderful romantic evening in Paris. The next day he had to leave for his own tour, and I had my gig at *Captain Video* that night in Paris.

For the past eighteen months my sister-in-law Sue had travelled on tour with us and I'd given her some jobs to do. One job was to shine a torch to guide me off stage after the song part of "Will You" finished when there was a total blackout of lights for a few seconds, at which point I would run off stage following Sue's torchlight beam, and the lights would come back on full for Wesley's sax solo. *Captain Video* was sold out that night. Some more of the Finchley boys had come over for the gig and there were many happy reunions backstage. Showtime came and things were going very well. When we got to the "Will You" part of the show, I finished singing, the lights blacked out, but I couldn't see my sister-in-law Sue's light beam. It was totally black on stage; I started to panic, looking for a gap in the curtains at the back of the stage. I couldn't find a way off. The lights came back on, and there I am standing at the back of the stage still grappling with the curtains. I ran off, cursing Sue. I found her in the dressing room chatting merrily away with our 'Finchley boy' friends, having totally forgotten to come and help me. I was fuming at the time as I felt such a plonker, but I saw the funny side fairly soon after, because it was funny remembering the sheer panic I'd felt looking like a fly stuck on a spider's web as the spotlights came full on to me.

I'd made no money for ages. Publishing money was coming in but went straight to Albion Records to pay the Tony Visconti advance: I was struggling financially. I'd been offered an acting job in a children's time TV drama called *Jangles*. The premise of the programme was this: A bunch of school kids spent their 'real' time in a club, called Jangles, with a God-like D.J. who put his tuppence-worth in every week. There would be live music per episode, and my character would perform one song a week.

I took the job. I needed the money. I also used this opportunity to record the backing tracks for the music with my brother at Martin Rushent's Genetic Studio. Martin was famous for producing such artists as The Stranglers, Altered Images, The Go Gos, and Human League. I really wanted to get to know him better. Our friendship stood the test of time and he was still producing records with me until his death last year. He is sorely missed.

During weekdays I lived in the *Holiday Inn* in Bristol. During filming and most weekends I'd fly off to some city in Europe to spend a few nights with Midge, who was doing a big European tour with Ultravox. I enjoyed acting again. It's lovely to get to know a group of actors, on and off the set. It's like a family for the duration. My TV mum was Sue, who is also Gail's mum on *Coronation Street*. My leading man was a gorgeous actor called Jesse Birdsall. When I first saw Jesse I was attracted to him, but he had an equally gorgeous girlfriend, but anyhow, I was 'in love' with Midge.

During the two months' filming in Bristol, Jesse and I became very good pals. He was no longer going out with his girlfriend and I wasn't seeing much of Midge, except for a night or so every two weeks. To be honest this was not enough for me. To get to see Midge was such a trial sometimes, like flying into Zurich Airport in a snowstorm. Strangely enough that day in Zurich the news on the radio said Lotte Lenya (the German singer who I'd been compared to in New York) had just died. I tried to keep my relationship with Midge alive but it was hard. Sometimes I'd find a ring, or some other kind of female jewellery in his hotel room, and I'd wonder if he was still shagging groupie fans, or was he faithful? I had my doubts about his fidelity because of the amount of jewellery and knick-knacks I'd come across. Maybe they're just things given to him by fans, like I get given to me, I'd tell myself. Meanwhile, Jesse and I became closer and closer; I wasn't unfaithful to Midge, but I wanted to be. To this day, I wished I'd just gone with Jesse. He was so kind, caring, and funny. We had a special buzz between us and he certainly didn't feel ashamed to be seen with me.

The last of my visits to Midge on his European tour came towards the end of my Bristol stint. I was to meet him in Paris, then fly on to Amsterdam for the weekend. I woke up in my Bristol *Holiday Inn* room on the Friday of my departure feeling very excited about our weekend plans. I'd had a terrible dream about trying to drive to Heathrow Airport in my VW Beetle with six people from my band and my sister-in-law Sue all squashed in with me. They all moaned until I stopped at some shops so they could buy some chocolate. 'Don't take long!' I'd shouted. 'I mustn't be late for my Paris flight. I'm going to see Midge.' They all disappeared for ages and I had to go into the shopping mall and collect them. When I drove up to the airport I saw my flight take off without me. I woke up very disturbed from this nightmare. 'Silly of me: it was only a dream,' I told myself, opening the curtains. The sight that met me haunts me to this day. The whole world had turned white. Blizzards had blown all night, the motorways were cut off, and there was one train going to London. All flights had thus far been cancelled.

I couldn't believe it. In fact I refused to believe it. I trudged through the three foot snowdrifts to the railway station (there was no traffic on the roads). I got on that one and only train at midday, which eventually got to London at 5.30p.m. – the journey would normally take two hours; maximum. The picture everywhere during that journey was blizzards and high snow drifts. I took a cab to my house and asked him to wait whilst I rang the airport to see if my flight, by some chance, might be going. Yes it was! I raced down to the cab and we drove high-speed to

Heathrow Airport.

I checked in and made my way to the gate. I thought, 'Ha, ha! So much for my dream of doom, I've made it; I'm on my way to Paris.' There was a huge queue at the gate, as the flight was continuing to India, and there was a baggage strike, so the bags were being checked in at the gate by hand. The flight was due to leave at 7p.m., by 9p.m. we were only just boarding.

I sat down in the plane and kept trying to figure out what time I'd get there, now that we were so delayed, as Paris was an hour ahead. If we left immediately I wouldn't get into Paris until around midnight. The captain kept saying, 'Sorry about the delay. We're just de-icing the wings.' He said this about four times, and the time had moved on to 10.15p.m. My nightmare kept playing in my head. What if it's an omen? I thought, at which point I stood up and asked to be let off the plane. The stewardess asked the captain to talk to me. He tried to persuade me to stay, saying that the bridge to the plane had already been taken away. 'I'm sorry to cause a fuss, but I must get off. I would arrive too late in Paris and I don't know where my boyfriend is staying. I only know where his show was but they'll be gone, and by the time I get there I'd have no money, and no clue where to go!' They brought the bridge back to get me off the plane. Quite a few people panicked and stood up saying, 'What's going on?' The crew tried to smooth things over.

The airport police met me as I'd come back into the departures area, and I had to be escorted by the cops into arrivals. I was so sad when I reached home. I eventually found out a phone number for Midge's hotel. I kept trying to ring to apologise for my non-arrival, but his phone was always engaged. Around 4.30a.m. I tried again, imagining he must be so worried about me. He picked up and I said, 'Hello, Midge, it's me.' The groggy reply shocked me: 'Who's this?' I put the phone down, really pissed off. He obviously wasn't very bothered about me. He didn't even recognise my voice.

The next day he left a message on my machine: 'Where were you last night? Bloody hell! A little bit of snow and you go to pot!' The cheeky bastard! A little bit of snow!! I had tried so hard to get there – twelve hours' worth of trying. I didn't talk to him for a few weeks. We sort of made up and he invited me to spend Christmas with him and his family in Glasgow.

The filming of *Jangles* finished and my feelings for Jesse remained unresolved. I was well chuffed about going to spend time at Midge's family home, but of course reality is always different from the cosy dream. His mum and dad were lovely, but he was distant and always watching TV like a couch potato. I thought he'd show me round his home town. I couldn't quite put my finger on it, but we were different. Maybe it was sleeping together in his little bedroom with his mum next door. I'd been getting funny vibes about him the day before we left, as he'd been doing the Christmas *Top of the Pops*, and I'd tried to ring him after, but his phone was always engaged. Anyway we spent a quiet time in Scotland in front of the TV. At night we kept our T-shirts on in bed as it was very cold in Scotland that Christmas.

We arrived back in London a few days after Glasgow. We spent the night in Midge's new Chiswick house. We stripped off and got into bed, both knackered from the days travelling. There was no hanky-panky, we just collapsed into sleep. He turned over from me as he fell asleep, and as he did I saw two hands worth of scratches going down his back. I traced my hands down the lines. It definitely looked like two hands had clawed him, and it wasn't me! All night I stared at those damn scratches, not knowing what to do.

The next day I asked straight up front: 'Midge, have you been fucking somebody else?' 'No, of course not,' he said. 'Well explain the marks on your back – they're fingernail marks,' I said. 'Oh those marks. It was Steve Strange's leather-studded jacket that I wore on *Top of the Pops* that did that – the studs scratched me.'

It seemed plausible, but then I remembered he'd worn a T-shirt under the jacket, and the scratches were finger-lengths apart. I didn't believe him, even though I wanted to. 'Whether you have fucked somebody else or not, I think we have come to a sad pass for me to even *think* that you had. I think it's over between us, isn't it?'

He didn't say much. He didn't take me into his arms and tell me he loved me and say, 'Let's work this out.' Of course I wished he had, but he didn't. I suggested that we break-up for five months – until my next birthday – and then see how we feel. Midge said, 'Okay,' gave me a lift home, set up the new stereo he'd bought for my Christmas present, and departed from my life.

I'd not been happy with Alan Edwards's response to Albion Records from the beginning, but that Christmas in 1981, he said that the head of EMI might buy my contract away from Albion Records. I thought I should have left Albion right at the beginning when they'd managed to get me to sign those contracts, without the presence of legal representation on my part, just before I landed the lead in *Breaking Glass*. I didn't want to be bought and sold anymore. I wanted to fight those people who I believed had cynically taken advantage of me, but Alan didn't want to. He wanted to get someone to buy me, but my market value had decreased since returning to Albion. I decided to take my life back into my own hands. I knew Albion wouldn't let me go without a fight, so a fight it would have to be. Alan Edwards didn't want a fight so I decided to leave him and go it alone. Leaving Alan was probably a mistake, because he had always given me two-hundred per cent and was a decent, honest, good guy. It was like a divorce; a very emotional divorce, and Alan was very hurt. For this I am eternally sorry.

I'd sought advice about terminating my deal with Albion and the first thing I was advised to do was to tell them I wouldn't make records anymore and that I wanted to pursue an acting career. This was to see if they'd just let me – their Golden Goose – go... as if they would!

The day I went into their office to inform them I was leaving, I was terrified; afraid I'd back-pedal, let them talk me around, and I'd not get round to telling them anything. So I sort of blackmailed myself by using my Walkman cassette recorder. My plan was to record the whole conversation I was about to have with them. I arrived at their offices for our meeting and slipped off to the toilet to switch on the record button then I proceeded to their room. I made my speech to them about not ever wanting to make records again, and I was moving to America to follow an acting career – I think I was braver because I was recording myself. At the end of my speech Derek Savage said, 'What do you think we should use for your next single?' Dai Davies added, 'We thought "That's Life"– Shall we go with that one?' They had totally ignored everything I'd just said, unless of course they were both deaf and stupid. 'I do not want to make records for you guys ever again,' I said, and left knowing we'd next meet in court.

I went to talk to my lovely accountant Peter Lawrence and he showed me all the final bills Alan Edwards had sent over. There were a few bills that were real stinkers, like a bill for £11,000 owed for non-payment of VAT on my last tour (Alan had failed to invoice for VAT on all my concert fees), or the £6,000 owed to a Van Hire Company because nobody checked the small print before we hired. The vehicle in question had been our crew bus which had run off the autobahn and crashed on Eastern German soil during our German tour; the small print said it would be charged to the customer everyday it would be off the road for repairs as a result of a crash. Our soundman Sheds was owed around £8,000, also for the last tour, and there was £5,000 owed to the cab firm we used. However, when I looked at the bills I also saw that £2,500 was Selector singer Pauline Black's taxi bills, whom Alan had recently started to manage.

Peter Lawrence was fuming that the VAT had not been invoiced. I was fuming about all those taxi rides that had nothing to do with me. The overall debts that Alan pushed over to me when I left him was over £30,000. I asked Peter, 'Do I have enough income to pay all these bills?' 'No Hazel,' he said quietly. 'You have £728 in the company account. I think you should file bankruptcy.' 'I can't do that,' I said immediately. 'My soundman Sheds is a friend. He has a house and family – I can't let him down like that! If I declare bankruptcy, he wouldn't get paid, would he?'

I didn't want to file for bankruptcy – fifty per cent was because of my pride and the other fifty per cent was because I really didn't want to let anyone down. I was determined to pay everyone back, slowly. £728 – not a lot to show for two years' hard slog!

After leaving Alan and Albion, I sought advice from a

wonderful man called Laurence Myers. Laurence was head of GTO Films; the company that had distributed *Breaking Glass* in England. We first met at Cannes Film Festival we got on very well. Laurence introduced me to a top legal firm called Russells, where I met with the head honcho Tony Russell. I had no money to pay for legal costs so I applied for legal aid. I was told that I must close my company, Hazel O'Connor Ltd., and show all my accounts. Social Services called me in for an interview, and I was interrogated as to where had all my supposed money gone – perhaps I had furs and jewels. It took a couple of hours to convince the Social Services' interviewer that I had no money and I had never received any great amounts during my two years of fame: I was absolutely skint.

I was granted a legal aid certificate (which means the state would cover legal costs and then I would have to repay them as money came in). A letter was sent to Albion stating that they'd breached their recording contract with me, and therefore I intended to seek a new deal elsewhere. Albion went to the court and asked for an interim injunction to stop me seeking new deals. This was the first of many court dates I was to attend. I had a fantastic barrister working on my behalf by the name of Mark Crann. Mark had told me in our first meeting that my gut instinct to walk from Albion – back before I'd made *Breaking Glass* – had been correct. It would be seen as a conflict of interests to own the publishing and recording rights of an artiste, plus the court was beginning to take a very dim view of the likes of Albion (and many other record companies) getting signatures on contracts without a lawyer being present. If only I'd made a bigger fuss two years before, I could have walked away from Albion, and maybe my life would have been very different.

My first day in court was very interesting. My friend Vickie came with me for moral support. Mark Crann, my barrister, was asking the court to lift the interim injunction. We won and the injunction was lifted. So Albion's lawyer put in an appeal, which was to be heard that same afternoon. The appeal court had three judges sitting and one of those judges really understood the music business; he asked wonderful pertinent questions.

Chapter Eight

Eventually the judges decided I should be free to actively look for a new record company, but the master recordings of this new album could not be released until the dispute between myself and Albion Records was resolved. If I was to lose against Albion, the hypothetical deal with a new record company would be negated and the new master recordings destroyed.

So I won, by getting the injunction against seeking a new record deal lifted, but it was an empty victory, as no major record company would touch me with a bargepole. They were afraid to invest in recording a new album with me, only to lose their investment if my eventual contractual court case with Albion went against me, and then I'd have to return to Albion Records. I was now untouchable – a pariah!

Over the next three weeks the same court official delivered a different writ every week. The first was Albion Records suing me for breach of contract (because I walked away from their contract). The next was Alan Edwards, who wanted to stop any money coming directly to me, and re-route it via him to pay back his debts. The third was Alan Edwards and Wesley McGoogan, suing for fifty per cent of my song "Will You". As the court official delivered the third writ he said, 'I'm sorry, Miss O'Connor, another one I'm afraid.'

So by March 1982, I was in quite a bad state; three court cases, no money, no boyfriend, no manager, no record company, and quite frankly I was feeling quite snowed under by it all. Alan Edwards's case against me was thrown out of court. He then came to see Alan Seifert (who had been Toyah Wilcox's manager, and still looked after Marianne Faithfull), who was trying to help me with management, asking for a £10,000 pay-off there and then, or the written promise of that amount at some later stage. He said if I didn't pay up – or promise to pay – he'd give evidence in my up-coming trial against Albion Records, on behalf of Albion!

Alan Seifert told Alan Edwards that obviously we'd pay him some money, but how much couldn't be quantified at that moment, because I didn't have any money at all, and maybe I wouldn't have any money for a long time. Alan Edwards was insistent: give him money, and he would swear evidence on my behalf, don't give him money, and he'd swear evidence on behalf of Albion. I was very disappointed in my ex-manager as this seemed to me to be tantamount to blackmail. Alan Edwards had been the person I'd trusted to deal day-to-day with Albion on my behalf, so most of my information for my case came from Alan, and if he suddenly changed sides I couldn't possibly win my freedom. It was very disloyal of Alan. Many years later, to his credit, he apologised for this stunt – he was also penniless and desperate after I left him, just as I was.

My new manager thought my ex-manager's behaviour was appalling; it was against all codes of conduct, and it was morally wrong. He told him there was no money so he couldn't promise any because 'Hazel O'Connor is penniless.' Some people around me thought I'd been mismanaged and that I should be suing Alan Edwards. I never thought he mismanaged me, he definitely made some huge mistakes due to lack of experience (like the non-invoicing for VAT, which cost me £11,000 as a result), but he was one of the nicest, most enthusiastic, and kindest human beings I've ever known. What he lacked in managing prowess, he more than made up for in creative ideas and great publicity.

When I'd had an audit done on Albion Records, it seemed they owed me a couple of thousand pounds, and I became quite hopeful thinking I'd finally paid off the £40,000 they'd charged me for the Vic Maile produced album, which never saw the light of day (pre-*Breaking Glass*). Maybe Tony Visconti's advance money had now been covered by my publishing money, so maybe I'd get a publishing royalty payment soon. The only thing I got was another court writ from Albion Publishing, suing me, Alan Edwards, and Wesley McGoogan! They were suing me instead of defending me over my song "Will You", on the grounds that I had not informed them that I'd written "Will You" with Wesley. I'd never even met him way back in 1977 when I wrote the song. Of course Albion knew all this, but it was a good ploy to keep me answering court writs and keeping me poor. The Performing Rights Society, on being informed that song was in dispute, froze all income generated by it, and would not release it until it was sorted legally. There was £85,000 due to come to me on that song; £85,000 frozen that would easily have paid for my court action against Albion and well they knew it – what a clever sneaky trick. All publishing contracts have a clause towards the end saying in effect that if a third party make a claim (as did Wesley and Alan Edwards) against the writer (Hazel O'Connor) the company (Albion Publishing) will defend their client (Hazel O'Connor) and pay legal costs, if needs be (which, of course, would be recoupable from Hazel O'Connor at some stage or other). Instead of defending me, they sued me. I presume it was so as not to have to pay the costs of defending me, and because they wanted to tie me in financial knots. I'd be unable to get my £85,000 from "Will You", and thus I was rendered totally penniless. It was a subtle way of getting back at me for suing their record company.

Those early months of 1982 were terrible. I missed Midge. I was so poor, I don't know how I managed to buy food and pay my household bills. I'd come out in a huge rash of acne boils on my back, and everybody that could put the boot in did so. There was a girl who used to work for Alan Edwards called Sunie Fletcher. She accompanied me on my first ever TV chat show. I considered her a personal friend and I let her into my home. This girl was now a music journalist, and she seemed to keep a steady flow of nasty snipes going in the music press on a weekly basis. For example, 'Hazel O'Connor was thrown out of the Simon and Garfunkel after-gig party at the Groucho Club in Knightsbridge, on the grounds of taste – not sexism.' I've never been to a Simon and Garfunkel party in my life! So she obviously fabricated stories like this to punish me! I'd never done her a bad turn, yet her press campaign against me was vicious. And here's the rub: The only court action you can't get legal aid assistance for is libel and slander. Most of the people I thought of as friends seemed to disappear. Paula Yates didn't call anymore, and to be honest I didn't want to see anybody.

Another libellous gem from that time was a tabloid piece which began life as a two-page fashion spread with interview. A fashion spread means you go out to the shops and borrow a bunch of clothes and model them for the piece, usually three or four different outfits are chosen, and a little interview goes with it. I did the photo session with a lovely and talented young photographer, called Chris Craymer, and the pictures looked beautiful. The interviewer, Noreen Taylor, arrived at my house, and we did a fine interview. I thought I was a bit down myself re men and relationships, but that was all. Later on, Noreen rang to ask could I do one more photo for the piece, as her slant on the story included my flatmate Sal, who was running the Hazel O'Connor business single-handed from her bedroom. So Chris Craymer came up to my flat, got Sal and I to sit on the sofa – her with a phone, me with a keyboard –and asked us to squish together for a head-shot. A couple of days later the piece came out. Sal and I bought the newspaper from our corner shop and sauntered back to the flat reading as we walked. I was quite excited because Chris was such a great photographer. I was convinced his pictures would look fab and Noreen had been so empathic – I was so sure her words would also be great.

Shock number one was an old busty modelling photo of me from when I was eighteen, on the front cover with a caption reading: 'My private struggles – an exclusive on Hazel's private life.' It didn't sound much like a fashion piece to me –more like an exposé of doom and gloom. Nothing could have prepared me for the second shock that hit us as we opened the centre pages. The title of the piece read: 'My soul mate Sal.' Underneath was a big photo of Sal and I looking like we were sitting in an embrace. This was the innocent headshot where Chris had asked us to squash in together, so he could get a good tight photo of our two faces. They hadn't cropped the photo to a headshot size, so it looked like I had my arm around her. Only one of the beautiful fashion shots made it into the piece. And then I read the article – It was such terrible bullshit. In the interview I'd said men didn't find me attractive. In reality, this was because I've always been down on myself in the attractiveness stakes, especially at this low point, as I was really missing Midge. Then the piece seemed to home in on my mate Sal – 'With Sal I can be myself; she understands me.' – Well of course she could; she's my mate! The whole thing made us look like lovers, which we weren't, and thus we found it offensive and very misguiding. I remember highlighting every slanderous, libellous sentence. 'I'll bloody sue them for defamation of character,' I said, sobbing and angry all at the same time. I phoned my solicitor and was then reminded that a slander/libel and defamation of character suit cannot be done on legal aid, and I had no money to fight back. This piece did terrible psychological damage to my already fragile state. It felt like a betrayal of trust. I was appearing at a music festival in Wembley later that day, and every time a female fan asked for an autograph I started getting very paranoid, thinking: 'Better not be too friendly in case they think I'm trying to seduce them.'

Chris Craymer rang, sounding very upset, saying the 'stitch up' had nothing to do with him, and how desperately sorry he was. I never heard from Noreen Taylor, so I presumed she'd masterminded the whole thing, and I hated her for it for the next fifteen years, until our paths crossed again.

This was the lowest I'd ever felt and I missed Midge loads. I asked my friend Sal to visit him for me, even though we had agreed to stay apart until my next birthday on the sixteenth of May, when we'd meet up and either stay split or get back together again Sal was hours later than she thought she'd be, and I sat up waiting to hear word of Midge. When she did come back, she was fairly drunk and the word she bought from him was, 'He loves you but can't be with you – Oh it's so sad.' She started crying. 'And he sent this to help you out.' It was a £2,000 cheque. That was it really – Sal crashed out, and I cried myself to sleep. It felt like I was being bought off.

The next day I tried to find out what had happened during her long visit to Midge, and why the money? But Sal kept being offhand with me. This is the moment I flipped. I shouted terrible abuse at her. I said that everybody had used me and must be pissing themselves laughing and now I was thrown away by all and sundry. I mostly remember the more crazy I became, the longer my room looked, and the smaller and further away Sal looked. I felt that the person shouting abuse and vitriol wasn't me – that I was only an observer, and not that crazy Hazel O'Connor woman.

When I came to my senses I found myself fully clothed, sitting in a bath full of water. I went to find Sal to apologise. 'I'm so sorry, Sal. All I can say is that it wasn't me shouting, I was possessed.' Hardly good enough when I saw the result of my mad outburst. I'd hurt one of the only friends who had stuck by me through thick and thin in these terrible times – I was so ashamed.

I went to see the doctor, and was told I was clinically depressed. He gave me pills for the morning and pills for the night. On my way home I took the morning ones, thinking they'd pep me up a bit, as I had the BBC interview team coming to film me at home. The pills did the opposite to pepping me up! It was a struggle to talk, think, or stay upright. When I saw the interview, I looked like an out-of-it heroin addict. I phoned the doctor and told him the result of his medication. He told me the chemist must have misread his writing, as the morning drug was actually the one for bedtime. I only took the pills for a while because a friend saw the name on the pill bottle and flipped. 'Haze, don't take this stuff, trust me, my dad is a doctor at a mental hospital and this drug, Largactil, is what they give the patients to knock them out, or to get rid of them.' I did so and thus ended any relationship with uppers and downers.

CHAPTER NINE

'Well, the dreams I've dreamed I shall dream again,
eternally speaking
Right now the face of eternity
looks blank into the face of time
It's just the thoughts of you lying in that fatal position
How can I speak, how can I speak -
when it cuts too deep'
"Cuts Too Deep" (*Smile*, 1984)

Granada TV offered me a small job, interviewing pop celebrities on a programme that Tony Wilson was hosting. Tony was the founder of Factory Records and the Hacienda Club in Manchester. Once a week I'd fly to Manchester and do my five minute 'pop slot'. The most exciting for me was when I was told I'd be interviewing Nico, the ex-singer of the 60s cult band, The Velvet Underground. I had been a fan of hers and the band since I heard their album in my early hippy days. In my punk days I'd been to see Nico perform at the Marquee Club in London accompanying herself with a harmonium only – I thought she was a class act. I hurried along to the makeup room to welcome her and discuss the interview. I always appreciated my interviewer coming to say hello before they interviewed me on TV, so I extended her the same courtesy. She didn't seem particularly interested in me or the pending interview, which, of course, is a big star's prerogative. I was a little worried when I saw how she was applying her makeup. She was piling loads of white powder on her face, which appeared very puffy and blotchy, not at all the blonde goddess of the 60s. I wanted to give her a hand with the makeup, as it was really looking bad, but she pooh-poohed me saying, 'Look, I'm fine, darling,' in her deep Germanic brogue. To be honest I thought she was stoned.

The interview seemed a bit of a disaster when we started filming, because all she wanted to talk about was the rivalry over her between Lou Reed and John Cole back in their heyday. I was very sad after that day was over. I felt that one of my all-time heroines was no more a goddess, just a mere self-obsessed mortal like the rest of us. I prayed – and do still pray – I'll never turn out like that when some fan interviews me. It was a good lesson on how *not* to be perceived.

After the Granada gig came to an end, I got another job singing jazz standards (and a few of my own songs) at a supper club in Knightsbridge, accompanied by a lovely piano player, called Bob Colley, and by Clare Hirst on sax. I'd first met Clare playing in the all-girl band, The Belle Stars, and we continue to work together on and off, right up to the present day.

Chapter Nine

I'd always loved these old standards of Gershwin and Cole Porter, and Billie Holliday's stuff, as Adrian had turned me onto them back in the 70s. It was a joy to get to perform in such intimate surroundings with no expectations on me to be the 'Punk Princess'. During this period I also performed and wrote songs with a great female pianist called Nickie Holland, who used to work with Funboy Three and Tears for Fears. Our repertoire consisted of songs like "God Bless The Child", "Stormy Weather", "Someone To Watch Over Me", "Let's Do It", and as I said, a smattering of my songs, like "Will You" and "Calls the Tune". This period was very important to me musically as I was forced by circumstances to develop as a singer.

I was offered the role of Candy Star, the hooker in the play *One Flew Over The Cuckoo's Nest*, which was to be performed at the Royal Exchange in Manchester: This was my first theatre job. The talent was superb: Linda Marlowe played Nurse Ratchett, Eve Ferrett was my co-hooker, Tim McInerney (who later played both Percy and Captain Darling in the *Blackadder* TV series) played Billy Bibbit, who my character comes on to the ward to have sex with, and John Sessions played another of the mental patients.

Laurence Myers (of GTO Films), who had been such a great help, introduced me to two fantastic pop business characters, namely Dick Leahy and Brian Morrison, and we got on like a house on fire. They were publishers who had a record company, and wanted to buy my contract off Albion, thus abating the looming court case I had with Dai Davies and Derek Savage. Albion still wouldn't let me go, even with a good offer of – money – it seemed like they'd never let me go until they'd fucked up my career entirely.

One day at Brian and Dick's office they played me their latest publishing signing – a young duo called Wham – which was when I first heard Wham rap. My mate Sal now worked for a PR company and did a lot of work at the Camden Palace Club. It was through her I met George Michael and Andrew Ridgley, which was a funny coincidence for me, as I'd already heard their music and all about them from Brian and Dick.

I was finally given a court date for the Albion vs. Hazel

O'Connor case. My dear friend Vickie came every day with me, which was handy because she's such a beautiful exotic bird. When I heard some garbage spoken by Albion's lawyer, I'd stage whisper to Vickie, 'He's lying,' just loud enough for the judge to hear, and he'd look across to me and Vickie and take note. There were some serious manipulations of the truth like: 'Hazel O'Connor received three million pounds in advances.' In fact, I only received the advance due to me in my 1980 re-negotiated contract, which was £12,000. They had received three million pounds in my name, but they never passed even a percentage of that amount on to me. Another good one was: 'Hazel O'Connor was a bit unhinged,' which I really took exception to, but on the whole I realised that when two parties go into a courtroom battle, there is no room for emotion: just facts, and interpretations of those facts.

The summer came, and the case was adjourned until after the summer break, which would be sometime in September. I was mortified. I had no funds to live on and no royalties coming in, as *Breaking Glass* record royalties were supposed to be paid to me via Albion, but obviously they were in no hurry to account to me. My publishing royalties were also routed through Albion, and the biggest 'earner's' proceeds, "Will You", had stayed frozen because of Albion's counter-action against me, Wesley, and Alan Edwards. It was a mess. I was penniless and still being mobbed!

Virgin Records showed interest in signing me. We had some meetings and a contract was drawn up: *if* I could get released from Albion. Albion were now saying they may release me and settle if they took a percentage of any advance money and sales that came from the new deal. Things really got serious with Virgin, and I was so excited, as it was such a brilliant company. I was put together with Culture Club's record producer, Steve Levine. What tracks to record? was the next question. Then Albion pulled a bombshell: they wouldn't release me for Germany. Virgin could have me for the rest of the world, but not Germany. 'Why the bloody hell not?' I shrieked, when I got the news. 'It seems they'd already contracted you to a new deal there, and they'd get sued by the Germans if they don't deliver a new Hazel

O'Connor album,' my new manager Alan Seifert told me. My mind was reeling. Knowing them they'd probably contracted me whilst we'd been in litigation to raise a bit of quick cash at my expense.

I will always remember the day when the Virgin deal was off, as I'd watched *Top of the Pops* on TV, hosted by Virgin Records at a club called The Roof Garden in Knightsbridge. My invite never arrived. I phoned Alan Seifert and said to him, 'They must have forgotten to post it.' 'No,' he said, 'they've pulled out from signing you.' The final settlement agreement with Albion was freedom from them for the world, except Germany, which was one of my biggest sales territories. When Virgin discovered Germany was out of the equation they withdrew their offer to me. It turned out that the head of Virgin in Germany was a guy called Ude Langer, who'd worked very hard on me as an act when he was with Ariola (Albion's last German licensee), and he had especially wanted me for his Virgin German operation. Anyway I was scuppered, the deal was lost, and Albion came out with zilch.

To be honest, the rest of 1982 is a bit of a blur, not because I was out of my head on drink or drugs, or nuts from the pressure, but because I was just trying to survive. I remember meeting Midge at a TV show in Germany that autumn and we spent a few pleasant hours together. We actually ended up getting quite romantic, the zing was still there, but I pulled away from him saying, 'What about tomorrow?' I'd just got over the hurt of our parting, so if we had a night of passion, would it mean we were re-united? 'Nobody need know,' he said, as he pressed his hard-on against me. I disentangled from his embrace and walked away – 'Goodbye you shallow man.'

I was asked to perform in a charity concert for the National Campaign for Civil Liberties in the West End of London at the Duke of York's Theatre. Ironically, right opposite on the same evening, in a theatre called The Coliseum, a concert was to take place celebrating the end of the Falklands War and Prince Charles would be coming. Therefore the whole street was fenced off. My friend and neighbour, Sheena Easton, was performing at the Falklands bash, so after my stint at the National Campaign for Civil Liberties, I climbed the fences across the road and went backstage to watch the end of Sheena and all the other celebrities show, and especially to get a look at the Prince.

Thames Television was filming and I saw a lot of crew I knew from a TV show that I had done recently, so I hung out in the darkness of the stage wings with a makeup artist friend, watching all the celebrities lined up on the stage, waiting to meet the Prince. Suddenly three or four big bodyguards started pushing us 'back-stagers' aside, saying 'Move back, the Prince is coming.' We all moved back, and there was Prince Charles suddenly strutting past us, he came level with me and stopped, looking me up and down, his rosy-cheeked, big eared self said sleazily, 'Mmm, little black dress. Do you have black underwear to match?' Then he moved on. I was gobsmacked. How *dare* he ask me such a smutty thing? Did he think that I, as a minion of his realm, would have been flattered? Think again mate! If I'd have been six feet further on, I'd have been amongst my peers all eagerly awaiting royal patronage, ready to bow and curtsey to this florid rude man. And Prince Charles would not have been asking about my undies – He would have said, 'Oh yes, Hazel O'Connor, mmm, *Broken Glass*, mmm, etc., etc.' I told the newspapers next day, I was so pissed off...

By mid-1983, my recording career was looking up. The producer, Martin Rushent said he'd like to do a demo with me to help me get a record company interested. We did an R & B up-tempo song called "Bring it on Home". The head of RCA, David Betteridge, heard it and wanted me to make an album. I spent halcyon days out at Martin's Genetic Studios in Berkshire, and when I wasn't recording, I'd take long walks along the River Thames. My brother Neil was also working as co-producer, so I saw loads of him and it was wonderful to re-connect.

RCA were ready and able to pay for a promo video. I asked George Michael if he'd be my leading man in it and he agreed. There was a tiny kiss in the video between us, so some tabloids had a field day: 'George Michael is moving out of his mother's home into the home of the more experienced Hazel O'Connor'. What was that all about? We just had a laugh when that kind of stuff came out. George was a good pal to me back then. We went

Chapter Nine

to see David Bowie at Wembley together, and hitch-hiked home doing Wham dances at the side of the road. As well as appearing in my video, he came to support me in my second theatre piece, called *Nightshoot*, at the Tricycle Theatre, London. In fact, via Sal's work at the Camden Palace, I'd met and made friends with a nice bunch of people: The Spandau Ballet guys, Shirley and Pepsi, George Michael and Andrew Ridgley, and the McGann Brothers.

I remember a bonfire party I had that year (I'd moved to a flat with a tiny garden), when George had brought a demo cassette recording of his first solo single called "Careless Whisper". The Finchley Boys were in charge of lighting the fireworks, and they lit a load of rockets at once, which looked very impressive until one of them turned round unexpectedly and crash-landed in George's 'bad boy quiff' hair. We all had such fun that night, listening to the new single, dancing and singing to Sister Sledge's "We are Family". New romance was in the air as Shirley and Martin Kemp were slow-dancing. When everyone left, I cleaned up , switched my doorbell off, and went to bed. I was awoken around 5a.m. by a load of shouting and banging on my window. I opened the front door to reveal George and his mate soaking wet and it hadn't been raining. 'Whatever's going on?' I asked sleepily. 'I forgot my demo, so we came back, rang your bell, got no answer, so we tried the others,' said George. 'Then that window above opened and a bucket of water was thrown on us.' Poor George, he'd been ringing and ringing the doorbell of my 'neighbour from hell' and she'd lost the plot. She hadn't been keen on my party earlier, and was shouting nasty things every so often from her upstairs flat. George ringing her bell was the last straw, so she dumped a bucket of icy water over him!

Just before my RCA album *Smile* was released, the man who had signed me – the RCA boss, David Betteridge – was offered a job he couldn't refuse, which funnily enough was with Virgin, heading their new V2 Label. There was nobody like him in RCA. He was the energy and creativity my project needed.

The first single got some airplay, but no big chart position. The second single "Just Good Friends" was getting a lot of airplay, then all of a sudden the BBC decided to take it off their play lists because it had a line in it saying, 'Manchester morning, Piccadilly calling.' The BBC guys took the view that this was an advert for the Manchester Independent Radio Station, Piccadilly, even though I was writing about Piccadilly Train Station. It just seemed like I was jinxed. My confidence was at a fairly low ebb, when out of the blue I was invited to a Cartier party in Tunisia.

The party was a great boost for my morale. Our table was such fun, with Elton John next to me – he is a great character, so was Alan Peron, the head of Cartier – who confided in me that *Breaking Glass* was a big favourite of his. I started to show them how to hang a teaspoon on their noses (something I had learned from kids' TV programme *Blue Peter*). We all laughed and laughed, then Elton kindly played an impromptu concert –he played "Your Song", and I was in ecstasy.

I went off to my bed at about 3a.m., as I had to be up early to catch the Cartier Celebrity Jet back to Paris. I always panic if I don't get my eight hours sleep. I woke around 9a.m. to find a note had been pushed under the door. It read: 'Dear Hazel, tonight was lovely – thank you so much for your presence. Anything, anything at all I can do for you, do not hesitate to ask. Yours, Alan Peron. P.S. I'm sending you back on the private jet directly to London with Elton. It leaves later so you can rest.'

When I came home from the party, I came down to earth with a bang. Mum was in hospital having serious surgery. My mum, who'd helped me through these fame years; who'd run the fan club after the friend who had been running it left, leaving me with debts. Mum answered every single letter that came to me. She helped so many fans with growing pains, sexual identity problems, and all the other rites of passage every teenager goes through: she was there for them all. To this day there's always somebody who was a 'Hazelnut' asking for Joyce, my mum. So now she was in hospital after serious surgery and in pain. I was so afraid I'd lose her, like everything and everyone else in my life. Thankfully, she recovered and God bless her, continued to be the link to my fan base for many more years.

As Mum recovered, my new pal Elton phoned and invited me to the Apollo in Hammersmith to see his friend Liza Minnelli perform. Without hesitation I said 'Oh yes, please.' I admired her greatly since seeing the film *Cabaret* and I loved her voice and her spirit. At the theatre Elton was hilarious. He kept looking at all the handsome guys. 'Look at her,' he'd say, meaning 'Look at him.' Elton hadn't 'come out' yet. I've never been bothered about gay or otherwise (except for when I was wrongly labelled), and to be honest it's nobody's business what another gets up to sexually as long as no harm is done to another. Anyway, the show was great and we went to say hello to Liza afterwards – I was so in awe – I felt like curtsying to her: a queen of musical theatre.

I was watching the newly launched Channel 4 TV station with my friend Vickie, and we saw a programme called *The Animals Film*, which was narrated by the actress Julie Christie. She was the very woman Brian Gibson always said I'd end up like: living alone up a mountain with lots of dogs. The film changed my life. After seeing all the cruelty involved in eating other creatures, I decided to no longer endorse eating flesh, because I could no longer be part of the chain of cruelty that it involves. So that day Vickie and I pledged to give up eating meat.

I guess it became known that I was a vegetarian, because I was asked to sing at a posh event at the Ritz, hosted by Lady Lothian, and it was a Vegetarian Ball. Neil and I were going to do an acoustic set. When we arrived to sound check before the ball began, I realised the place was crawling with Hari Krishnas because X-Ray Spex singer Polly Styrene had joined the Hari Krishnas and her Krishna Band were also playing. I was filled with fear, dread, and hatred, remembering the rape of my face as a runaway teenager living in hippy Amsterdam so many years before by a so-called 'Krishna monk'. Grrr! I felt myself baring my teeth. Then out of the blue one of those shaved-up, saffron-robed boys stepped in front of me, trying to hand me a veggie cook book. 'Hi, I'm Amimisia. Can I give you this cook book?' I didn't even look at his book. I just blurted out, 'I'm already a vegetarian, and I was raped by one of your lot when I was sixteen, so leave me alone!' His robotic expression changed and he looked stunned. 'I'm so very sorry,' he said.

We began to talk, and he introduced me to his mother: a

beautiful, classic raven-haired beauty, with a white sari, and lavender coloured eyes. 'This is my mother Ritashia.' I melted. They seemed so exotic, yet so sincere and nice. I accepted a dinner invitation to Ritashia's house in London's Maida Vale area.

Ritashia had been a model and had dated the world's sexiest men. She was the daughter of a countess or some such who lived in Palm Beach, and her stories were so interesting; she'd come to Krishna consciousness after her son introduced her to it. After eating pasta together, she took out two copies of the Bhagavad Gita and said she'd sing the Sanskrit line, then we'd recite the English together. She started to drone a tuneless line of Sanskrit verse. We recited the translation, then she read the explanation of the verse – then she droned the next Sanskrit line – ouch! Meanwhile I was reading on ahead, and the actual meat of the verses touched me in a profound way, but dear Ritashia was murdering it. I politely asked if I could take the book home and read it quietly, then we could meet next time to discuss it. She agreed – Phew!

I read that holy Hindu scripture, which is the middle part of a much bigger Indian classic called the *Mahabharata*, and I loved what I read. The premise of the story is that the rightful dynasty, the Pandava Brothers, are about to fight their own cousins on the Field of Kurukshetra, and Arjuna, one of the Pandavas, is surveying the field of impending battle. He starts to lament to his cousin and chariot driver Krishna: 'How can I fight all these Kings and family?' At this point Krishna reveals to him the meaning of life and the universe. He talks about the soul being the thing that drives the body, and when the body dies, the soul does not. It struck many chords in me, as I'd always tussled with the idea of a Revelations type of judgement from my Sunday School days, when billions and zillions of zombies are lined up waiting to be judged, which in itself could take an eternity! Whereas I read in the Baghavad Gita that the soul moves to a new body at death, unless the soul has become realised, and thus would be going back to heaven, paradise, Godhead, or whatever you want to name the place where God resides. I read that every action we make in this life is encoding our 'Karma chip'. We are shaping our own destiny, our journey, with free will to do good or bad.

I chose to go back to Ritashia and Amimisia's house and a few weeks into our friendship they invited me to a big dinner party at the Hari headquarters in Letchmore Heath, a place they called Bhaktivedanta Manor. We drove north on the M1, twenty minutes from London, and arrived at a big country manor house, bought for the movement by Beatle, George Harrison. The place was swarming with saris and shaved heads. It was doing my head in. We moved up the grand staircase and were let into a normal sized room, stuffed with Hari Krishnas. On the opposite sofa to me was Sir John Mills, his wife Mary, and their daughter – my childhood idol – Hayley Mills. I was gobsmacked. Then the guru guy came in: Srila Gurudev. He looked very clean and shiny, a touch surly, but a handsome, youngish man. He talked, we listened, then we sang Hari Krishnas and my teeth started gnashing, because I had so much hate for the Haris en masse. I suppose that's why I went and stuck it out because I needed to put the ghosts of the past to bed. I thought at the time that he answered questions quite pompously, but what did I know of holy men? His mentor and bringer of the Hari Krishna movement to the West was definitely a devout lover of God. His name was Srila Prabhupada. After the talk we went to the dining room, elegantly decked out to Ritashia's requirements, and we enjoyed the most beautiful, sumptuous feast that I've ever eaten. I started chatting with Hayley Mills and really enjoyed her company. I began to incorporate Krishna consciousness into my life bit by bit. I became friends with that guru and Hayley Mills over the coming years. I met Chrissie Hynde again, as she was also a vegetarian, and going to the Temple.

My career was strange and interesting as usual. I did a two-week sell-out at Ronnie Scott's Jazz Club in London. A promoter from Budapest, saw me and got me to go to Poland for a TV show, then on to Hungary for two shows at the Budapest Opera House. The plan for the Polish leg of the trip was to fly to Warsaw, meet with our interpreter and a mini-bus, then drive four or five hours to Poznań.

We arrived at the Hotel at 10p.m. and hoped to get some

food. The waiter said, 'Yes, you can have dried fish or peach sundae.' I chose the peach ice cream and went to bed. This was poor Poland during Soviet times. The band was more or less the same gang from Ronnie Scott's club, plus sax player Clare Hirst from The Belle Stars. Now Clare liked to party, so that on the eve of our departure to Budapest, Clare went dancing and vodka drinking with the boys from the band. As we began our journey the next day to Warsaw Airport, Clare was dead to the world. After three hours' driving she suddenly woke up: 'Oh bloody hell, I've left my passport in the hotel room in Poznań!' Panic ensued. We couldn't go back as we'd miss our flight at Warsaw which was still two hours or more away. Someone had a brainwave. We took a few song reference cassettes and pasted my photo on the front, then wandered into the next police headquarters, where we sobbed and pleaded, offered them my album, and could they please help us? It cost a $100. The police in Poznań went into the ex-hotel bedroom, went to the drawer where she'd put her passport, then a cab driver drove to Warsaw Airport hotfoot to try to deliver her passport before we had to leave her behind to get on our flight to Budapest.

    Warsaw Airport was a bit grim in those days, with lots of grey-coated soldiers, police types, and wooden tables denoting the Gate, and us trying to delay boarding the flight until the last minute. Finally I had to go past the table gate to board and just then a man came running through the terminal waving a brown paper bag in his hand. 'Clare Hirst? Clare Hirst?' 'Here!' we waved. She got out her passport and boarded giggling as she looked at the other contents in the bag, which was her undies – She had stashed her passport in her underwear drawer then forgotten the lot! Budapest was superb. We did two sell-out shows and I discovered that *Breaking Glass* had made a big impact there. I continued to do huge gigs there for the next few years.

    Back home in London, I couldn't catch a cold, let alone get a record deal so I decided to sell my London flat and move to the Hertford countryside. I found a house, moved in, and now lived opposite fields and close to the Hari Krishna manor. Alan Seifert and I parted company, and at one point there was talk of John

Chapter Nine

Reid – Elton's manager – looking after me. One day John's assistant Julie rang me to arrange a meeting with John, when she said out of the blue, 'I am a friend of Walid Ben Saud. He's been my boyfriend's best mate ever since they were at school together.' 'Wow!' I thought of Walid in Beirut, both of us teenagers, escaping off to the hills in his sports car; it seemed like a million years ago.

Julie put me in touch with Walid and we went out to dinner, and filled in the gaps for each other in our life stories. He was now a respectable married wealthy businessman. I asked him where had he disappeared to that last time I'd been with him in Beirut. Apparently the Saudi Secret Service had an idea something was afoot, i.e. an imminent air attack from Israel. So the minute he arrived at the Palace in the early hours of the morning he was put aboard the Saudi Royal Yacht, with the rest of the Saudi Royals, and sailed away to safety.

I invited Walid up to Nottingham to a comedy TV show I was filming. My mum also drove over from Coventry in her three-wheeler Reliant Robin to meet us. We decided to go out for dinner before returning to London. Walid's assistant John drove Mum's three-wheeler so she could travel with us in the white Rolls Royce Walid had hired. We looked like a strange convoy: a big beautiful white Rolls with a silly little three-wheeler car hot on our tail. Eventually it was time to depart. Mum left to drive back to Coventry, and Walid, John and I were taken to a small airfield where a private jet waited to take us back to London! We had a few glasses of champagne and hey presto, we were back in London in no time at all. Unfortunately I didn't see much more of Walid, as he had to whisk his brother back to Saudi. His brother had got into some sort of trouble and poor Walid's house was being staked out by the press.

Clare Hirst and I were playing some jazzy gigs with the third member of our trio, Nickie Holland, on piano. Nickie was a fantastic musician and she did all the string arrangements. I felt truly blessed to sometimes get to do gigs with such great musicians as Clare and Nickie. An A & R man (talent scout) at Island Records heard us and paid for us to demo stuff. This was the first time my song "Driftwood" was recorded. We also recorded quite a lot of popular jazz standards like "Stormy Weather", "Summertime", and "Someone to Watch Over Me". But, as usual, we were a bit ahead of the times, and Island declined to take it further.

I'd been invited to a film premiere 'do' and dinner after and, as I hardly ever went out, I thought, Yes, I'll put on my glad rags. I can't remember the movie, but I do remember the dinner – or should I say, some of the dinner guests. There was a guy in white trainers and a sort of put-together black-tie look, and to top it off he wore glasses. I made up a story about him in my head: 'He's a rich movie producer, very eccentric, who got his assistant to hire his bad dinner jacket and frilly shirt, and he wore his trainers 'cause he didn't give a shit for convention.' We kept catching each other's eye across the sea of tables. Then the speeches at the end of dinner began, and the speaker started mentioning the celebrities present. As he did this, the celebrity in question was expected to stand up and take a bow. The speaker said, 'Hazel O'Connor, star of *Breaking Glass*.' Up I stood, bowed, and sat down again as soon as possible. I saw Mr Eccentric smiling at me. The next minute Mr Speaker introduced 'Christopher Lambert, star of *Tarzan*,' and up stood my eccentric film financier. I was crestfallen, as I try hard to steer clear of attractions towards actors, 'cause you never know who they'll be next, and the ones I've known are often unfaithful to their partners. In my mind, I had to stop looking over at him once I knew the truth about him.

I danced the night away and decided to leave around 3a.m. As I walked off the dance floor to leave, he, Christopher, put his arm across the aisle to block my departure. 'You are going?' he asked, in that gorgeous French accent, and before you could say Jack Robinson I was sitting down and chatting with him. Within half an hour we were sharing a taxi to pick up my car. Once inside the taxi he just started kissing me. 'What a brave man,' I thought, as I hadn't been kissed for ages. Being a star intimidated men, so nobody approached me unless they were seeking to use me as a trophy, and I certainly didn't want to be kissed or manhandled by a trophy seeker. But this Christopher Lambert was my equal and he was so sexy. We arrived at my VW Beetle and I was going to drive him back to his hotel. We got into my car and drove off, but at the first traffic lights he started kissing me again. I had to push him off as the lights changed or else we could've had a nasty accident. Finally I drew up at Blake's Hotel where he was making his home through the duration of the filming of *Highlander*; we did a bit more kissing, then I left. There was no way I was going into his hotel yet – Next time, I thought.

Next time came a few days later when he invited me to dinner at Blake's. I agonised over what to wear, and eventually arrived my usual half-hour late, flushed and panicked. As I walked towards the table, I realised the other two guests were Julie Walters and star of the *Chariots of Fire* movie, Ian Charleson. I felt so flustered again because I'm a big fan of Julie's. She was so funny, so nice, so perfect, and I shrank more and more.

After dinner we went to Christopher's suite to drink some champagne. Whilst waiting for the boys to open the bottle, Julie turned to me and said, 'Oh Hazel, I'm such a big fan of yours. I love that tea and coffee song. You write lovely songs, and your performance in *Breaking Glass* was really good.' This opened the floodgates 'Well I'm a bigger fan of yours – you're brilliant, and I'm sorry I've been so quiet, but I felt shy around you,' I blurted out. I had the best night out for ages with Julie, Christopher, and Ian. We ended up going to Ian's flat singing jazz songs around him playing the piano until 8.30a.m. the next day. And, yes, eventually I did have a little thing going with Christopher and he was a great lover!

Julie and Ian had told me about a film they were producing and acting in called *Car Trouble*. With director David Greene's say-so, they ended up giving me a small role in that movie.

At a TV quiz show, a few months later, I met a fellow called Mike Smith in the green room. He told me he knew of a BBC script that was about to go into production to be a five-hour drama series. He wanted my permission to put me up for the role. Before I knew it I was meeting the producer Chris Parr and the director Paul Seed. I decided I wanted this role, and was perfect for it. The series was called *Fighting Back* and the story followed the trials and tribulations of Vivienne and her two children, a white boy of eleven and a sixteen-year-old mixed-race girl.

At the end of the meeting I put my cards on the table: 'I think I'd be perfect for this role and I really want it, so I'd work very hard for it. I can relate to the underdog fighting back.' They both looked a little taken aback. We parted company and in a few days, Mike Smith phoned to tell me I'd got the part.

Again I was lucky enough to be acting with some of the best. My husband was played by Derek Thompson (He played Charlie Fairhead in *Casualty* and had also appeared in *Breaking Glass*). The father of my mixed-race daughter was played by Malcolm Fredericks, a founder member of the Black Theatre Group. I wrote the theme tune for the show, and recorded the voices of many of the extras all coming from the St. Paul's area of Bristol (where we were filming). We called the gospel group The Arts Freedom Singers. What a buzz to hear all those great naturally talented singers together.

Whilst filming in Bristol, I made friends with Derek – *Fighting Back's* director Paul Seed's nephew – better known as 3D. He was a graffiti artist, loved Robert de Niro, and rapped in a hip hop crew called the Wild Bunch. The Wild Bunch later re-named themselves Massive Attack. I had lovely times hanging out with 3D. He did a great graffiti of my name, and gave me one of his beloved pictures of Robert de Niro.

The Live Aid single was released in November 1984, organised by Midge Ure and Bob Geldof, and I wasn't surprised not to be asked. All the people singing on it were better known than me. I understood that concept, but would have liked to have sung in the chorus, to have done service for such a great cause, but Midge (my ex) or Bob (my boggle mate) never asked. It was a great achievement raising so much cash for Ethiopia. Bob was a brilliant catalyser and a moving speaker. By the time Live Aid took off, I'd done my fair share of good causes, such as Youth CND, Anti-racist gigs, Greenpeace record, concert against Sizewell B (nuclear reactor), and an anti-heroin record which I co-promoted with the wonderful Paul Weller and Princess Diana.

I'd made friends with a lady called Bridget Stopps, whose

husband David managed Howard Jones, and we were all committed vegetarians. By the time the Live Aid Concert at Wembley kicked off, I'd also made friends with Linda McCartney, re-met Chrissie Hynde and her husband Jim Kerr (Simple Minds), and Dave from the Eurythmics – we had an association of like-minded vegetarians called Reprieve. We wanted to use our various talents to educate people about the cruelty of slaughter houses and meat eating. Chrissie paid for a film to be put together, and I narrated it.

The Live Aid concert was planned for the summer of 1985 and various mates kept asking me: 'Are you going to Live Aid ? – Are you singing in it?' I would just change the subject because I wasn't going. I still had no money, no record deal, no support, and I was definitely not in fashion. As they say in the wonderful world of showbiz, You're only as good as your last 'hit'. I couldn't afford to buy an artist's ticket. Even though loads of my mates were playing, I felt very much an outsider again. Then dear Bridget Stopps rang and said, 'You're going to the ball. We bought a block of tickets – or rather, Howard Jones has – and we want you to be there.' I was so touched – Thank you Howard, Bridget, and David.'

At Wembley that day, the playing artist enclosure was packed, and there was also a royal top-notch box area, and a backstage village. For both of the latter, you needed an extra-special pass to get into, and I didn't have one. My mates in Spandau Ballet couldn't believe I didn't have passes to go to the box or backstage, so they made it their mission to first take me to the Royal box, then decided they'd bring me backstage, so in we went. I saw David Bowie first: 'Hi Dave!' 'Hi Haze.' Then Pete Townshend of The Who, whom I'd watched sound-checking years ago at Coventry as a young teenager. Alison Moyet and Linda McCartney were there, and my mate Clare Hirst, who was about to play sax with David Bowie. Clare and I agreed to meet after the gig, and go to the party together.

Finally the concert was closing with "Do They Know It's Christmas?" all my various musician mates, like Spandau Ballet, David Bowie, and Linda McCartney, said, 'Come on, Haze – Everybody's going to sing it.' So I went on to the Wembley Stage

Dancing with Elton John on the beach at a Cartier Party in Tunisia, 1983
(Richard Young / Rex Features)

Showing Elton how to hang a spoon on his nose. *(Unknown)*

Opposite page:

Clockwise:

Fighting Back BBC TV mini series, 1986. *(Unknown)*

Just before leaving to live in America. *(Chris Craymer)*

With director David Green on the set of *Car Trouble*.

Nightshoot at the Tricycle Theatre. *(Christopher Pearce)*

With David Easter in *Girlfriends* in 1987. *(Unknown)*

With Clare Hirst and Martin Braithwaite in *Sing Out Sister* at Riverside Studios in 1987. *(Unknown)*

CLOSE ENCOUNTER: Ex-Brookside actor David Easter and pop singer Hazel O'Connor has one of the title roles in Girlfriends, a Second World War musical opening at London's Playhouse Theatre tomorrow.

TODAY, THURSDAY, OCTOBER 15, 1987

With Kurt Bippert my new husband arriving at Heathrow. *(David Parker)*

Wedding day, Venice Beach, California, 1988.

At home In LA in 1990 with Siobhan MacGowan and Kurt.

Sandwiched between Mark McGann and Joe McGann at the Pink House.

Singing with Joe McGann and Neil Morrisey in Kinsale, Ireland.

Actress Julie Graham and I at the Pink House.

With Kurt and mum in Howth, Ireland.

The Cuchulaín Cycle flyer in my big dangerous dress.

Right: With my harpist, Cormac.

Below: With Sabrina Winter and Bananarama's Siobhan Fahey in the back garden at my place in Ireland in 1997.

Meeting Tony Visconti again, in New York, 1999.

Both these shots are from the photo session for the "To Be Freed" album, 1993.
(Jim Rakete)

5 in the morning. (Tim Jarvis)

With Cormac and Mr Pelvis & Mr Damage - puppets from the *Beyond Breaking Glass* stage show.

First steps in house building with pretend cousins Steph and Ju, and right with Malachy.

Work in progress – the house takes shape.

Party at Evan's after Brooklodge gig, with Viva, Evan, and Brian Kennedy.
(Malachy O'Loan)

Here & Now Tour 2009 press launch at the Soho Revue Bar with Boy George and Kim Wilde.
(Brian Rasic / Rex Features)

From top to bottom:

Winter 2008 Mum with Geoff at the time of her cancer diagnosis.

Mum visiting my Walk of Fame Star outside the BBC, Coventry 2010.

Mum reunited with grandchild Louise.

Mum reunited with grandchild Charlie.

2009 Our last Christmas together at the hospice.

"Re-Joyce" recording session at Womb studios.

Toyah Wilcox, me, Vince Hill and Pauline Black. *(Pete Chambers)*

Left to right: Vince Hill, Pete Chambers, Kev Lomas, Pauline Black, Roger Lomas, Toyah Wilcox, Mark Roberts and me. *(Pete Chambers)*

Backstage at the "Re-Joyce" charity concert and record launch.

Back row: Roger Lomas, Ranking Roger, me, Mark Roberts, Andy Shortland, Rob Arnall, Tony Dangerfield, Kevin Lomas, and Steve Tombs.

Front row: Neville Staple, Carol Decker, Toyah Wilcox, Vince Hill, Pauline Black, Sarah Fisher, Bob Brolly, and Clare Hirst. *(John Coles)*

Left to right: Ranking Roger, Toyah Wilcox, Vince Hill, Carol Decker, mum, Bob Brolly, me, Neville Staple and Pauline Black. *(John Coles)*

With Pauline Black receiving our Wall of Fame in Two Tone Village, Coventry, 2011. *(Unknown)*

Performing at the Jazz Café. *(Will You Prod)*

My Bluja Project with Sarah Fisher and Clare Hirst. *(Will You Prod)*

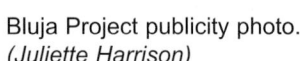

Bluja Project publicity photo. *(Juliette Harrison)*

With my dance teacher Sean. *(Will You Prod)*

and stood amongst my peers. I stayed at the back, next to Alison Moyet, and sang my heart out with the rest of Wembley Stadium.

When the final song finished, the heady array of music stars disappeared back to their waiting Limos, and I said my farewells as they melted away. I was looking around for Clare and I sat on the now empty revolving stage with some of the crew looking out onto the now equally empty arena. As far as the eye could see there was only the audience's rubbish left behind, plastic bags, bottles and cups, and probably loads of money and drugs, dropped and lost during the euphoria of the concert. When I did festival cleanup as a teenager, we found loads of money and bits of hash on the ground when all the fans had left.

The following year, the BBC was about to show the first episode of the *Fighting Back* drama series. I bought a newspaper just to look at the TV listings, and was very surprised to find that it was 'pick of the day'. I must confess, I was so excited I bought all the other newspapers to see what they said, and every different newspaper gave a good review or chose it for 'pick of the day'. My photo was on the front cover of the *Radio Times*, which would have made Nan very proud. With these kind of reviews I figured the phone wouldn't stop ringing with offers of more acting work. Well the phone didn't even begin to ring; there were no more TV or film offers, but I did now have a top acting agent – Dennis Salinger, the head of ICM. Dennis had been Michael Caine's agent for years and he was a great man in his field.

Eventually I auditioned for a musical called *Girlfriends* written by Howard Goodall. The piece was set during World War II, and was about the lives of the WAAFS (Womens Auxillary Air Force). There was to be twelve women and one guy – David Easter – in the cast. The show was to re-open the Charing Cross Playhouse that had been closed to the public for forty years. The part I was trying for was a 'chop girl' –meaning a girl whose airman boyfriend is shot down, and she has a jinx attached to her, so other airmen would be discouraged from dating her, in case they got shot down too.

Anyway, I got the part and was very excited to be involved in

Chapter Nine

a West End musical, as this was my first experience of musical theatre. On the first day, the cast, musical director, director and writer, got together and the director told us, 'The first week is for going through the material, so we don't expect you to know it this week, but next week we will.' 'Phew, thank God!' I thought, as I'm useless at learning lines or music from reading them; I have to learn audibly. For instance, for all my harmony parts and songs, I would record on my cassette tape and listen back and learn that way.

A lot of the cast had worked with Howard Goodall before and they all seemed very pally. David Easter and I became great pals, and I was looking forward to the process of becoming a musical actress. The learning of the music was hard, but I diligently taped every part I was required to sing. At the end of the first week, I had a private learning session with Howard and the director was also there. They seemed a little exasperated that I didn't know all my parts yet. I said, 'I thought you said that we were allowed to use this week for learning?' I decided to speak up for myself - the director told us to try to be friendly and rational: 'Look, I'm the kind of person who learns slowly, but once I learn I'll never let you down.' The director said, 'We are a bit worried about you actually.' I tried to remain calm, replying, 'I understand your worries. We're all doing firsts with this show; my first musical, your first West End show. Of course you're worried, but I promise you, the day we open I'll be a credit to you.' The director was like a dog worrying it's toy. He wouldn't let up gracefully: 'Well you need to work very hard to come up to standard, Hazel. We don't have a lot of time.'

This lack of support after only five working days together pissed me off. I realized they probably didn't even want me in their musical, as my part was not that big; I only had one proper song to do, the rest was choral work. They probably had to have a star for their show, but I felt they were under-working me; not using my talents to the full. So I replied, 'When this show has it's press night, I will do you proud, you just see, but I bet the press will say, "Why didn't we see more of Hazel O'Connor?" ' The guys were flabbergasted now, and I was in tears of anger. I tried to be one of the team with them and they treated me like an idiot. I was right about the reviews though. *Time Out* Magazine said, 'We didn't see enough of the staggeringly talented Hazel O'Connor, which was a shame.'

Girlfriends did okay for a while and then audiences started to drop. Whilst everything was going well, the bitchy members of the cast were amiable enough, but once we'd had notice that we'd be closing in a few weeks time, they reverted to the nasty stuff. The biggest and best example of musical theatre bitchiness was this: I go to my position for the opening scene along with all the cast members; the 'opener' is a big choral song, everybody in different harmonies. My character is a mechanic. So there I was pretending to fix an aeroplane and singing out my harmonies, when I espied a piece of paper stuffed into the pretend equipment that I was fixing. I kept singing, but took out the piece of paper, unfolded it and read, 'Fuck off Hazel O'Connor.' I thought it was a joke from one of the backstage crew being silly, but we were mates, so it was okay. On my first opportunity off-stage I asked all the crew as I saw them, 'Did you leave a joke note in my stage props?' 'No!' was the reply from everybody I was friendly with. So I presumed it wasn't a harmless joker, but a very nasty person who'd done it.

By the end of the last song of the first half, I had a stage fight with a girl who I believed may have been a part of the 'fuck off' note. Every night she would fail to support her own weight in our mock fight, and I'd nearly break my back trying to hold her up. This night I couldn't hold her weight any longer, and as usual she wasn't holding her own weight, and down she went with a puzzled look in her eye as her head hit the stage. By the end of the scene we are all wearing tin hats. The iron curtain came down, and the audience went out for half time. The girl who bumped her head turned to me: 'Darling, what are you doing? You let me fall,' she whined. 'No, you didn't hold yourself up, that was the problem,' I shot back at her. She started whining again: 'Well darling, you are so unprofessional...' She never finished her speech 'cause I was seeing red. I took off my tin hat and hurled it at her feet – She jumped back a shocked expression in her eyes.

'Why don't you just fuck off, you little bitch! Fuck off back to your kennel with the other bitches!' I screamed. She ran off towards a crew member, hiding behind him, and said, 'Help me, Hazel's gone mad!'

The stage manager came up behind me trying to calm me down. I pushed his hands off me. 'Get away from me!' I said. 'Don't you dare touch me! Don't you dare!' He backed off. I ran to my dressing room and sobbed my socks off. At the end of the show I apologised to the girl, because maybe she didn't do it, but I think her and her coterie had dogged me long enough. Everybody heard about the 'fuck off' note and made allowances for my behaviour that day. I wasn't proud of myself for losing my temper, but nobody gave me any trouble after that.

The show finished and I was already working on my own musical script called *Sing Out Sister*, about three girl musicians/singers in the forties touring US bases in Germany just after the Second World War. The characters were based on my real experiences with Lady Luck and the German GI tour from those early singing days. A new friend of mine called Barry Langford, whom I'd met on the flight coming back from L.A. earlier that year, helped with the show's publicity. The Riverside Studio in Hammersmith was going to run it for three days. Charlie Hanson, the Riverside director and founder member of the Black Theatre Co-op, ended up directing *Sing Out Sister* because I just couldn't. I thought I could, but thank God Charlie said he would help. My pal Clare acted in the show as well – bless her. *Sing Out Sister* sold out for three nights, and received glowing reports. I felt good that I'd proved it could be done on a shoestring – and with a lot of help from my friends.

During all these trials, tribulations and triumphs, my relationship with Krishna consciousness grew, and I tried to be less attached to and therefore less hurt by events. I would go to the temple on a daily basis, made easier by my move closer to Bhaktivedanta Manor (Temple). I lived in 'Wham land' also – as George Michael's family home was just up the road. We'd often go for walks across the fields when he was at home.

One day I went to the Temple to find that my Guru friend

Srila Gurudeva had run away. I was devastated. In the dead of night he'd left with some lady devotee and they'd moved to the U.S. What a letdown he'd become; for the past three years he'd been preaching his celibacy and purity, then he ran off with a guru groupie. What hurt was that he couldn't behave like a man of truth and say: 'I've fallen in love, so I can't keep my vows anymore.' I realised slowly that one can't be attached to God because of personal cult, and all humans are fallible. But I did want to ask him why, so I went to look for him in L.A. I didn't find him but I decided to move to America for a new adventure.

    I had some things to finish up in England before I could leave. I'd been dating a guy called Bash, whom I'd met while working on the musical *Girlfriends*. He worked backstage but his main love was playing guitar. I'd asked him to play in the band for a tour of Ireland that my old pal Louis Walsh had put together for me. The pressures of touring together finished the romantic relationship, but he decided he might come to L.A. for a while, so we could do some acoustic gigs together.

    In my last few months in England I'd arranged to give my house to my friend and her kids to live in and I was trying to fix the house up before I left. Some of the guys I'd known as monks at the Hari Krishna temple had now left, and they were coming over to my place helping with DIY. One guy in particular sent my heart hopping. I remembered seeing him in civilian clothes at a big Hari Krishna festival two years before and he'd sent my heart racing then. His name was Kurt Bippert. During the next few months Kurt told me about his plans to move to America, probably L.A., as he was born in the USA and he held an American passport even though he had been brought up in London since he was four years old. I was so thrilled that we'd be seeing each other in Los Angeles again. They say in Krishna consciousness, 'God fulfils all desires.' So, I wondered, was Kurt God's gift?

****

PART THREE
A NEW LIFE

CHAPTER TEN

'Did you ever get the feeling you've been here before
Well I do – You see a face
Ya know a place
Maybe it's déjà vu
You better believe in the freedom
You know the next line
You better believe in the feeling
Time after time, am I dreaming
You dive down into life's ocean
You're riding on the crest of a wave
A big momma come a-crashing down on you
You spin around, hit the ground
Rise again and spit the sand and say
Heh ho I'm still breathing
Heh ho I'm alive'
"Still Breathing" (*Beyond the Breaking Glass*, 2000)

Moving to Los Angeles represented a fresh start and freedom from the confines of being 'Hazel O'Connor'. I wanted a personal life and more adventure. I wanted to busk on the boardwalk of Venice Beach without people saying, 'How sad, she's reduced to busking.' I wanted to sing jazz in 'hip' little clubs, and mostly I wanted to see if I could 'cut the mustard' without any reference to *Breaking Glass*, which hung like an albatross around my neck.

Fame had curtailed all of the freedom I'd had, and then it was over in a flash and I had to work with the fallout. There was a huge amount of money from "Will You", that could have made the difference between one life and another, but I couldn't touch it. It's no good having fame and no money! But, really, I could just as easily take the bus as get a limo. It is fun sometimes to take a limo, and to feel spoilt, but I didn't really miss the trappings. All I wanted to do was to be able to continue to sing. In the USA all this was a possibility because *Breaking Glass* hadn't been a huge hit there, so nobody knew me, but it was a cult classic. Looking back I achieved everything I went to America to create – and more. It was a financially poor time but emotionally rich, as I was having some fun again and making new friends. It was a very happy time for me.

Kurt ended up in Los Angeles a few weeks after I got there and within a few months we'd moved into an apartment in Venice Beach together as friends, our rationale being we were both vegetarians and Hari Krishnas. Our relationship became romantic and eventually we married in a Hari Krishna ceremony on Venice Beach, July 22nd 1987.

All our friends were there, like actor David Rappaport, who was Kurt's best man, and David Wakeling, a singer from the Beat and General Public gave me away. It was a lovely day except for forgetting we'd left the champagne in the freezer, and the bottle blew up. We had our reception in our apartment, all our new Venice Beach friends were there and a great music session ensued.

The morning after I was having second thoughts about the

marriage – we had got married rather quickly. I left Kurt asleep and wandered along Venice Beach, and I sobbed my heart out. 'Have I made a mistake?' I wondered. I needn't have worried; our early-married days were wonderful, full of fun and adventure. I did note, however, that he could get into an awful temper sometimes and throw his weight about, and he seemed to be forever in debt. But most of the time we were happy.

Kurt and I decided to move out of the town and up into the hills of Topanga Canyon about nine miles from the edges of L.A. We bought a mobile home in an exclusive village at the top of the canyon. We had lemon trees, a swimming pool and Jacuzzi, with views of the sea if you looked in one direction, and the San Fernando Valley with its ever-gathering smog clouds in the other direction. We ended up with two rescue dogs Babes and Whiskey.

Kurt was doing courier delivery work and one day I accompanied him on a job to Santa Monica. Poor Kurt tended to be absent minded (he was an artist, and that was his main love), and on this day he'd forgotten to put the cap back on the radiator, and he had pushed the bonnet of his car down on the radiator cap which had jammed the bonnet down. When we came to Santa Monica his car was violently overheating, and the bonnet was jammed, so I offered to deliver the letter to the Outrageous Fruit & Grain Company. The boss – a tall blond woman called Pam Hanson – took an instant shine to me and the big bow around my head. 'What a great accent you have,' she said. 'Do you want a job here answering phones?' 'I'll phone you later to talk about it,' I replied.

I actually really did need a job as the original plans for L.A. had changed a lot. For instance, when Kurt and I were newly-wed, we'd gone to my new L.A. manager Barry Krost's house, where we'd met Sarah Brightman, loads of the crew from the film *Blade Runner*, and a lot of high-flying agents. Barry wanted to network me – I drank much too much champagne and ended up entertaining a bigwig from CAA (Creative Artists Agency – One of Hollywood's leading talent agencies) with the story of our wedding. They were so impressed that I was in CAA within the week for a proper meeting. This meeting was the first one I'd had since knocking on Hollywood's doors, where I was given bagels and cream cheese and jam and hot chocolate, fizzy water, and anything I asked for actually.

CAA wanted to create a TV sitcom based around me, so we discussed who was to write it. There was a big choice of writers at this time as there was a writer's strike going on in Hollywood, so some of the best writers had time on their hands. Everything had gone great. Afterwards I visited my *Breaking Glass* producer, Davina Belling – who now lived half the time in her Hollywood Hills home – to tell her about it. It had been Davina who had put me in touch with Barry Krost in the first place. She was still one of my biggest supporters. I also went to tell my other supporter, director Brian Gibson, who now lived full-time in Hollywood. Unfortunately, just as we were about to begin, the writers' strike finished, and all the top writers went back to their original jobs, which were very backlogged, so my project went on to the back burner.

I had made a few good contacts after doing some interviews on Oscar night with some of the British actors in Hollywood. From that evening I'd got together with a publisher called Tim Hollier, and was given a lift home in British actor Charles Dance's limo. So when Pam from the Outrageous Fruit and Grain Company asked if I want a job – I simply said yes, I did – I needed a job because as yet I had no money coming in. Yes, I did many gigs at this time, and yes, I busked on Venice beach, but no, these were not big money-spinners. I phoned Pam Hanson later telling her I'd love to work for her, but for how long I didn't know, as I was a singer/songwriter about to sign a new deal. In the meantime I could give her some months of my life. I wanted a normal job to prove I could do it.

Kurt and I decided to go back to England for a visit. We returned to Hertfordshire where we'd first met and had a religious ceremony at the Hari Krishna temple where I'd spent so many happy hours and Kurt had been a shaven-headed monk. Now we could have a wedding with all our family and friends. I wore a borrowed red wedding sari, as did my mum, who'd phoned the night before and asked if I'd mind her wearing a sari that a friend had given her for the occasion. 'Mum, that would be lovely, you'll look so beautiful.' It was a beautiful day. We were married in the temple room, in a traditional Hindu Fire Ceremony – a fire which many things were thrown into, like rice, a banana, and each thing is seen as a sacrifice, with the congregation chanting together. Kurt and I were then tied together by our clothing and walked around the fire seven times. The only blot on the day was the tabloid press trying to get in for a good photo. One guy gave my friend a ready-loaded camera for her to take shots – she refused, of course. The one photo that did get taken was of Kurt throwing the banana into the fire, so the stupid caption was: 'With this banana, I thee wed.' The devotees cooked a wonderful feast.

We returned to the States shortly after, very glad to have shared the moment with our close friends and relatives. Back in L.A., gigs were going very well for me and I seemed to have a sub-cult status in America because the film *Breaking Glass* never took off on the movie circuit, but it did play on the Art-Movie-Theatre circuit. Then it was shown on cable and lots of rebellious twelve to twenty-five-year-olds saw it – and were hooked.

Sometimes we really struggled financially, which wasn't helped by Kurt getting a credit card and spending, then getting into huge debt, which the American system likes because they hammer you with interest and, at worst, take your home from you. Since losing my home as a child I've always been terrified of dispossession: funny that, as most of my life has been littered with dispossessions.

So Kurt and I had some massive arguments. He got so mad one day he stuck a knife through the face of a painting he'd done of me. Sometimes he'd not bother to let me know he'd be late home from work, and I'd worry, then we'd fight. In fact we should have seen the writing on the wall and quit while we were still ahead, but poverty at the level we were at can be blamed for many things.

Louis Walsh in Ireland asked me to go and do another tour there. So Kurt came with me, as did my writing partner and guitarist Major Black. That month in Ireland was the best time I'd spent with Kurt. There was a heat wave and all the pale-skinned Irish men were stripped down to the waist, turning salmon pink. We fell in love with County Wicklow with all its mountains, valleys, and lakes. 'If we ever get rich, let's move to Ireland,' I said.

Back in America we survived – just. That Christmas in 1989 was a very lean time. We'd been selling plastic poinsettia plants to earn some money and arguing more and more, then I saw in the paper that George Michael was playing a big concert in L.A. at the Forum, so Kurt and I went along. George's office had arranged great seats and backstage passes. The show was fabulous, backstage was even more fabulous, and there were two holding areas for celebrities and friends. A big bar room held around three hundred people, one of them being Midge Ure. We had a brief, polite chat and moved on.

The other room was small, holding about thirty people at most, which was a very select room – Well actually it was all the real mates, including both George's and my lawyer, Tony Russell (who'd led my legal campaign to free me from the clutches of Albion Records seven years before). George's family were there and I felt so happy to be in the 'very special room'. Also I don't like big rooms full of people. George invited us to a big party his manager was having in Hollywood some days later.

The party was stuffed with guests and lots of really famous people. I saw Bob Dylan sitting in the corner, which really impressed me. Eventually we caught up with George who was continuously surrounded by twenty to thirty people wanting his attention. I popped into the twenty or thirty people and said, 'Hi, George.' 'Hi, Haze. How are you?' he said with a big, beaming smile. What a nice guy, I thought. He shed the crowd for a five-minute yak with Kurt and me. 'This is my husband, Kurt Bippert.' They shook hands and during their conversation they found out they'd both attended the same school in Kingsbury, London. They had been taught by the same teacher. 'Do you remember Miss Smith?' gushed George. 'Oh yeah,' said Kurt with a wry grin. For five minutes my mate George was just George, then the twenty or thirty people began swirling like hornets around a nest and that was our time gone. 'See you again sometime, George.'

Kurt and I now turned our attention to the fruit mountain on the table ahead of us. There was so much stuff, beautiful things, strawberries, loganberries, peaches, avocados – everything – and we wanted to take some home, but didn't want to be noted taking a pile of fruit. 'Tie the sleeves of your jacket Kurt,' I whispered to him, and I did the same. We then filled our sleeves with fruit and left. I'd never done that before and I know I could have just asked, but my pride was stopping me. How do you tell your big pop star friend that you (another supposed star) are hungry and penniless!

Eventually the finances eased. I signed a new songwriting deal with Tim Hollier's Company, Allied West, and I had money to live on again. Kurt started using his artistic talents to make money and things were on the up and up. I also saw saxophonist Wesley McGoogan in L.A. – he was playing with Billy Ocean. We'd long since buried the hatchet (if there ever was one), and talked about trying to get the money for "Will You" out of the deep freeze. Seven years it had been sitting there, helping neither Wes nor myself. It was good to see Wesley again, as it reminded me of our good times during the heady days of fame.

Louis Walsh rang to tell me the Olympia Theatre in Dublin were doing a run of The Willy Russell musical *Blood Brothers*, and would I be interested in coming to Ireland? I loved that musical. I'd seen it in London's West End, with Barbara Dickson playing the role they wanted me for. I agonised over the decision – I couldn't do it: I was newly married and my life was now in America with my husband.

A month later I noticed that the old birthmark on the back of my leg had started to grow two tumours. They itched at first and then started to hurt. A socialite friend of mine who lived in Walt Disney's former home said, 'Oh darling, that could be skin cancer, you need to get a skin biopsy.' She gave me the name of a skin hospital and doctor.

Kurt came with me to see the lady doctor I'd made my appointment with. She told me as she cut the two tumours away that my birthmark – a lateral verrucous nevus – is not a common thing and would very rarely be cancerous. She then asked if I'd minded showing my leg off to her students at some future date. I was happy to do so and agreed immediately.

The following week I went in for the biopsy results. I told Kurt he didn't need to hold my hand as the doctor had already told us it couldn't be cancer. I sat in her office waiting for her to come in. I was all smiles, but the doctor came in with a very long face. 'I'm afraid I don't have very good news for you,' she said. 'We found two types of cancer: basal cell and squamous, cell carcinoma.' I'd already read up on these two sitting in the waiting room. Basal cell is usually confined to the skin and doesn't metastise (travel to other organs). Squamous cell is a bit more tricky, as it can move into the underlying muscle and travel.

Life all at once became crystal clear. The word cancer frightened me. The memories of Nana dying from it came back to me. If I were to die where would I want that to be? Not underneath clouds of brown smog in Los Angeles, no way! 'Then I think I shall go and live in Ireland – less worry of the sun there,' I said. The doctor looked worried and said, 'You don't have to do anything so drastic. There's lots of ways to treat it,' she said.

But I knew this was one of those pivotal momentous moments – a kick in the pants – move and grow, follow your dreams. I had dreamed of one day living in Ireland and I knew that's where I must go. I phoned Kurt, I told him it was cancer, and that I intended leaving America and settling in County Wicklow, Ireland. 'I can't expect you to come as we've made a life here, but I have to go and if you want to be with me you're welcome to come too,' I told him. 'I'll come with you, Haze,' he said simply. I loved him so much for his support at that moment.

We organised a major move, put our luxury mobile home up for sale, prepared shipping and quarantining our dogs, and Louis Walsh, bless him, organised a chat show appearance on *Kenny Live* on Irish TV, which gave me a flight and a couple of nights in a hotel. So my mission was, do TV show day one, day two go to Wicklow with my friend Billie Webster (who'd sung on the last Irish tour with me) to look at property and find one, so that day three would be spent organising my mortgage and departure.

Billie and I searched and searched until it was turning dark and nothing suited. Then there was one that we'd overlooked. We arrived at a lovely bungalow cottage on a half-acre of land with outbuildings for Kurt and I to have a studio each, and a stream running down the side. We shook hands on a deal. The next a wonderful mortgage broker, John Lowe, who Louis put me in touch with, gave me the mortgage.

By the time we left California around two months had elapsed since the diagnosis. I learned very quickly not to tell people about the cancer because of their reactions. The best example was, when I saw my neighbour Marie, just hours after leaving the doctor's office. 'How did it go at the hospital?' she asked. I felt a bit silly saying cancer, as it didn't seem real, and I tried to say it smilingly. 'Well actually, it's skin cancer.' 'How awful for you,' said Marie, and her face went down-turned and morbid. 'Why are you giggling about it?' she added. "Cause I'm scared,' I said, and walked on. Lots of people did variations on that theme and I couldn't handle their 'Oh, poor you, sad looks' and their own fear of their mortality, which was prompted by even talking to me!

I'd always promised myself that if I was told I'd got cancer, I'd try alternative therapies and I'd heard of a special healer in Topanga Canyon, a mile up the road from our place – She had a great curing ointment for skin cancer. I went for a consultation and, to my surprise, she started dowsing me with a crystal pendulum. At the end of my appointment she said, 'I'm not reading cancer, so I can't give you my ointment; your adrenal glands are very depleted so it's your thyroid. I'm going to give you herbs for these things.' I thought, 'She's got to be wrong because the biopsy already told me cancer at the hospital.' Nevertheless, I took her potions daily.

A very sad thing happened during these last months. The best man at our wedding – small person actor David Rappaport, famous for roles in *Time Bandits* and *L.A. Law* – went into Laurel Canyon Park and shot himself dead in the heart. It was very sad, indeed tragic – and not knowing why.

On the last week before we left, my skin doctor phoned me: 'I've got great news for you, Hazel. Remember I said it's so rare to get cancer on your type of growths? All the doctors here looked at your biopsy results and concurred; but there was one test we don't do here, so I sent your biopsy on to a lab that does this test, and my hunch was right – it's definitely not cancer. It's something called keratinoid kartoma, and it's not malignant.' I was so relieved, and I realised the dowser/herbalist had been correct. The whole episode had launched Kurt and me into a whole new adventure in Ireland.

CHAPTER ELEVEN

'In a top flat in Bayswater
Rebecca would be doing my hair
We had so much fun
She knew all the words to my song
As it played on the player.
She'd give me her bed for the night
She would feed me, clothe me and such,
I'd laugh and I'd say when the light hits that way
You remind me of Shirley MacLaine
When will I see you again?
When we sing silly harmonies into the night?
I try and I try but I can't help this missing you
I wonder - where you are now?

We had us a dream back then
When we got back the things that were stole
We'd have us a party, orchestra, long gowns,

And we'd be the Belles of the Ball
And we'd dance to the Emperor Waltz
Because that was your favourite tune
I'd laugh and I'd say when the light hits that way
You remind me of Shirley MacLaine
When will I see you again?
When will we sing silly harmonies into the night?
I try and I try but I can't help this missing you
I wonder - where you are now?

Are you an angel, have you been re-born?
Didn't you find your Buddhahood?
Was it worth all the toil?
I write 'cause I miss you and
there's nothing more I can do
When will I see you again?
When will we sing silly harmonies into the night?
I try and I try but I can't help this missing you
I wonder - where you are now?

Now the top flat is empty
But our rare old times call from the walls
And I hope that wherever you are
You're alright – and I'll still have our Ball
And we'll dance to the Emperor's Waltz
Because that was your favourite tune
I'd laugh and I say when the light hits that way
You remind me of Shirley Maclaine
When will I see you again?
God Bless Rebecca – I miss you'
"Rebecca's Song" (*5 In the Morning*, 1997)

1994 had brought major changes for me. The unravelling of my marriage had begun four years earlier when we moved to Ireland. And now I was to face three major losses – the loss of a friend, a husband, and a manager. I was feeling very sad and mixed-up, but luckily I was able to continue getting counselling at the Catholic Marriage Advisory Service, even though Kurt had ceased coming with me. Our counsellor, Sandra, continued to see me, until she felt I didn't need to see her any more.

1st June 1990 was to have been a new start, with a lot of help from Louis Walsh, who had found me a bank manager, car insurer, accountant, and a long string of gigs to earn money until the end of the year. Then I realised I was carrying a new life in my body. Kurt and I were happy and scared. I was doubly scared, worrying how would we pay the mortgage when I couldn't tour anymore? Pictures of me waddling on stage six months gone did not appeal to me at all. We began a very tense time full of arguments and hysteria. Sometimes Kurt would threaten me with violent behaviour – but he'd never hit me. I would run off down our pretty country lane sobbing and fearful of the future. I realised I must take care of baby first and foremost.

Our tense times lessened as did my morning sickness. I started to look and feel great. I was positively blooming and doing five gigs a week on average. We were now looking forward to our baby coming. I'd passed the dodgy three months term and I felt safe. Disaster struck at almost four months gone, when I caught a virus that made my throat and glands swell. My doctor couldn't give me antibiotics, because they'd hurt my baby, so he gave me something to try to ease my throat, and we drove the three hours to Cork to do my gig. I recovered from the virus a few days later. A week later I was singing at a wedding party in Poulaphouca ('place of the Púca' in Irish. A Púca is something between and goblin and a fairy), on the border between Counties Wicklow and Kildare. I began to bleed and my tummy was hurting terribly, but worse was the instinctive knowledge that I was maybe losing my baby. The person in my belly, who I'd be having a relationship with, was maybe leaving me.

Chapter Eleven

Kurt and I went home and I lay down and waited until the morning to phone the doctor. By morning I was still bleeding and in a lot of pain. I phoned the doctor, who said he was sending an ambulance, as I needed to go straight to hospital. 'I'm losing my baby, I can feel it,' I said, and put the phone down.

I didn't wake Kurt, as I didn't want any fuss. I clutched my belly and packed a few things for hospital. Kurt woke up and came into the kitchen. I was quite calm. Then I did what I'd done to my brother Neil all those years ago. I'd very practically told him that Mum was leaving Dad, I was going with Mum, so what was he going to do? Knowing he'd be the good guy and say, 'Well I'd better stay with Dad then.' This time I delivered the 'fait accompli' to my husband, the father of our baby. I said,

'I think I'm losing the baby. The doctor has sent me an ambulance which will be here quite soon now and I'm going to hospital.' 'Why didn't you wake me?' he said. 'I just wanted to be left alone,' I said, shutting him out.

At this point the wolfhound dog Fionn (a dog we'd rescued a few months before) must have felt the tension and got himself wrapped up in the phone wire and it pulled the new answering machine smashing to the floor. I shouted at Fionn, Kurt shouted at me, I shouted at Kurt, and for a split second his eyes said, 'I hate you.' My eyes held his and said, 'I hate you too – and I don't care about any of this – the only thing that matters is already on its way out.'

At that moment my womb must have let go. I pushed past him, ran to the loo, and there most of my baby left me. I sat on the toilet screaming with fear as the blood splashed up the walls – and rage – primal rage. I wanted to rummage down the toilet to try to find my baby. Kurt was holding my hand and crying as well as me. 'I'm sorry, Haze,' he said. 'I'm as scared as you.'

The ambulance arrived and stretchered me out. Kurt and Fionn followed in our car. I was still losing lots of blood, but to be honest, I really didn't care about that, I was just wracked with guilt – it was my fault. 'Maybe the baby decided not to come to Kurt and I because we were always arguing,' I thought. And the clincher was: 'I'm useless as a woman – I can't even do what our bodies are made for – I can't grow life.'

I sobbed quietly to myself as we bumped over the mountains into Dublin towards the hospital. The lovely ambulance lady, as if psychic, said, 'It's not your fault, love, it's not your fault, things happen sometimes, they just happen, it's not your fault.' But the voice in my head kept saying 'It is my fault – I am guilty of losing my child.'

I was admitted to a very sad ward in Holles Street Maternity Hospital in Dublin city. All the women were either in for scans, as it was feared their babies were dead inside them, or, like me, they had already started miscarrying. Kurt sat holding my hand. Our road manager Jay came in, and then I was left to sleep. I woke up to a searing pain in my belly. I thought I needed to pee. The sister gave me a bedpan and stepped out of the curtained area to leave me to it. That's when my last part of baby – or afterbirth – left my body. Goodbye sweetheart. That was 13th August 1990. I came out of hospital frail and pale and in great sadness. The doctor thought the baby had probably died quite a few days before. Perhaps the virus had killed him/her.

A week after coming out of hospital our wolfhound, Fionn, collapsed with 75 per cent kidney failure, and as Kurt went off to the vet's with him, I pleaded: 'Please don't let anything else die.' Through a lot of alternative therapy we brought Fionn back to health. I then went to my friend Siobhan McGowan's parents' house, where her mum Theresa nursed me. They were so kind to me, Theresa, her husband Morris, and Siobhan. They knew all about the pitfalls of life and the music industry from first-hand experience, with their son being the amazing Shane McGowan.

Within three weeks of the miscarriage I was contracted to perform at a big outdoor festival in Poulaphouca again. Bob Geldof was top of the bill. After the gig I was eating in the dining room next to Bob, and we spoke about my miscarriage: 'Oh go for another one straight away,' he said blithely. 'That's what a friend of mine did.' And then he said, entirely guilelessly, 'What's up with you and Paula? Why don't you just ring each other and make friends? Like you used to be.'

I threw myself into work for the next four months. I secretly loathed myself, and my face became a patchwork of eczema sores. The doctor gave me antidepressants, but I didn't stick with them – they stopped me feeling anything.

By 1991 I was working really hard and was touring with my Irish band all over the UK. I found a new manager, Peter Lyster Todd, a man full of integrity, a true gentleman of Rock. Tim Hollier, the publisher, stopped my publishing advance so I presumed our contract had voided. I did an acoustic unplugged tour at the beginning of 1992, the wages from which I was lending to Kurt to make a print of one of his paintings. A thousand were made from two months of hard graft on the road, and nine hundred and sixty are still in my attic to this day! However, the unplugged tour showed me other possibilities, creatively speaking.

When I got home, after two months away, Kurt kept going on about a new friend he'd made whilst painting at a local beauty spot called Glendalough. Her name was Viva. He said her name every other sentence and I thought, 'Who is this other woman?' Kurt's mum Shirley had come all the way from Australia to stay with us, so she and I went out to meet Kurt and his new lady friend. Well, I met the most wonderful human being – Viva – and I knew straight away she wasn't shagging my husband. We quickly became firm friends.

My granddad died that year which marked the end of an era, and Mum moved back into Nan and Granddad's house. Heading to Christmas 1991 was very tough, as we were still very poor, and for entertainment I wrote a modern fairytale set in L.A. and Ireland. I asked Viva if she'd play a part, and I asked a friend called Mary, who had a keen interest in acting, if she'd like to be in it. Slowly I arranged a group of actors. I met a really exuberant professional actress called Kathrina and her husband John. Kathrina was pregnant, so she couldn't commit to act in the play because she would be too far advanced in her pregnancy, but she could direct the play for us all. So *Meetings in Time* was born. We had so much fun getting it together. Each member had at least two acting roles, and also a crew job, like Kurt, who played my husband in L.A. (who gets killed) and an Irish lad in 1842 (who also gets killed). Viva played a fairy musician and an old lady called

Anne Doyle. Viva and I both made costumes, and Kurt painted the scenery. Kathrina did a great job getting performances out of us all. Then we performed it for three nights at Roundwood Parish Hall to packed houses.

In 1992 a young German man, called Jorg Dogondke, approached Peter Lyster Todd to make a record deal with me. Kurt and I moved house to a falling-down 17th-century stone cottage. Kurt set about rebuilding it, whilst I went to record in Germany. Sony Records Germany wanted to sign the record and me to their label. I also did a writer's deal with them. Suddenly I'm doing loads of PR and TV and photos. We made a pop video for the single called "My Friend Jack." My hairdressing friend Rebecca came on set and looked after my hairdo for the duration of filming. She did this free of charge, just to make sure I was looking my best. Rebecca had been doing my hair for years since I'd been going to Trevor Sorbie's salon, where she first 'did me'. After being at Trevor's, she opened her own salon with her husband, and lost it all when her marriage split. She always did my hair for free, gave me a room to stay when I was in London, and fed me. She was one of my only friends who didn't think I'd gone loopy when I started going to the Hari Krishna Temple. As my life and career were getting better, Rebecca's was too. She'd become a Buddhist, a top fashion designer, had funded a wonderful new salon, and she seemed to be getting her life back.

Meanwhile I went back to Germany to record a live album. My Irish band came over, plus the extraordinary German keyboard player, Wolfgang Grassekamp whom I'd met in Ireland, and who became one of my band's most favourite fixtures. To top it off I'd invited Wesley McGoogan to record with us – I wanted to build bridges. We all stayed at my German agent's house, where we rehearsed, and after the gig was recorded we'd stay to mix.

After recording in Stefan's house I came back to Ireland to rehearse my first musical on the Dublin stage. It was a great piece written by a school teacher, Sean Purcell, and directed by a highly talented Dublin director, Michael Scott. The play was called *The Raven Beckons*. I played a woman whose life and marriage unravels after her fifteen- year-old-son commits suicide.

My relationship with Kurt seemed to be unravelling slowly, ever since the miscarriage, and the woman I played provoked a lot of buried feelings in me. The old 'life imitating art' syndrome again! I threw myself into that show and enjoyed all the people. There were no nasty bitchy types in *The Raven Beckons*, and of course after my last experience of a 'big' musical being *Girlfriends*, I was a little cautious. Michael Scott was so helpful to me as a director and he treated me as a creative equal – and did so with all his cast and crew.

I worked again with Michael when he work-shopped W. B. Yeats's plays *The Cuchulaín Cycle* (a series of five plays based loosely on stories about Irish mythological hero Cuchalaín). I'd never done any classical acting things before, and the W. B. Yeats's stuff has a lot of spoken verse, and his plays have overtones of Classic Greek Theatre. So I was very happy learning new things and meeting new talents. The musicians Michael Scott had arrayed for this workshop were phenomenal: Rossa Ó Snodaigh from folk/world music band Kila on whistles and percussions; Colm Mac an Iomaire of the band The Frames on fiddle; Aengus O'Connor on cello, and a gorgeous smiley harp player called, Cormac De Barra.

I was soon back on the road touring Germany and discussing my third album for Sony with my artist development person, Evelyn, in Sony Frankfurt. Evelyn had become much more than a work acquaintance, she was a new friend. In fact all the women I worked with at Sony were brilliant and I remained friends with them all even after my relationship with Sony ceased.

On the home front, Kurt and I seemed to be leading separate lives. He was working as a production manager for a theatre company, and I was always on the road touring, or flying back and forth to Germany. We were always arguing about money; we'd gone to counselling about a year after the miscarriage, and tried to stay together, but we were falling apart.

I began recording my final album for Sony Records aptly called, *Private Wars*, with U2 engineer/producer, Paul Barrett, in his Dublin studio. During that recording time the "Will You" publishing mess was finally resolved. Wes got twenty-five per cent of the song, and unfortunately out of the £85,000 that had sat doing nothing for twelve years, most went to pay for the legal costs. I received £18,000. Kurt and I were trying to buy an old run-down house in Dublin, so this money went straight down as a deposit. My manager Peter got an offer he couldn't refuse in Australia, so he was just tying-up loose ends for me and for the album before we parted. Fionn the wolfhound died. Before the album was finished, Kurt and I had separated, and he went to live in the Dublin house. It's ironic that the final proceeds of my famous love song we used to facilitate my marriage split.

Terrible news then came from England. Sal rang to tell me that Rebecca had collapsed in her new hairdressing salon. The hospital had found cancer in her kidneys, and she wasn't given a good prognosis. She spent her last months with her family. I wrote to her and we spoke on her birthday, but she was leaving. I hoped her Buddhist faith sustained her. Within three months she had died. I was stunned, as were the hundreds of friends who attended her funeral. She was a very special gal, our Rebecca. After her death I felt compelled to write something about her in celebration of our friendship, and "Rebecca's Song" was born.

A friend from my London days – a poet called Brendan Hickey – moved back home to Dublin with his lady Annie and new baby, Saoirse. Brendan invited me to the songwriters' club in the International Bar in Dublin, run by that great facilitator of Irish songwriters, Dave Murphy. Dave's club was like being in the living room. There were no mics, no electronics – apart from a couple of spotlights – and raw talent. We'd all pay in £2 and new songwriters would get to air their songs. As the audience was mainly made up of songwriters, they would be very supportive, with lots of sing-along with choruses and harmonising.

My first night at the Songwriters' Club was nothing short of an epiphany. Besides seeing loads of talented, enthusiastic young songwriters, I saw a few guys who made me sit up and take double notice. One was a Northside Dublin singer/songwriter called Damien Dempsey, with a great song which everyone seemed to know, titled "Do You Feel Alright Tonight?" Another was Mundy Enright, with an equally memorable song – and voice

– titled "Where's My Friend?" Going to Dave Murphy's Songwriters' Club, next to marriage guidance counselling became my most important fixture of the week. I began having acupuncture for my eczema and depression, which led me to Tai Chi courses. At home I finished all the unfinished plastering and building projects. I bought a drill and a saw, and got on with it. One funny observation struck me, as I toiled away one day taking down one of Kurt's many stone walls, which he'd erected in our garden: I liked to build pathways and terraces with the stone from our land; Kurt liked building stone walls.

That year I received my first-ever record royalties for *Breaking Glass*, with the help of a wonderful lady lawyer called Helen English, and a manager called David Morgan. Because Albion Records, as I discovered, had gone bankrupt in 1987, A & M should have been paying me directly. So finally in 1994 David Morgan and Helen English managed to get A & M to pay me directly, and not via Albion (which was the original agreement). However, Albion still turned and bit me on the bum. Even after the company went bust in 1987, they had managed somehow to continue to collect my royalties and presumably pocket them right up until 1993.

I also found out via Helen English that Albion had sold all its assets, including me, before they liquidated. But of course my contract said in the case of Albion ever going bankrupt, all master recordings of my three albums (*Glass Houses* – the first shelved album – *Sons and Lovers*, and *Cover Plus*) would become my property. My contract also had a very clear clause about assigning rights to another company. I had to be notified and they needed my permission. Well naturally, none of that happened. To date, I have never received one penny in royalties from the Albion albums.

The weirdest thing I experienced now was the amount of allegedly unlicensed copies of my old albums, which were out there in the marketplace. One of the guys that worked for Albion, had stolen and used *Cover Plus* and a makey-uppey compilation called, *Writing on the Wall*. Then a German company called Line Records, carrying the defunct Albion logo, released *Cover Plus* and

Sons and Lovers. To cap it all, my ex-publisher, Tim Hollier, licensed that demo of 1989 he'd paid for to try to get me a record deal, and this came out as an album called *L.A. Confidential*! And not one of these bastards paid me a penny for my work, or even accounted to me. I did find out that Dai Davies's new company was being accounted to from Line Records. Where do the royalties go, you ask? So did I, and so do I. Managers and lawyers, all along the way, would send letters and try to help me, but Albion and Line have categorically ignored me and my representatives. I guess if I had some money I would have chased and sued them, but I was still living hand to mouth, as I always have, and these kind of scams are engineered with the knowledge that the artiste couldn't afford to take them to task.

I'd had a knee injury which my doctor thought came from that old first tour injury, when I'd busted my ankle ligament; now I'd busted my collateral knee ligaments. I used to do a lot of step aerobics at the local gym in Wicklow, but when my injury got bad I had to stop and have physiotherapy. Towards the end of the physiotherapy a friend told me of a Karate club in Wicklow Town, and I went to try it out, to help strengthen my knee. I wasn't very good at it, but I enjoyed the exercise of it, and I loved 'Kiai-ing'. *Kiai* is the shout and exhalation one makes on the final execution of a punch, block, strike, or kick. When I punched, I pictured the face of anyone who'd done me wrong in the past. When I kicked, it was those Albion guys I pictured. When I blocked it was symbolic as well as physical – nobody getting past my block to take a swipe at me anymore. Karate slowly, and sometimes painfully, taught me always to be aware. Once, the day before a German tour, I was training with a group in a circle. One nice young guy in the middle was to kick, or punch, all the people in the circle, and our job was to block and counter-attack. I lost concentration for a second and felt a great pain in my ribcage. He'd kicked and I hadn't moved. It turned out that I'd cracked a rib, and that is a very painful injury to do a two-week rock tour with!

The theatre side came back into my life later that year; Michael Scott staged his production of *The Cuchulaín Cycle* in a

Dublin theatre, and I got to work with all that gang again which was bliss. I got to play Queen Emer, Cuchulaín's loving noble wife, who offers to renounce her husband's love if his life can be spared. He gets to live and she has to renounce him. It was a very moving piece, and my big six-foot long dress was a masterpiece, designed by Synan O'Mahony. Not very practical though when walking past the musicians. I'd sweep in on my dramatic entrance, and twenty paces later, I'd realise that I'd gathered in my skirt: Cormac's music sheets, Aengus' newspaper, Cliodhna (our fiddle player's) sandwiches, and Rossa's drum stick! My frock and all its layers of net were like a hoover, or a big sweeping brush.

Whilst performing every night in *The Cuchulaín Cycle*, I was rehearsing daily for a musical going into the Olympia Theatre Dublin for the Christmas period. We were performing Gilbert and Sullivan's *Pirates of Penzance*. Working in theatre over the Christmas was great fun, and one evening backstage I had a surprise visit from my *Breaking Glass* producer, Davina Belling, and her husband Larry. Dear Davina and Larry, still taking an active interest in my career and my life. We'd catch up on all the *Breaking Glass* gossip. How was Brian Gibson? Still in Hollywood? I'd seen him the year before with a new love in his life and his first baby daughter. Had they seen or heard of Phil Daniels? Still married to Jan (of Alan Edwards' office) with children? Wasn't it great Jonathan Price was doing so well, and what about Mark Wingate, a leading actor on TV's *The Bill*?

Not long after seeing Larry and Davina, I saw Alan Edwards whilst he was in Dublin with David Bowie (who was now one of his long list of clients, along with the Rolling Stones, and in the not too distant future – The Spice Girls). We sat in his hotel room and talked. 'I remember the first time I came to Ireland was when you were on the first Irish Tour, and you demanded I got my arse over here to sort stuff out, and I drove at breakneck speed to get to you. Then the road got blocked by a tree struck down by lightening. Life with you was dramatic, Haze,' he told me, smiling. Time does heal all wounds. I thought, this guy was, and is, an important brother to me. We went through too much to not be able to forgive one another. Alan told me how broke he was spiritually and literally when I left him. I reminded him of our difficult parting, as I like to when I want to see him squirm. 'I'm not very proud of that. I'm sorry,' he said. 'And I'm sorry too,' I added, 'for all the bad things I may have done to you, wittingly and unwittingly.'

I heard tragic news about Wesley McGoogan, the sax player. He had been working on a kitchen (he was a fantastic builder with wood and often built kitchens and cabinets for people) and was cutting a particularly hard wood with his circular saw, when the saw hit a knot, jumped up, and cut a couple of fingers and a thumb off. They were stitched back on, but there was serious nerve damage, and it finished his sax-playing days. But Wesley is a very dynamic person, and he works on the production and writing side of music. I was glad that we got to record his superb sax playing on the live German album and I was glad we'd re-built our bridges before this happened to him.

I started to do quite a few acoustic gigs in Dublin, often asking Cormac, the harp player I met while working on Michael Scott's theatre projects, to join me. I got Mundy, or Damien Dempsey, to play a support slot. Cormac was a wonderful human being, as well as a fab musician. He was the first musician I ever met who refused payment, saying, 'No, I don't want it; I know you made nothing tonight, pay me back one day – if you like.'

I bought my friend Sal a flight to Ireland for her birthday present with the express hidden agenda of introducing her to Mundy. Sally had now worked in the music biz for many years, and lately in very successful outfits. She was part of Deacon Blue's management, then she managed Mica Paris, and her last venture was to start a label called Nude and find the band Suede, then she got sickened by the underhand dealings that can go on and she left the biz. I felt she still had so much to offer as a manager, and I wanted Mundy to have an ethical, committed, experienced manager, and I felt that my mate Sal was that person.

Sal loved Mundy's talent. He got on well with her, and she with him, and Sal got Mundy sorted with a big publishing deal and a record deal with Sony. It was very exciting for me as they started having success after success, and I was so glad that I had engineered the plan for them to meet. Mundy's song, "To Thee I Bestow", was used in the soundtrack for the Baz Luhrmann's *Romeo and Juliet* film, starring Leonardo Di Caprio. Yesss! Hurrah! It's good to see someone getting ahead in this business.

I had a great electric band these days with a didgeridoo; a guitarist and singer, by the name of Darleen Sovran; a fiddle player, Cliodhna Quinlan, singers Billy Webster and Liz Gormley, with Davie Watson – who played with me in L.A. – on bass, and on drums, a fellow Taurean, Paul Moran. He'd always check how late it was when we stayed-up jamming on tour, and I'd see him counting the amount of hours of sleep he'd get – as I would be doing – if he went to bed then (eight hours sleep being optimum for us Taurean folk). Billie Webster had suggested a fine guitarist by the name of Ger Kiely, who was also a guy who knew where he was going and what he wanted.

He said to me one day, 'Let me produce an album for you. I can help you write some good songs and then you can sell it on.' I think he thought that I had secret supplies of money (most people did) because I was still fairly famous. At this point in time my teenage admirers were in their early thirties and lots worked in TV and radio productions. During the recording of this album that Ger produced, I tried to re-mortgage my house to pay for it. Ger asked me to pop up the road with him to a music party. He wanted to introduce me to some of the members of Clannad. Clannad were a Gaelic band who'd carved a niche in the market with their lush harmonies and beautiful melodies and Irish lyrics. They have contributed songs to films such as *The Last Of The Mohicans*, starring Daniel Day-Lewis, and *Patriot Games*. They have sold millions of their albums around the world.

When we got to the launch, Ger introduced Clannad's beautiful, raven-haired vocalist and harp player, Moya Brennan. I was thrilled to meet her, as Kurt always loved Clannad, and we had shared the early days of our marriage with their music and Moya's lovely voice. Moya seemed very thrilled to meet me too. She introduced me to her husband, the brilliant photographer Tim Jarvis. Then I met Moya's brother Ciarán and his lovely wife

Lynda. I discovered Lynda and Ciarán lived five minutes up the road from me. From that day on the Brennans have had effects on my life, and they have embraced me into their 'family circle'.

When my album, *5 in the Morning*, was finished I was in serious debt. I didn't really get the kind of support I needed – and foolishly expected – from Ger. Once the master-mix was done I hardly saw him. I had no idea how to licence an album and no particular contacts in the Irish music biz, whereas Ger gave me the impression he knew everybody.

I knocked on many doors, and eventually a friend introduced me to an acquaintance of his from the London music biz, and this guy said he'd try and find a company who'd like to licence the album. About a month before, I'd licensed a live recording of a Berlin concert from the previous year that Wolfgang Grassekamp had recorded and cleaned-up for me, but a studio album needed a big commitment to marketing, because it owed me a lot of money that I was still paying off a loan for.

Eventually a company called Mystic Records licensed it from me for three years. They released one single, called "Na Na Na Na", which received lots of Scottish airplay. I toured to support the album-selling campaign in early 1998. During that tour I met the woman who I had blamed for the last sixteen years of doing damage to me.

I was playing my big London gig at the Shepherd's Bush Empire, and after soundchecking, I was to spend an hour in interview with the editor of the Mail newspaper's *Femail* Magazine. The interviewer walked into my dressing room and gave me her card. The name on it was emblazoned on my memory: Noreen Taylor – she'd done the 'My Soulmate Sal' lesbian-slant tabloid piece that had so shattered my life back in 1982.

All the things I'd wanted to do and say to that woman came flooding into my head as I read her name, and I thought, What do I do here? Do I pretend I don't remember, and just do this interview, and forget the past? Do I say, 'You fucking bitch! You ruined my life!'? Or do I acknowledge that I knew her, and remembered what she'd done, and ask why? Lately I'd been reading loads of Louise L. Hay books on healing and forgiving, letting go, and moving on, so I said, 'Why did you write that pack of lies all those years ago, Noreen?' She looked at me and said, 'I didn't know if you'd remember me. That's why I gave you my card, because I want to tell you what happened.'

She told me her side of the story, how as a young journalist starting out, she'd taken the story back to her then features' editor, who was none other than Ms 'You-are-the-weakest-link-Goodbye!' Anne Robinson. Her features' editor did what all good tabloid features' editors do, and that was to reshape the piece until it took a spectacular shift entirely and – in this instance – into Hazel O'Connor and her soul mate Sal gay slant. When she read her much-changed interview she'd complained, and was promptly told, 'This is how it is; like it or lump it, you can't change it.' Noreen had discussed with a colleague whether to write me a letter of apology. Her friend told her she mustn't ever do that. Welcome to the real world of journalism!

I remembered something my ex-guru from the Hari Krishnas had told me years ago, how we can be attached as strongly in hate as in love. I didn't want any more bindings in hatred because it harmed my soul. I said, 'Noreen, we've both lived with this all these years, you with your guilt, and me with my hate, and we don't need that. Thank you for telling me the truth and I forgive you and let us both let it go. We hugged, did a fantastic interview, and during that piece she apologised as well. I think we both grew that day.

A new drama shortly overtook my life that so shook me that I realise, in retrospect, it was to be a building block of a brand new chapter.

CHAPTER TWELVE

'In the alone of my night
When the angels have all taken flight,
Monsters come out fighting
No need to fight, if I can talk
No need to run
If all I need to do is walk on the path enlightening
And will I go where life leads
Though the road be far and wide
Through the broken dreams of yesterday
With time on my side and with faith as my guide
I will walk on through
Though I don't know where I am going to
To find my way back home at last
Heh I'm gonna walk on walk on
Though I'm crumbled and cracked
Walk on walk on
Won't be looking back in anger
I'll walk on beyond the breaking glass.'
"Beyond the Breaking Glass" 2002)

Chapter Twelve

I trained hard in karate and whenever I was home in Ireland I went to our local club, and up to the Dorset Street Dojo (gym) to train with our *Senseis* (Karate Masters) Tommy McGrane and Paul Hickey. After Dublin training I'd go down the road to my new hairdresser's house for a chat or just a cup of tea. I really liked him. He lived with his boyfriend who I'd met through Siobhan Fahey who had been one of Gary Tibbs girlfriends when we shared a flat back in '78. Siobhan had gone on to fame in Bananarama and Shakespeare's Sister, and had been married to Dave Stewart. I'd invited Siobhan to my house and my hairdresser's lover had been her driver.

I loved having those chats and cuppas and I soon met their friends and neighbours. One of the neighbours had an eleven-year-old daughter who was a brilliant singer. I gave her some singing lessons and I wanted to help her talent. One day, out of the blue, their neighbour rang me to tell me that my hairdresser and his boyfriend had been accused of sexually abusing one of the boyfriend's family members ten years before. The family member had been ten-years-old. The neighbour was as shocked and as bemused as I was.

The police were brought in and eventually the two guys went to the police and gave their side of the story. The child abuse team wanted to take a statement from me about the guys and their babysitting of the neighbours' kids. 'I sometimes got my hair done in the neighbours' house when the guys were babysitting, but I never saw anything improper.' I told the police this because I didn't see anything. The police were now investigating sexual abuse of the neighbours' kids, including my singing pupil! At first I was in denial. I couldn't believe it possible. How could anyone abuse a child's trust? Then the train of thought took me back to my own experiences when my Mum's ex turned up out of the blue when I was fifteen and tried to snog me, and how I'd been a rape victim, more than once. Sexual abuse ruins lives. All these feelings had been safely buried for years, but now they came flooding back with a vengeance. I started to feel very unwell. I couldn't sleep at night, and only when dawn came did it feel safe to fall asleep. I slept with a small axe under my bed and didn't want to see anyone. I cried and was feeling frightened all the time. I went to my doctor and she sent me to a psychiatrist.

Mr O'Sullivan, my psychiatrist, listened to my tale, then gave me a book to take away and inwardly digest. The book was about posttraumatic stress syndrome. Seemingly posttraumatic stress syndrome can raise its ugly head at a much later stage than when the actual shock or stress happened. I was a textbook case, certainly. Causes of this illness can include being in a war zone. I thought about the bombs raining down on me years before in the Israeli air raid on Beirut. Another cause can be verbal abuse at a young age (my Dad saying I wasn't his child). Another is violent sexual crime (rape). Mr O'Sullivan explained to me how these terrible and scary things can be locked down in the memory somewhere and buried, but can be re-awakened by a trigger situation. My trigger was the betrayal of trust, and thoughts of how sick it is to hurt a child.

It was May 1998 and I decided to have my birthday at my dear friend Vickie's house with her daughter – my goddaughter Sara – in Brighton. I needed to have a week away from thoughts of what my hairdresser may or may not have done, police questions, and my own ghosts. Whilst I was staying at Vickie's, my old mate Herbie Flowers – who played bass on David Bowie's "Space Oddity" and on Lou Reed's "Walk on the Wild Side" – phoned to say hello. I'd not seen him since the year before when he'd come over to Ireland to play on my *5 in the Morning* album.

'Hey, Hazel,' he said. 'Why don't you do a show at the Edinburgh Festival this year? Tell your stories – sing some songs. It's great fun. I do it every year and I know there are still a few time slots available at the venue I'm at. It's a great venue – part of an old church. It's called Graffiti.' 'I'll phone you back,' I said.

I promptly phoned Irish harp player Cormac De Barra and asked him if he fancied getting a show together with me, featuring my stories and songs; just the two of us to do it. Cormac said he was up for the challenge, and by the end of that day I was booked to play two weeks at Graffiti in the Edinburgh Fringe Festival.

Chapter Twelve

I began noting my stories down and I went to my actor/director friend, Kathrina Shine, and asked if she would edit my stories with me for a 'One-woman-and-a-man-on-a-harp-show', and might she direct us? She said she would, and thus *Beyond Breaking Glass* was born.

We all worked very hard putting that show together. We intended to use slides, tell stories through narration and little drama vignettes, and I'd sing all my most well-known songs to harp accompaniment only. Kathrina did a great job directing us. My costume designer friend, Fiona Roberts, made two life-size puppets that Cormac worked, and these two guys were called Mr Damage and Mr Pelvis of Shaft Records.

Meanwhile, I had heard through the grapevine that my now ex-hairdresser and his boyfriend were being charged with child sexual abuse. They were eventually convicted and sent to gaol. I've never seen those guys since. The whole story was very tragic, especially for those guys' close family members.

In the middle of August Cormac and I drove through Dublin en route to Belfast to catch the boat to Scotland. I was pulled over by a big motorbike cop in leathers and impenetrable sunglasses. 'You'll lose your licence for speeding like that in this country. You were driving like a maniac'. 'I'm sorry, but I was in a panic. We've got to be in Belfast in two hours for our boat 'cause we've got a BBC TV show first thing tomorrow morning in Edinburgh.' He looked deadpan at me. 'Prove to me that you are booked on the ferry.' I ran to the car to get the fax confirmation, which had my name on top. He read it and then said, 'Okay, Hazel O'Connor, what film was she famous for?' What a daft question, I thought. '*Breaking Glass*,' I answered. 'Correct,' he said. 'You may go.'

I couldn't believe it. He was so angry with me at first, and then I thought he thought I had the same name as 'that Hazel O'Connor bird', and now he was letting us go on our way. He followed us all the way out past the airport though to make sure I drove slowly. It was bizarre. We missed the boat anyway, so we went to the movies in Belfast and caught the next boat. I drove through the night, arriving in Edinburgh at 6.30a.m., with a live TV broadcast booked for 8.30a.m. Hello Edinburgh Festival –

Goodbye all the shit back home.

We went to do our TV appearance on the top of Carlton Hill in Edinburgh. It was cold and windy on the top of that hill at 8.30a.m. and I was knackered from driving all night with no sleep. There were only three people doing the outside broadcast for BBC 2: The director, who also worked the camera, the producer who helped move the cable for the camera and the interviewer. We only had one microphone between us and for the interview we sat on the grass. Then my brief was to take the mike over to Cormac and his harp and begin a song with the microphone hopefully picking up the harp, my voice, and Cormac's voice. Halfway through the song, I saw the director's hand motioning me frantically from behind the camera to move in more – or so I thought. As we were live on TV, I tried to move slowly and subtlety closer into Cormac and to keep singing. A few seconds later the director made the same signs with his hand from behind the camera. I kept moving slowly inwards, and kept on singing, assuming that was what he wanted. I was nearly on Cormac's lap by this time! After we finished I asked, 'Did I move enough for you?' 'Oh God, I wasn't signalling you; I needed more cable!' replied the director.

Later that morning we moved into the flat that we'd rented. Lots of people who live in Edinburgh rent their homes during the Festival time, as they can make a good deal of dosh! Edinburgh is a very beautiful city with the old castle dominating the centre and the wonderful medieval buildings lining the royal mile all the way to Holyrood Palace. Set just aside from Holyrood is a big mound called Arthur's Seat, and the view from the top is splendid.

The Arts Festival circuit was a whole different ball game from rock bands on the road. I thoroughly enjoyed the new learning curve. Kathrina had written a lighting cues script, and also cues for slides to pop in and out of the show. Luckily she was with us for the first few days to help sort out any hitches. After the first night, we realised that having a slide show running in tandem, or in the spaces of live monologue, actually distracted from the spoken word. Also using a slide projector gave us one more piece of equipment that could go wrong, like a projector light blow-out.

Chapter Twelve

The second night we decided to show all the slides at the end of the show, as Cormac and I performed the final song, "Beyond the Breaking Glass". Whilst Cormac played a solo I was to ask the audience to turn their heads around to the left side of the wall and they could watch my photograph album of slides, starting from childhood pictures, hippy days, through Lady Luck, into *Breaking Glass* times, and beyond. I said, 'If you'd like to look to your left ladies and gentlemen,' and the audience dutifully did as I asked, but the slide projector didn't go on. So again I said: 'And now if you'd like to look to your left,' hoping the backstage crew had understood it was time, but nothing had happened again. There's an expression in theatre called eggy moments (as in egg on your face) and I felt this was the most supreme eggy moment I'd had for a long time. Poor Cormac couldn't keep the music going much longer –then suddenly eureka! The slides started to roll. When we came off stage Kathrina was really cross, saying, 'We decided not to show the slides.' 'When was that decision made?' I asked. 'After you started the show,' she replied. 'Well how on earth could we have known unless you paraded in front of us with a sign, or if we were psychic?'

Anyway, that's the fun of live theatre; you never know what might happen next. We all settled down to enjoy a very successful run of the show. Before we'd left for the festival, Cormac and I had asked my old mate actor/musician, Mark McGann if he'd produce a cassette of the harp and voice songs from *Beyond Breaking Glass* for us to sell in the venue's shop in Edinburgh. We thought it might offset some of the enormous costs of staying there. Mark did a brilliant job, but we hardly sold any for the first few days. Then I spotted Tina, who did a jazz set before us. As soon as she came off stage, she sold and signed her own CDs. 'Don't you feel embarrassed selling your own records?' I asked later. 'You must be joking, Hazel,' said Tina. 'I sell loads this way and people get me to sign them. They feel like they've got something special and personal. If I painted pictures I would be selling paintings. That's what artists do, Hazel. You are an artist and your records are your sellable art.' I suppose I'd been so 'put off' by my early days of fame where I would be put in a chair behind a table after a concert and sign autographs – hundreds of them – and yet I really never got time with any of the fans – I just found it all so false. But that was then and this was now! I asked Cormac if he fancied selling our cassette with me after the show. 'Of course, it would be a laugh,' he said.

That little conversation with Tina changed my life: 'One more turn of the screw' for the better. The first time Cormac and I opened our 'record shop' after the show, we couldn't believe how many people flooded around us wanting to buy any Hazel O'Connor records. I became more self confident because I realised I was very much in demand, even though the music industry with its ten-penny view of pop stars had nothing to do with the music career I had now carved for myself, and maintained –with a lot of help from all my talented friends like Kathrina, Cormac, Laurence Myers, Peter Lyster Todd, Davina Belling, and so many more. I further realised what a lot of bullshit the straight music industry is – and a dying industry to boot because of technology. How much profit is skinned from the back of its talent, and what a disgusting, immoral business it is. I had been essentially out in the cold since 1982, and yet I'd never given up singing because that's what I love doing and now –sixteen years later – I was triumphing by my own efforts, selling records myself, and I rejoiced.

One evening, just before the show, I saw some very colourful guys with pink Mohicans, tattoos all over the place, and piercings everywhere. I thought, 'Oh dear, they look like they've come to see me and I bet they think I'm with a band.' So I went over to talk to them. 'Hi, guys.' 'Hello,' they all said, looking very chuffed. 'I just wanted to tell you I'm not with a band, you know, it's just me and Cormac De Barra on Irish Harp, and I'll be telling stories as well.' I said. 'Hazel, we don't care, we just want to see you, and whatever you do we'll be interested.' they replied. They came back with more friends a few days later, and became good pals to Cormac and me.

We met a booker for a theatre in New Jersey in America, who thought the show had a wide appeal and could do well in his theatre. We met all sorts of people young and old, from all corners of the earth, who felt really touched by our *Beyond Breaking Glass* show.

When we returned to Ireland we were very excited at the prospect of trying to get an English tour of the Arts Theatres. Already a new friend, Liam Rudden, had put us in touch with his pal who booked the Hemel Hempstead arts theatre. Liam also said he'd help get some PR for the show.

Then I began cold calling arts theatres and venues where we thought the show might work. My patter went like this: 'Hello, my name is Hazel O'Connor. You may, or may not know me, but I was quite well known in the early 80s from a movie I starred in called *Breaking Glass*.' At this point the person would either respond with, of course they know who I am, or they would say nothing, meaning they don't know me at all. Then I would just carry on with 'Well, myself and my top Irish harp player, Cormac De Barra, have just come back from a successful two weeks at the Edinburgh Festival with a show called *Beyond Breaking Glass*. Would you like me to send the reviews to you, as we are trying to book a tour of it around England now?' I got more yesses than noes, and though it was pure torture trying to sell myself, I persevered. It seems we'd missed the Autumn '98 theatre season, but Spring '99 was looking good. Cormac and I decided we would do whatever we were offered at first, as long as the fee paid both our flights from Ireland and small car hire.

The first mini tour I organised that autumn brought us close to where Wesley McGoogan lived. He came to see the show with his 16-year-old son Lester, named after our original Finchley boy Lester Purdy. Wes liked the show and wasn't perturbed that I'd talked about him and Alan Edwards suing me. We were all friends again, and all that shit had been a long time ago. It was so great to see him with Lester. How fast and furious time passes, I thought.

I'd briefly been managed by actor Joe McGann's business partner and manager a couple of years before, and had remained friendly with Mandy who had worked for him. I showed Mandy the list of theatres and asked if she would phone them and help us put a proper tour together. Mandy came up trumps and booked a great three-week theatre tour for Spring '99.

In January 1999 I went to Los Angeles to act in an Internet drama called *The Soul Patrol* for my old mate David Koenigsberg. Cormac happened to be in the States at the same time so we decided to link up in L.A. and do a *Beyond Breaking Glass* show at the Cat and Fiddle pub in Hollywood. I'd played quite a few successful gigs there ten years before when I was living in L.A. The owners, who were ex-60s' Brit pop star Kim Gardner and his wife Paula, had always been very supportive of me, as had their Irish-born manager, Brian McCaffrey. They offered us a room to perform our first *Beyond Breaking Glass* in America.

At this stage, Cormac had become an expert at manipulating our life-sized puppets of music executives, Mr Pelvis and Mr Damage, that play a part in the show. Tony Visconti and his wife came to see us. He was now divorced from Mary Hopkins and had married May Pang, and was living in New York, but was down in L.A. for the Grammy awards. It was great to see Tony again after eighteen years. He looked well, but his once Italian black hair was now white. We examined each other's faces for wrinkles and smiled; we had both aged well. I invited them to the show, figuring it would really interest Tony to hear our old *Breaking Glass* songs performed on an Irish harp. I wondered what he'd make of our stripped-down versions of the hits he'd created with me: Cormac and I rip into "Eighth Day"! Tony ended up mixing the sound that night. Tony and May loved the show and I asked him if he might help us make the album of the show's songs. He agreed, and we decided to go to New York in April and begin the project with him. We made contact with an Irish pub in New York who wanted us to do a gig at the same time so it seemed we had two good reasons to go to New York. I was so pleased that Tony loved what we had done, especially because Tony Visconti and Brian Gibson helped me to become creatively what I am today.

We stayed and recorded in Tony and May's New York flat. It used to be May's spinster flat, prior to her marriage to Tony, and now that they had kids, they spent most of their time in their house in upstate New York. The fab bit about my bedroom was that May must have slept in the bed I was sleeping in with none other than John Lennon. John, you see, had left Yoko Ono during their marriage and gone to live with May Pang for a while. I used to crash out thinking, 'Mmmm... I wonder if I'm on John's side of the bed?'

The night we arrived in New York, Tony asked us to come to a Placebo gig at the Irving Plaza. He was recording with Placebo at the time, and he told us David Bowie was going to perform a couple of songs on stage that night with them. We were quite knackered but hey, couldn't miss a night out like that! The venue was packed and seething with expectancy (even though David's appearance was a 'best kept secret'). It was such an exciting night, hanging out with my musical mentor Tony, my favourite musician and human being Cormac, and David Bowie, one of my all-time favourite songwriters and performers, at a great gig from Placebo.

Here we were, happy in New York. At the end of the performance David was rushing off but stopped for a quick natter and introduced us to his beautiful wife Iman. He seemed the happiest and most relaxed I'd ever seen him. As I shook his hand, I got a little kiss on the cheek, and I cast my mind over all our little meetings during the course of my choppy career. That first time in Tony's Good Earth Studio in 1980 cutting his hair, chatting in the pub after the first *Breaking Glass* film preview. How he turned up at my gig with Iggy Pop at the Music Machine, like he said he would. The odd bumping into each other in studio canteens over those first few years of my fame, when he'd offer pearls of wisdom like, 'Look, Hazel, chances are most people will know more about you than you would of them because of your fame, so I try to balance it up by getting to know a few facts about them, starting with a name, where they are from, and so on. Then you are not at such a disadvantage, and people tend to relax more then.' He had told me this when I was struggling with being on show all the time. And I've put his advice to good use ever since - thanks Dave! I think the last time I'd seen him was in the backstage bar at the Wembley Live Aid concert and now here we were again. Cormac, Tony, and I hang out with the Placebo boys backstage for an hour after the gig. We had a great laugh, but jetlag was getting the better of me, and even though a further drink with Placebo was very inviting, as they held the Limo door open for me, I was knackered, and so back to the apartment and bed had to be the choice.

The New York recordings went very well. Then, after we had completed our parts, I went down to Los Angeles to see all my old mates again. The two best mates I stay with in L.A. are Denise and her daughter Sara in Venice Beach, and Margo and her family in Beverly Glen. Both of these households are very interesting. Denise was one of the first friends I made when Kurt and I lived in Venice Beach. She had done very well for herself, with a clothes shop in the heart of Venice, called 'What She Wants', and a fabulous funky apartment two minutes from the beach. Margo is the ex-wife of my first American writing partner, Major Black. Both used to live by the L.A. Hari Krishna temple when Kurt and I first came to L.A. and I had stayed in touch with Margo. She is an amazing character, as are her family and friends.

Through Margo I'd met a wonderful American guitarist and Grammy-winning record producer. This guy was a recovering crack addict, who'd been staying at Margo's when I was there, and we became pals. I'd often go to the A.A. and N.A. meetings with him. I found the testimonials of ex-addicts very inspiring and realised how the twelve-step program was applicable for any addiction, from chocolate to cocaine. I heard such tragic life stories, which were turned around with the help of A.A. meetings and the twelve steps to sobriety (and freedom). Our friendship became romantic, which was foolish as he was only a couple of months clean, and A.A. suggests an addict in recovery shouldn't get involved in a romantic relationship for the first year of their clean-up. I hadn't been with a guy for a couple of years and I was vulnerable.

When I came back to Ireland, we'd be on the phone every night and he would lay on the 'love stuff' extremely thick, like, 'Oh baby, I miss you so much – Hurry back to me baby,' etc. Within a month he came over to Ireland to hang out and do some recording on the album. When we got back to my cottage from the airport, he was a little remote: I put this down to jetlag. He

Chapter Twelve

stayed for a week, during which we walked, talked, and recorded his guitar parts at Ciarán (Clannad) and Lynda Brennan's studio. But my boyfriend was not the same loving guy I'd last been with in L.A. I couldn't quite put my finger on it.

He went home to L.A. and I was to join him at his mum's house a few months on for the summer of '99. The trans-Atlantic phone calls were kept up, but not the same volume, even though the 'Baby, baby I miss you' stuff continued. Summer came and I was going to L.A. via New York to stay a few days with Margo's daughter. Whilst in New York, Margo rang me about this 'boyfriend' of mine – she said he'd been shacked up with a new bird for the past month. My first reaction had been to run away back to Ireland, or go to my brother Neil in Montreal. Then I thought, 'Bollocks to that – I'm going to squeeze this bastard and make him squirm.' So I turned up at L.A. Airport where he met me in his mum's white open-top Corvette, and I pretended to know nothing. His opening gambit was, 'It might not be so cool to stay at our house because my mum has been partying all week, taking loads of cocaine, and she's a bit crazy at present.' 'So are you telling me I can't stay with you then?' I asked. 'No, no it's just a bit un-cool at my place as my mum's been partying all week, blah, blah, blah.' He repeated this sentence about five times, never telling the real truth, and I kept badgering him with, 'So are you saying I can't stay after travelling half way around the world, or what?' We went to his house for a cup of tea. He just didn't have the capacity for basic honesty, eventually I cut to the chase, and asked, 'Have you got a new girl in your life?' 'No, you're my girl,' he lied. 'What about the girl you've been working with? I heard you've been shagging her. Is that true?' 'No of course not,' he lied again. By this time I'm counting my blessings that I'm not 'his girl' – what a big bad liar he was. 'Cut the crap,' I said. 'I know about Christine.' 'She's my friend,' he said. 'You're a liar, and I hate liars. You know what you can do – Go fuck yourself. Goodbye and good luck.' I walked away and never saw him again.

A few weeks later, I met Tony Visconti's lawyer in L.A. who didn't seem to be having much luck hawking the stuff we had done together. The whole project was marred with bad vibes from what had happened between me and the guitarist. Cormac and I were quite despondent because by now the *Beyond Breaking Glass* show Spring 2000 tour was booked out in the UK, and a second season was booked that August at the Edinburgh Festival. We needed the show album to be finished and ready to sell on the tour and we had nothing.

I decided to stay in L.A. for the summer of 1999, and I began work on a documentary about the stage show *Beyond Breaking Glass*. The director was a very talented film editor called Fernando Villiers, and his boss, Chris Heffernan – who owned a production house in Venice Beach – gave us all our post-production facilities for free. During that summer I caught up with John Taylor of Duran Duran and he gave us an interview for our documentary about Duran Duran's early days on the road as my support band. It was great to see John again. It had been at least fifteen years since I'd seen him and there was a weird coincidence regarding his Hollywood Hills home. He'd purchased it from my mentor, *Breaking Glass* director Brian Gibson – Small world, eh!

Back in the U.K, various friends of mine did little drama snippets with me for the documentary. The actor Charles Dance played the two baddie record company guys from the fictional record company 'Shaft' from the *Breaking Glass* show. Charles and his wife Jo threw open their house in Somerset to all six of us – Fernando and Cormac and crew – and we had a ball shooting our scenes and jamming into the small hours – Charlie is a proficient banjo player! We shot scenes from the documentary on and off over the next couple of years. Other scenes we shot in Brighton. Joe McGann (*The Upper Hand, Truckers*) played a manager, Julie Graham (*At Home with the Braithwaites, William and Mary*) a lawyer, and at the end of every day we'd have a massive sing-song together.

The *Beyond Breaking Glass* documentary was nearly completed and I took the opportunity, whilst in London doing a TV show, to go and see Mohamed Al Fayed. I wanted to ask if he would allow me to show some clips from the original *Breaking Glass* film in my documentary. I hadn't seen him in twenty years or more. As I entered his beautiful office upstairs in Harrods, he stood up and shook my hand, and saying, 'Hazel, what happened to you? We put three million into you, and you disappear.' 'It's a long story,' I said. 'I'm so sorry for your loss of Dodi.' 'Ah what can we do? It's not in our hands.' He looked very sad.

We smiled gently at one another. I told him about my film and asked if I could have some clips from *Breaking Glass*. 'You can have what you want,' he said. How very kind and how lovely to have seen him again, I thought, as I left Harrods, into the rainy London night. Memories of my beginnings and of Dodi Fayed, the young, rich film producer, coming on to the set of *Breaking Glass* daily – keen and enthusiastic. Dodi Fayed, Princess Diana and their sad end together. My losses seemed trivial to Mohamed's loss of his son.

So we decided to record a low-key *Beyond Breaking Glass* album in Ireland with Cormac's brother, guitarist and engineer/producer, Fionán De Barra in a box-room studio and pulling in all sorts of great acoustic players with favours and deferred payments. With sheer tenacity we re-recorded our entire album. I asked Angolan percussionist Mario N'Goma to play, as he had recently begun performing with Cormac and me. Robbie Malone (bass player with David Gray) donated his performance as a present. The wonderful Eamonn De Barra (of Slide and Damien Dempsey) played flute and whistles. Aidan Roberts on guitar and Cliodhna Quinlan on fiddle – who had both toured with me for the last two years – also played. I was so lucky to get such a talented bunch together to work with me on the album. We had taken a risk to re-record the whole album from scratch, with only acoustic musicians and to keep the concept very simple. We had Fionán doing all the clever stuff mixing it on the computer, and with Cormac and I steering it through, we pulled it off – Phew! To top it all, Cormac and Fionán's brother Ruairí De Barra did our cover artwork using one of the beautiful photos that Tim Jarvis (Moya Brennan's husband) had done a couple of years earlier. I'm thinking of changing my name to De Barra, because the whole family took me in and were so generous lending their amazing talents to the album.

CHAPTER THIRTEEN

'Big brother beware 'cos some of us do care.'
"Big Brother" (*Breaking Glass*, 1980)

Chapter Thirteen

In 2001, we returned to the Edinburgh festival to play the Komedia venue at the Southside run by Marina, who had given us our first chance to play *Beyond Breaking Glass*. On one of the nights, the space was jam-packed with around 700 people and I was in the middle of telling the part of my story where 'Mr Pelvis' and 'Mr Damage' the fictional record company executives force me to sign the record deal without a lawyer present. I notice Laurence Myers in the audience: Laurence was the film producer who put the *Breaking Glass* film out in England and who championed me during my court battles in the early 80s. After the show we strolled down to the Balmoral Hotel for afternoon tea and a good old chat. Oh, it was so good to see him.

We took *Beyond Breaking Glass* to the Dublin Fringe Festival, where it went down very well. The Dutch impresario Hans de Visser came to see the show and immediately invited us to do a tour of the Netherlands. We realised that we needed distribution firstly. We worked in Ireland through a distribution company called Gael Linn, but we were responsible for PR. Of course we had no budget. Thankfully, Sally, my friend who managed Mundy, put me in contact with a wonderful PR company in Cork, run by Niamh Berkowitz. Niamh said she would help out for expenses only. She gave her time and talents for free and she was brilliant. But alas, we couldn't sustain a campaign for long as we just didn't have the running costs. We had to keep gigging to keep food on the table. But my profile was going back up as we noted the amount of radio interviews and music sessions that were coming in, and I was finally earning a decent wage – Let's say I was getting for a gig what a builder would get for a days work! Soon after, we could take Hans de Visser up on his offer, and we were on our way to the Netherlands.

In Amsterdam, Cormac, Mario, and I turned up for sound check at the theatre a few streets away from the squat where I lived in 30 years previously. We sorted out the lighting cues, then went for a bite to eat. As we walked back through the front of house for show time, there in the lobby were my old friends from London, Al and Annette. Back in '75 they had the studio next door to mine and Adrian's: at first I didn't know who this grey-haired, smiling man was, but of course it's Al – I knew his eyes. They had two young men with them – the children were all grown up! Maureen, who'd lived just around the corner all those years ago, was also there. She had run a theatre company back then and it had been her who had proposed me for Actors Equity when I went to Japan and Beirut to work as a dancer. When I saw her, I thought, 'Now *she'd* make a good manager.' Maureen was a determined person, and very trustworthy, and she ended up becoming my manager after that chance meeting. We all hugged, then I went off to put my stage clothes on.

After the Dutch tour, we had a number of dates booked back in Ireland. We were due to play in Wicklow and we found out just before the show that Mario N'Goma – our percussionist – was stuck in Portugal and couldn't get a flight back, so Cormac and I had to wing it. Maureen Simpson was now managing me, and Al and Annette had come over from Holland, while my brother Neil travelled from Canada. I was so happy to see him. I looked at our Neil and thought about our life in music: all he taught me, all the gigs we've played, all the countries we've been in together. How lucky we are still to be making music as our job. I start to sing:

'In my heart in my soul in my darkest hour
Through rivers deep, lonely roads over mountain towers
Through the driving rain and the sunlit lane it's you I embrace
Through the echo on the wind it's your song they sing
I'll see you again'

The spring tour in the UK was a sell-out. We played the Guildford Rock Festival during the summer on the huge acoustic stage. That day was funny, as Cormac and I turned up in my Honda Civic with Matilda the harp in the back. We went to the backstage gate for the acoustic stage and asked where we could park for unloading. The security man was very curt. He told us we would have to drop our gear backstage and then head off again into the vast car parks to try and find a space. 'Rolf Harris had to park over there – So did I,' he said. 'Well I'm not Rolf Harris, and I'm

Chapter Thirteen

not you,' I said. 'Well, who are you then?' he said. 'Hazel O'Connor.' He went very red, at the speed of light. 'I'm sorry, Hazel, I didn't realise it was you,' he said, opening the gate. It was my fault really because I should have simply said at the beginning of our exchange: 'Hello, I'm Hazel O'Connor. Where can I park?' But I hadn't.

The stage was absolutely massive – with only Cormac, Matilda the harp, and I to fill it – very scary! What a buzz that gig was. Well, we started the set terrified with about five hundred people idly watching and by the time we finished, we'd gathered about three thousand cheering fans. They all seemed bowled over by Cormac's fantastic harp playing mixed with my husky blue vocals: we were on the up and up. After our appearance, we went over to the main stage to watch David Gray as our mate, bass player Robbie Malone, was in the band. The set was great and it was fab to see my lovely pal doing his wiggle-bottom bass players dance. Elated after the gig I popped over to their caravan asking, 'Is Robbie 'wiggle-bottom' Malone in there?' Poor old David Gray came to his dressing room door looking at me like I'm a nutty fan, so I quickly stick out my hand and say, 'Hi, David, I'm Hazel O'Connor. Great gig, thank you. Is Robbie in there?' David's face changed from a look of, 'Who is this loudmouth at my dressing room door?' to one of genuine gladness to make my acquaintance. It was all very heart-warming as we shared a glass of champagne, old mates and new.

We went back to Brighton to stay with our pals. Cormac was always billeted with actors Joe McGann and Julie Graham, in their place which everyone called the 'Pink House', and I would go to my old pal Vickie and goddaughter Sarah. We had so many wonderful music parties there. Also at the Pink House, we met *Men Behaving Badly* star, Neil Morrissey, who thought his company might be able to help me finish the *Beyond Breaking Glass* documentary. As a result of our chats, Neil invited Cormac and me to play at a festival in Kinsale, County Cork, where his production company met up every year.

We made the trip to Cork and arrived in Kinsale, about half and hour's drive from Cork City. At the Lord Kingsale bar we were chatting to Maureen, one of the owners, who said, 'I think you know my son.' It turned out she was David Austin's mum – Dave featured on many of Wham's albums and was one of George Michael's oldest pals. It was great to see him after a gap of 25 years. As we come to the end of each show, I always like to get my audience to do some singing with me – it was something special that night to have actors Neil Morrissey and Joe McGann singing on stage with us – 'Heh ho, I'm still breathing.'

Moya Brennan invited us to play as her guest at the Frankie Kennedy Winter School in 2001/2 in Gweedore. This festival takes place over the New Year period and is a huge gathering of traditional musicians. It was founded in 1994 to commemorate the life and work of the legendary flute player Frankie Kennedy. The members of Clannad (all from the Brennan extended family) grew up in Gweedore, an Irish-speaking area, and they have made it their mission to bring the language and music of their roots to people all around the world.

We stayed as guests of the Brennan family for the duration of the festival and a couple of days after our own gig, we all got together in the Brennan family pub (Leo's) for a massive session. I sang "Rebecca"; the song I wrote about my friend who passed away. I always have this song in my set list and singing it is my way of bringing to mind the friends who have gone and honouring their memory:

'When will we sing silly harmonies into the night?'

As a result of touring *Beyond Breaking Glass*, I decided it was time to write down my stories before I forgot them. I didn't want to write at home, because I thought the 'ghosts' of my past might haunt me in my house. Luckily for me, only five minutes up the road from me was Ireland's first and only fully organic Hotel and restaurant, Brook Lodge. I wrote every day in the hotel in beautiful surroundings and got to know the owner and staff very well.

Evan Doyle, the owner, asked us to do a show in the Chapel in the grounds of the hotel and we ended up doing several, and used it as a venue to shoot the video of our cover version of George Michael's "One more Try". I remember one particular gig where there were lanterns lit all along the pathway and over the bridge to lead the people to the Chapel doors. All my friends and neighbours were there in the audience – Jill who's been typing this book, Fred and Freda, Viva, Evan, Ciarán and Linda Brennan, Moya Brennan, Brian Kennedy, Cathy Jordan (from Dervish), and my manager Maureen. We came to the end of the show and Moya and Ciarán Brennan, Cathy Jordan and Brian Kennedy came on stage with me and we sang "Beyond the Breaking Glass" – then the audience joined in: 'Walk on walk on beyond the broken glass.' We all know we'll have a great session at Evan's house afterwards.

On the road again – this time back to Brighton. I love playing Brighton, it's my second home. All my London friends seem to live here now. Sally, Vickie, my goddaughter Sara, Julie Graham, Joe McGann, and loads more. We organised a fan club party at the Komedia and Mum and Geoff came down from Coventry. Lots of my fans there knew Mum from the days when she ran the fan club for me. Mum – Joyce O'Connor – was their friend and their Agony Aunt – and there was no better woman! I finished the show with "Driftwood" and I felt the great depth of emotion in the room that night. My goddaughter came on stage – she is now a beautiful teenager – and sang with me.

'Sitting on the sunny shoreline
See some driftwood come to rest
Worn out by the tides torn up by its endless rides, never free, just a bit like me
I've been that piece of wood I've been tossed about on the ocean of illusion, confusion brittle and twisted like waves lashing out at the rock
Well now I know
I've just gotta find
That shoreline Oh yeah
That little peace of mind
And let the sun shine in'

Back at the hotel after the show, over a cup of tea and some biscuits, Cormac and I count our earnings. We've started making good money. 'Where do you keep your cash, Cormac, when we're travelling?' 'In my old sock,' he replies. 'Ha! – So do I.' He then lifts his cash-laden sock and whirls it over his head singing, 'We're in the money!' Money sprays all over the room. We collapse laughing. 'Oh shit, I didn't expect that to happen – I thought I had the sock by the ankle bit, not the toe!' We laugh and collect up the strewn money.

A day's work on tour is a long day let me tell you. Up and out of the hotel by midday, drive for two hours and get some food, drive another hour and find the gig venue, unload, move into a dressing room, set up a sound check and focus the lights. Then we'd get a cup of tea and maybe eat, but if it was under two hours left before the show time, I'd eat after the show in case of stage flatulence. 8.30p.m. is stage show-time and we would finish around 10p.m., then sell a few CDs, sign loads of autographs and say hello (a lesson I learned from the Edinburgh Festival). It would usually be around 11.30p.m. or midnight before we would hit the road looking for our next Travel Inn. So yes, it's a long day. And yes, "Beyond the Breaking Glass" needed UK, and wider distribution. I asked Richard Rogers, a guy who'd produced an album of Bowie covers, to which Cormac and I had contributed a version of "Rock and Roll Suicide". Richard suggested I talk to the guy he was doing the Bowie project with, Charlie Kennedy, of Invisible Hands Music. I phoned Charlie and he said he'd catch a plane over and visit me to chat about distribution. Bless him, he took the plane to Dublin Airport, the taxi to Dublin train station, and I picked him up at my local mountain train station. 'Charlie Kennedy?' I shouted to the dark-haired young man in his denim flares and a haversack over his shoulder. 'Yes; hello, Hazel!' he said. He looked to be in his late twenties. 'Jump in,' I said, opening the car door. 'Sorry about the hairs and dog smell, I have two dogs and one is a big hairy wolfhound.' Charlie took it all in his stride, and I thought, 'Yeah, maybe we can do business.' And we did; Charlie released four album titles of mine at once, and slowly my work started to appear in the record shops again.

Chapter Thirteen

Cormac and I had added one Mario N'Goma to our *Beyond Breaking Glass* show by now, and the trio sounded fab. I had phoned the organisers of Glastonbury Festival to try to get a gig there and I was referred to a lady who ran the theatre tent, one of the smaller stages. It's nearly impossible to get to play the main stages, as the agent that runs them generally puts their own acts on. It's totally sewn up, the usual really - big money begets big money. Anyway, the theatre tent booked us for three nights, and it was a roaring success. We had great fun except for the last day. I'd driven from my B & B in Shepton Mallet by the usual route, to get on-site parking, but the route was closed, and the entire one-way festival traffic had been reversed in preparation for getting the punters out as quickly as possible, with that night being the Grand Finale. Security men kept waving me on at every gate. I was in danger of missing my gig. I was beginning to get upset, and every time I tried to explain my situation, stressed security would wave me out, sometimes very rudely shouting, 'Don't fucking care, just move, you're blocking the traffic.' Finally I got out of my car in tears, collared by a security man who phoned the security office, who phoned the production office, and eureka! After being given the run around for the past hour and a half, I was led into and through the festival by a security van; a journey which usually took five minutes taken three hours when I finally reached our stage, just in time to go on.

CHAPTER FOURTEEN

'Somebody told me your spirit had gone
But I don't believe it's true 'cos it was you
Who said the spirit goes on and on
Somebody told me it was you – you know
If it don't kill you it'll make you strong.'
"Strong" (*Hidden Heart*, 2005)

Chapter Fourteen

My mum became very ill: she'd contracted pneumonia, and having bad lungs all her life, it was very serious and frightening. I rushed over to England to do my best as her nurse. Being a health food freak, a vegetarian, and a believer in a holistic approach, I tried to make good healing foods for her. I'd studied Reiki so I tried that on her. I massaged her feet and I'd have danced on my head if I thought it might help. My mum is a very special person, full of spirit, and she fought to get well.

It was discovered that her heart was in bad shape, that she needed a bypass, but she had been told that because her lungs were weak, there was a fear that she wouldn't survive the operation. But if left unattended she was a walking time bomb and could 'pop her clogs' at any moment. At first Mum said she'd just wait till her heart blew, then she changed her mind and said she'd take the chance and go for a bypass. Around this time my dear dog, Babes, who'd been mine and Kurt's dog in L.A. (and had stayed with me after the marriage split) died. I became so aware of death and impending doom and I was frightened and very sad. I shared my time between Mum and touring.

In the beginning of 2003, peaceniks of the world, like myself, did not believe in the Bush administrations war on terrorism, as they trained their gun-sights on Iran. On 15th February 2003, I joined with the rest of the peace-loving democratic world, to say No! to American war-mongering. I sang on the peace stage in Dublin all afternoon singing a rotation of three songs: Bob Dylan's "Masters of War", Bob Marley's "Redemption Song", and Hazel O'Connor's "Eighth Day". The Irish Peace Movement expected 20,000 people – We were delighted to see 120,000 demonstrators. That day I was proud of the millions of fellow peace-loving brothers and sisters worldwide. We all said No! to the Bush war-machine.

In March the U.S. and British Coalition invaded Iraq. Bush had publicly refused to be swayed by 'minority' pressure groups. I decided that I would not go back to the States until the Bush administration had left the White House. Hopefully they wouldn't blow the world to smithereens in the meantime. No weapons of mass destruction had been found in Iraq, but thousands could be found in America in the hands of a very dangerous 'God on our side' right-wing government.

A month later, I received the call I'd been dreading from England. Mum's heart surgery was happening the next day, and I had just enough time to hop on the boat from Ireland, and drive like the clappers to see her before her surgery. I arrived at 6a.m. and was allowed to hold her hand until she was wheeled away to surgery at 9a.m. I was terrified she would die under the knife, but I also knew my mum had a very strong spirit.

I went back to Mum's house for a few hours sleep, and returned to meet up with Geoff, my step-dad and Mum's long-term boyfriend. Dear Geoff had sat outside the hospital since the operation had begun. It was now 12.30p.m., and she was alive and kicking, but still unconscious. I stroked her head and kissed her. 'I love you so much, Mum,' I whispered. 'Stay with us, stay with us, please stay.' Some hours later she sort of came round, but she was in a state. She'd told me prior to the op that if she had a stroke, she didn't want to be revived. She also told me of how afraid she was of waking up with that tube down her throat, and hoped she'd be sedated until that was taken out. The minute I saw her moaning, I remembered her wishes. 'She needs pain relief. Please don't let her be conscious until that tube is out else she'll panic and choke.' I called her anaesthetist, and he upped her morphine. A few hours later the tube was taken out and she was semi-conscious. So far she'd survived. She came out of hospital a week later, and I tried my nursing skills again. We had some great laughs at that time, like when I just couldn't seem to roll those tight surgical anti-embolism stockings over her ankles. Mum always sees the humour in a situation. Me, I was ever grateful for the opportunity to do things for Mum ever since I came home from running away to Amsterdam. I'd wanted to be a model daughter, to be a good daughter, and eradicate the guilt I've felt through the years for hurting her so much back then. Mostly though I was so happy to be there for Mum because I love her.

Within a few months of Mum's heart operation, Cormac and I were off for our first tour of Australia. We'd decided to go via

Malaysia and to have a few days in Kuala Lumpur on the way out. Australia was a blast and I was able to see my ex-mother-in-law Shirley at our first gig in Brisbane. She'd told me about her new grandson, and how thrilling it was, and how Kurt and his new wife were well and happy. Of course I felt great pangs of sadness for the child Kurt and I had lost, and for our dead marriage, but it was so good to hug Shirley. I knew she still loved me even though I was now the ex-daughter-in-law.

Our gig in Sydney was a roaring success and we were getting a lot of radio airplay for tracks from our "Beyond the Breaking Glass" album. Unfortunately we discovered there were no albums for sale in the shops, even though Charlie, at Invisible Hands Music, had led us to believe he had distribution sorted out. In fact it negated the whole effort of going so far away to tour if people couldn't buy your album after seeing the gig. As usual it was a *fait accompli* – we just had to get on with our tour. When Charlie met up with us in Oz, of course I let him know how pissed off I was, but it was all too late – another missed opportunity! We recorded vocal and harp in a little studio in Melbourne for our forthcoming single, "One More Try", by George Michael. Within two weeks our tour was over and we returned home via Penang, Malaysia, where we stayed for a week's holiday. I would have loved to have stayed a lot longer in Malaysia to go and see the orang-utans in Borneo, but needs must. I had more touring to do in Britain, Ireland, and Holland, and the reality of my life has been: don't gig don't eat. Existence has been on the level of hand to mouth for years now.

My wolfhound Oisin was diagnosed with cancer and he was quickly slipping away and my heart was breaking. The birthmark on my leg had grown tumours on it again, like when I lived in California, and I was scared. And still I had to keep leaving home in search of work. Oisin died on the 5th of November. I held him as he died. I felt his spirit leave. The hospital phoned in the middle of his dying, and tried to get me to come in fairly quickly. I couldn't discuss anything right then and there because I was wrapped around my giant hairy friend who was in his final death throes.

Eventually I went into the reception area of St. Vincent's Hospital in Dublin a few days before Christmas. As I turned the corner to the skin clinic I was shocked at the amount of people waiting to see the specialist. I was just back from three gruelling weeks on tour in Holland, and I asked the nurse if I could make another appointment for the New Year because I was so tired and I just wanted to go home. She said she'd check my notes. The nurse came back and took my arm steering me through the back door where I found myself in a cubicle – miraculously at the front of the queue. 'How could this be?' I wondered. The nurse didn't do this because she was a fan – she didn't know me from Adam.

A few minutes later Ms O'Donnell the specialist arrived. I thought I was just there to discuss getting the whole of my birthmark removed and I began blabbering, 'I'm really sorry for wasting your time; I was quite happy to come in another time. I wasn't trying to jump the queue or anything.' She stopped me mid-sentence: 'You have squamous cell carcinoma.' My mind reeled. It was the same diagnosis as I'd had in the States, and the reason I'd moved to Ireland. Then I was told it was a mistake, and I had been telling my audience about this cancer mistake for the last five years, and now it had caught up with me. I felt I was being punished for being so glib, and for all my words and songs, nothing came out of my mouth but, 'Bollocks! Bollocks, Bollocks, Bollocks!' This lack of articulation lasted about a minute, followed by the practical, 'What's to be done? I'd like to remove the whole area as soon as possible.' Ms O'Donnell replied, 'Within the next three weeks.'

I left the hospital bemused. I didn't want to tell Mum yet because she was still recovering from heart surgery, I remembered how afraid I'd been back in 1990 when I was told I had cancer. I'd babbled to some people whose faces immediately looked negative and sorry for me, and that had made me feel even more afraid, so I decided I would tell only a few, and only positive people who'd uplift me – not to bring me further down. I told Viva my best friend and neighbour, I told Maureen my friend and manager, and I told Cormac my friend and accompanist.

I immediately phoned the Bristol Cancer Centre, which

Chapter Fourteen

specialises in normal and holistic approaches to cancer. I ordered books, tapes, and videos, and started to research my disease. I began doing my Yoga and Tai Chi every morning and tried to calm down and meditate. I took stock of my life. Eventually I told my mum, after asking her if she would want the truth from me, no matter what. She said she would want the truth from me, the same as I want from her with regard to her health and well being.

On the eve of my operation in St. Vincent's Hospital in Dublin, I had decided to treat myself and go up the road from my house to one of my favourite places: Brook Lodge. Evan, who ran this place, had already done so many favours for me. He had promoted a show in the summer for Cormac and me, and let us use the hotel for the promo video of the single "One More Try". So I went for my supper at the Brooke Lodge before leaving for hospital.

I sat in my favourite spot in the empty Cherry Orchard Café, eating alone, frightened about the upcoming cancer surgery. I became aware of a smell, like when the handle of a pot is burning. I asked David – who'd served me – if he could smell it. Was there a fire perhaps? He came running back out of the kitchen saying, yes, the kitchen was ablaze. Very quickly the room I was in filled with smoke. I moved out, and suddenly it was all go. I helped to get fire extinguishers, unravel the water hose, and saw my friend Evan and other members of staff running in and out of the kitchen with cloths around their faces, trying to fight the blaze. It was all so shocking, and I realised disaster can hit any of us at any moment, and nobody is exempt – it is a part of life. The fire engines finally arrived and my local DIY shop attendant, Peter, was one of the firemen now dressed in his blue uniform. The fire was eventually extinguished. I didn't know if this incident was a good or a bad omen, but I was very shaken.

The next day I went into the operating theatre, wide awake, and armed with my Paul McKenna hypnosis CD and player. Ms O'Donnell said I could have the op with local anaesthesia, unless things got complicated. The offending flesh was chopped away. I was stitched-up, and by 1p.m. that day, I was allowed home. My manager, Maureen, collected me and brought me home. Two weeks later I went back to hospital to have the stitches removed and Ms O'Donnell gave me the best news I'd had in a long time. In her opinion, even though the original biopsy read as cancer, she felt that the tissue they'd removed during my operation was not cancer, and the cells from the original biopsy were actually something that looked like cancer, but wasn't. I leapt and ran out of the hospital, immediately phoning Mum, Maureen, Cormac, and my good friend and neighbour Viva, to give them the good news.

I had been visiting Mum and she'd read in the newspaper that Brian Gibson, the director of *Breaking Glass*, had died of bone cancer. I was mortified, as I didn't even know he was ill. I phoned Davina Belling in L.A. and she and her husband filled me in on what had happened. I was lucky enough to be in England, so I could go to the funeral. I couldn't believe my acting mentor was dead. He'd always said, 'You're going to end up as a recluse, living with a bunch of rescued dogs halfway up a mountain like Julie Christie or Brigitte Bardot.' Whilst I was married, I thought, 'You're wrong, Brian, I do live up a mountain, yes, I do have rescued dogs, yes, but I'm a happily married woman – not a recluse.' Of course that was no longer true. I saw Jonathan Pryce on my arrival at the chapel, and we hugged and cried. So many people came to see Brian off. The most poignant was his wife Paula and their three-year-old daughter. My heart went out to them, but I was glad Brian had, had such love. I remembered Brian Gibson, my Svengali, trying to get me to cry all those years ago during rehearsals for *Breaking Glass*, and me, dumbly asking, 'Do you mean real tears?' 'Yes, Hazel,' he said patiently. And now twenty-five years later, I sat in the chapel staring unbelieving at his coffin, and I couldn't stop the floods of real tears. 'Goodbye, Brian, my mentor.'

I had been invited to appear on the Avalon Stage at Glastonbury 2004, but unfortunately Cormac was busy touring with Moya Brennan. Cormac's brother Eamon played in a young traditional band called Slide, and I was to be touring with them in May, but they weren't free in June to back me for the Glastonbury Festival either. I couldn't believe it – A rock artiste's dream is to

Chapter Fourteen

play Glastonbury, and here was I being asked to, but couldn't accept the gig as I had no one to play with me.

Whilst in Coventry, I asked the advice of Two Tone producer, Roger Lomas. I'd known Roger since I'd turned hippie at 14-years-old. Roger had been in the 60s band The Sorrows, when the Two Tone movement happened. I was happy to see Roger producing Selector, The Beat, and many others, so I figured that he would know some musicians that could play Glastonbury with me. He suggested a band called The Subterraneans. He added that he wasn't being nepotistic but his son Kevin played bass in the band. I went to see them, thought they were great, and asked if they were up for it. The Subterraneans were refreshing as they'd been there, nearly done it, and definitely got the T-shirt. Now they just wanted to play without the bullshit. They started rehearsing my stuff – plus Roger had suggested we make a live DVD for a company he did work for. So now the Subs and I had a small tour, a DVD to film, and a great slot at Glastonbury.

The only downside to all this was very little money was coming in and my debts began to mount. The DVD and Subs tour went great. The Slide tour went great. Then Glastonbury came around. As luck would have it Cormac was able to play with me and the Subs at Glastonbury; he was going to fly into Bristol and Maureen was going to pick him up and bring him the rest of the way.

I had decided to camp this time, as we'd done a three-night stint at Glastonbury Theatre tent two years before and stayed in B & B at Shepton Mallet. Trying to get on site on the Sunday had been a nightmare, so I thought, This time I'll buy a bloody tent, an air mattress, and bring pillows, sheets and duvets. My friend Viva was co-driving with me and she had bought our cheapo dome tents from Lidl some weeks prior to departure. Viva had suggested I put my tent up in the garden to make sure it all worked, as she had with hers, and it helped to make sure all the parts were there. Of course, I didn't practice putting my tent up, so when we eventually got to Glastonbury, found our camping space and began erecting our tents, Viva's was up in a jiffy, as she'd practiced, whereas mine went up and down three times – I started at 9.30p.m. and finished at 2.30a.m. I should have followed Viva's advice. Around 3a.m. I attempted to sleep. Of course this was impossible, as the ground was booming with bass beats from the dance tent and late night gigs going on all around. Anyway it was okay, as I was so excited to be there, to be actually camping, something I had not done for over twenty-five years!

The next day was hot and sunny and Phil Jackson (aka Phil Didge) came to call for us and help make my tent a little more secure (Phil was the consummate camper!) Viva and I went over to Phil's camp. It was a didge workshop which he and his other didgeridoo adepts ran every year, teaching and jamming, and always guaranteed a roaring fire, a hot cuppa tea, and a warm welcome during the cold evenings.

The stage manager at the Avalon stage warned us it was going to rain and suggested we buy a tarpaulin – Lucky we did, as the skies opened and it poured all the next night. It also poured most of the next day. Myself and the Subs were en-route to play a radio session before our 5.50p.m. gig, but we had to abort as Glastonbury was turning into a quagmire and it was taking hours to drive half a mile to the on-site radio station.

My Wellington boots had collected water, so I wore plastic bags over my feet like socks so I didn't feel the soggy rubber boots. At 5.30p.m. Saturday, I thought maybe I'll just do the gig in my wellies, as it would be easier – and that's what I did! The Subs plus Cormac, plus Phil 'didge' Jackson played a blinding set. Afterwards I ran over to the CD shops to sign CDs and say hello. The queue went on for three hours. It was a great success that night, and to top it off Cormac, Phil, and I played a gig at the Small World Café where everything was solar powered. Then Cormac and Maureen departed the festival site, and I went back to my now very soggy tent. The next day the Subs and I played a live set on Radio Avalon. The sun was shining as we drove there on an open truck – On the way back, the heavens opened again and we all got drenched. I had intended to watch the legendary James Brown, but the deluge changed my mind. Viva and I drove out of the festival site, and took a couple of rooms in a motel en route back to Ireland. We watched the highlights of the festival from our hotel rooms, dry and warm.

I'd met up with my old friend record producer Martin Rushent (producer of the Stranglers and Human League, to name but a few – he'd produced my 1983 album *Smile*). We'd not seen each other for about fifteen years, but had felt in touch with each other's lives up to a point, because my brother Neil had come with me to record at Martin's Genetic Studios and had ended up staying there and working with Martin for the next seven years. Martin had come to one of the spring gigs I'd done with Slide, Cormac's brother Eamon De Barra's trad band. That night I'd gone back to Martin's house for a cuppa. 'You have a great blues voice now Haze,' said Martin. We chatted into the night and decided to start work on a long-term electro-blues project together, which we named 'Rush-Haze' for the time being.

In January 2004 I had started work again with Paul Barrett (engineer/producer of U2, and my 1995 Sony album, *Private Wars*). For my next album he'd put me in touch with his nephew Gavin. I wrote two songs for the new album and we started to collect all the material together for a September recording schedule, as September was my only month off from touring. By August 2004 I'd met with Charlie Kennedy and Maureen, and planned to release my Paul Barrett produced album in February 2005 to coincide with my February Tour with Cormac De Barra. I found out in late August that Paul Barrett wasn't able to record in September, and as that was my only free time I had to do some quick and fancy thinking. I asked Cormac his opinion. I hoped we could record at my house with Cormac's brother Fionán engineering, and record all the acoustic instruments in Ireland, and then ask Martin Rushent if he would add percussion and mix it at his house in England. All the people said yes, so we were on! I also wanted to do a few duets, one with Moya Brennan (Clannad's lead singer) and a blues one with Rob Reynolds, who has a brilliant R & B voice. He was also in Invisible Hands music and had toured a good few times with Cormac and myself already. I wanted to re-record an acoustic version of "If Only", from *Breaking Glass*, with the Subterraneans and Tony Dangerfield (Subs vocalist), dueting with me.

It was such fun to record in my living room at home, with my daft dogs trying to get into the act all the time. A lot of the musicians that Cormac had played with in Moya Brennan's band joined us, and also acclaimed fiddle player, Maire Breatnach. The work was sent to Martin in England, and with the help of many talented musicians at his end the album continued. Martin was very excited about this recording, as it was sounding so beautiful.

Funnily enough my first love Adrian had bought a house quite close to Martin's home, so I asked if I could stay at his whilst working with Martin. Dear Adrian was so kind to me, and the first few nights I stayed there – a little inebriated – he said how sorry he was that he had left me alone at the hospital all those years ago, when I was first diagnosed with malaria. I'd never given it a thought before so I told him not to feel guilty, I held nothing against him; the opposite, in fact, as he was the foundation and teacher of everything I went on to do in my life. We reminisced together over those next few nights – listening to Maria Callas singing "One Fine Day". 'We should have married, you know that, don't you, Haze?' – Yes, I knew that, but now sitting like two old codgers, looking back over what seemed another lifetime, we'd both lived a hundred lifetimes since then. When I finished my work there and was departing back to Ireland, when he asked if I'd need to stay again in the near future. 'Probably,' I said. 'Then have a key to the house. You're welcome anytime, Haze.' So we'd come full circle: Adrian, Martin Rushent, and I.

Sadly a young fan – Jo, who'd been knocked out at the CND concert all those years ago and with whom I'd gone to hospital straight after coming off stage – young Jo, now a 36-year-old woman, turned up at a gig and told me she was in the secondary stages of cancer. She died towards the end of 2004.

I bumped into a drummer who played with me the first year I came to live in Ireland (he'd been poached by Bob Geldof in 1999 and for the last fifteen years had played in his band). He told me that Bob said, 'Tell Hazel that I still have that fan letter she wrote to me all those years ago.' Like I said, life moves in a circular motion.

Martin Rushent was so enthusiastic about the album *Hidden*

Chapter Fourteen

Heart, he believed it was one of the best he'd ever produced. I really enjoyed the process and we wanted to see if it would sink, or swim. The radio response was great, and to be honest, my life had long since ceased to be ruled by a records being a hit or a miss – I just love to sing. Of course the extra money a hit brings in could fix the numerous holes in my roof, or I could get a gardener to mow my unruly acre, instead of always coming home knackered from touring, then immediately pushing the bloody heavy mower all over the place, and I could get a person to paint and decorate my cottage.

Just before the release of *Hidden Heart*, I was asked to appear on a British TV show called *Hit Me Baby One More Time*. It was a kind of competition for singers from the 70s, 80s, and 90s. And besides performing the hits which the artists are most famous for we had to choose to cover a hit song made famous be somebody else in the last five years. I chose to do a jazzy version of Kylie Minogue's "Can't Get You Out of My Head", as I thought my gay fans would like it, and I remember seeing a TV profile on Kylie where she said I was one of her favourite pop stars from the past. It was a hoot doing the show. My fellow competitors were Sinitta, Hue and Cry, China Black, and the Real Thing. Just before the show, an old mate of mine gave me a photo of myself, her eight-year-old son, and Sinitta – taken twenty years ago. Her son was now a grown man of twenty-nine! At the press conference I looked for Sinitta to show her the photo. I was wondering if she had aged well, and then I saw who I thought she was, but it turned out to be her mother. Sinitta then joined us and she looked just fantastic, as did her mum. We laughed at this photo from so long ago.

Just before it was my turn to appear on the stage there was an accident. Usually all the artists had to appear on a lift, with smoke bombs and mad lights going off all at once. I was already dreading the lift because I had slightly elegant shoes on, and this made walking off the lift and going the stairs towards the audience very difficult. (I can only walk in flat shoes because of my strange feet.) The Subterraneans – who we'd wangled on to the show – and I are being hurried to the side of the stage to be ready straight after the Real Thing who were standing in position above the lift shaft. Suddenly one of the Real Things fell down the eight foot lift shaft right in front of me. This was live TV so it could have been disastrous – they cut to a commercial break, then the guy who fell limped on to the stage, and being the true professionals they performed their hit "You To Me Are Everything" as if nothing had happened. The doctor was waiting straight after. I felt sure he had broken a leg or an ankle. I followed them doing my most famous hit "Will You". Of course I didn't win, I didn't expect – or want to, especially as the winners thus far had been Shakin' Stevens and some other MOR acts. It wasn't really my thing. I've never been a light entertainment act and wouldn't want to become one after all these years of being a rebel. I really enjoyed being part of the show though. The other artists and the crew were great, and I got to buy some new clothes.

Within weeks of doing the TV show I began my UK tour to promote *Hidden Heart* which doesn't get released until I've nearly finished the tour, and I have a foreboding feeling of déjà vu. Not only is the album release late, but Charlie, the head of Invisible Hands Records – that great guy who took plane, train and automobile to Ireland to do business with me – is in Canada busy with his other artist. He doesn't have to be so literal with the invisible bit! I feel my faith and hope slowly draining away. Then I check myself. Reality Check: I am fifty. I am singing. I am doing what I chose to do with my life all those years ago, because to sing makes me happy, and I know I have made other people happy. I believe in loyalty and truth, so do my team mates Maureen and Cormac, the most fantastic musician I've ever worked with. So if Charlie is too invisible from my career, I will tell him the truth, but I'll also endeavour to be loyal, because he has backed me without contracts for three years now.

Just before Christmas 2005 Blondie with support by Hugh Cornwell were at the Olympia Theatre, Dublin. A theatre I have a history of friendship with, from gigs Louis Walsh organised back in the 80s, to performing in *The Pirates of Penzance* in the 90s, and always staying in touch with the king of backstage, John Brogan, and the king of theatre executives, Brian Whitehead.

Chapter Fourteen

Charlie invited me to the gig as he also handles Hugh Cornwell. I went to say hello to Debbie Harry in her dressing room. Twenty-five years ago I'd sat in her and Chris Steins apartment in New York with my first manager, Alan Edwards. Dear, sweet, and beautiful as ever, I didn't want to bother her, as she was due on stage any second, but she gave me her time and we remembered our past. I sat and chatted with Hugh Cornwell, as dry and witty as ever. I hadn't seen him for twenty-five years either. It was good to see them but I had to go before the end of the gig as I had a radio show to do.

January 18th was the date my nan died thirty years ago and Mum was very depressed that week. January 24th 2005 my dad died so I was glad I'd seen him one last time a couple of weeks before. My father in my mind's eye is always the raven-haired Galway man who sang and played piano by ear, who joked, drank and smoked. My father wasn't the old, knackered white-haired fellow I saw in the hospital bed. I'd held his hand: Where had my dear daddy gone? Dad was very feeble but glad I'd come. He died of heart failure in the night a few weeks later.

CHAPTER FIFTEEN

And the carol singers singing
in the bleak winter and it's dark,
Don't be afraid my arms will hold you
hold you forever in my heart,
"Re-Joyce", 2010

Chapter Fifteen

In 2006, I realised Mum and I had never been on a road trip together, so we decided to go to the Languedoc area in the South of France. Mum's best friend Hilda (my 'Auntie' Hilda), and one of her daughters, Steph, lived there with her husband Ju. We went to stay with them for a couple of weeks. I was fascinated with the history of the region, especially with the story of the Cathars. The Cathars were a Christian sect that was more or less wiped out by the thirteenth century, when the pope declared them to be heretics. He granted permission to the King of the Franks to clear the Languedoc region of the Cathars and take their land. The King gained huge areas of land in return for his pious deeds, which included the burning alive of 20,000 citizens of the town of Beziers because the Catholic half of the citizens refused to hand over their 'heretic' neighbours. The Cathar beliefs were very simple: they didn't believe you needed a church to worship God and they objected to the selling of indulgences and so-called holy relics by the clergy. They believed in God and Jesus but didn't revere the cross as an emblem, as they didn't want to worship the instrument of Jesus's torture. They believed in the transmigration of the soul, as do the Buddhists and Hindus, and that we are put on this earth to perfect our spiritual knowledge through many incarnations until we are perfected enough to go back to God. Similar to Eastern religions, they were herbalists and vegetarian... I think I would have been one of them had I lived in those times.

Anyway, Mum and I loved the Tarn region of Languedoc where my 'pretendy' cousin Steph and her husband Ju lived and ran their gîte (holiday home) business. I got it into my head that I would love to live in the area. Mum told me not to pick somewhere so close to Steph's that I would burden them by asking for help, as Ju and Steph were great builders and designers. They had built two lovely gîtes as well as their own house and totally inspired me. I dragged Mum around on a day of property viewings, which was daft really, as I had no savings and no money other than when I did gigs. Luckily the houses we saw were crap or overpriced so that was the end of that little dalliance... Until the very last day of our hols, that is. We'd gone for tea in the beautiful monastery town of Sorèze; a gorgeous place, full of little half-timbered medieval houses with shuttered windows. In the half-timbered estate agent's window, Mum saw 'Le Chenil'; an empty shell of a building on 4 acres of land all river frontage with its own private gated bridge. The estate agent took us two kilometres up the road to a tiny but very busy little village famous for centuries as a coppersmithing centre. The house hit all the right spots – but it was an empty shell. A dirt floor, no interior walls, no doors or windows; no kitchen, no bathroom. No nothing but four good walls and a fine roof. A blank canvas. I wanted it. I could see myself there.

I dreamed about it all night then woke up on the day of departure entirely depressed, berating myself: How could I – who lived from hand to mouth all my life – imagine I could afford to buy it? It wasn't even expensive, but get real, Hazel. You can't do as all your peers do (as in buying a house here, a house there). I was off in la-la land... I remembered the talking to I'd given myself back in the *Breaking Glass* audition in 1978 at United Artists films and I started to dream a new dream. Unbelievably, with the help of my French pal Frederique back in Ireland, I put an offer in for the house and it was accepted. Then the mortgage broker that Louis Walsh had found for me when I'd moved to Ireland in 1990 managed to raise cash on my Irish cottage and suddenly I was the owner of a derelict French house!

I had a friend in Ireland who was a builder and he would do as much as he could for me at a 'friends' price. He managed to get a staircase, a front door, and a window fitted before some family trouble hit and he had to go back to Ireland and I was off on tour. I was stuck. How the hell could I, on my own, do the build ahead of me with next to no money? What on earth had I got myself into? Well, my prayers were answered when my friends began to step in and help. My friend Viva and I cleared the land. My good friend Malachy came over and with his and my wonderful pretendy cousins we laid the cement floor. Then Patrick my painter and decorator pal from Ireland came over and helped me knock through doorways and build interior walls. We camped out

Chapter Fifteen

in the dog sheds outside until we both got food poisoning, and after one cold March night of projectile vomiting and the runs with no loo and no running water except for the torrential rain, I decided it was time to find a B & B.

Steph told me about a woman called Veronique who had a B & B close to my house. I called at her house, but no one was there, so I tried the sprawling property next door. 'Hello!' I shouted, and out from a shed popped the most fantastical woman I had met in quite a while. She had colourful hippy artisty clothes with a red bandana and red hair, with a pair of red Dame Edna Everage glasses on her happy smiling face. 'Looking for Veronique.' I said. 'I'm Veronique', she said, and I just felt I had to give her a big hug. Funnily enough, I found out years later that she wasn't the Veronique I'd gone to find at all, but they gave us really cheap rooms with bathrooms and a kitchen. Oh it was luxury! And the best bit was that she and I were just destined to meet in this lifetime, as she has become one of my closest friends since then. Isn't life great?

After Patrick came over, Johnny, a friend of Cormac's arrived and he helped put up doors, kitchen units, and loads more. Martin Rushent's nephew Dan came and put in all the plumbing. Others came: Mags did some painting, Harry the woman built a dam in the river so we had a splash pool, Malachy and I dug out the back of the house by hand to put in a damp course, as the mountain backed straight on to the back wall, and water was coming down the hill into the house.

So many friends have helped over the years and it feels like it belongs to them as much as me because of their Herculean efforts. The funniest things for me was trying to buy building materials in the French language, as I only spoke rough French years ago that I had learnt back when I was in the French cabaret in Beirut. But with the help of a little home-made booklet Steph and Ju gave me for building words in French, I managed to get my supplies and the men in the builders' yards were always ready to help this mad, cement-covered, word-bumbling, middle-aged woman giving it a go. Mum and Geoff came out to join me in 2008 and they stayed at Veronique's. Mum wanted us to talk with Geoff about his memory losses and the diagnosis of dementia. That was our last time together in France. Geoff helped me with some plumbing and we strolled down the aisle of DIY shops together as that was our 'thing'. Mum cooked in my still dusty, crumbly kitchen with its second-hand fridge and chairs and crockery, courtesy of Steph and Ju. We had a blast, but Mum was not well either. Her energy was going.

In December that year I'd just got back to Ireland after touring in the UK, when I got a call from Mum in hospital in Coventry. Her test results would need a next of kin there when the consultant would tell her, so I turned around and got on the boat straight back to Coventry. At 7.30a.m. on the 19th of December the consultant arrived in with a kindly nurse. We sat around a table in the family room. He told us it was cancer in peritoneal cavity: large and inoperable. They could offer her chemotherapy which might prolong her life. Her life expectancy at that point was two to six months. Mum came out with her wonderful black sense of humour, sharpened no doubt by fear. She laughed a little and blurted out, 'Well thank God for that! At least it's not my lung disease that's gonna get me!' The nice nurse who was there to give support at this kind of devastating news looked a little aghast... No tears. Mum and I clutched each others hands and we laughed. Of course the laugh was the same as crying, and inside I screamed, but the O'Connor way was to laugh in the face of adversity.

She came home for our last Christmas Day together with Geoff in my grandparents' house, which was now Mum's home, and then she was back in hospital for another few weeks. I was very lonely in those times, but was lucky enough to be befriended by a guy who used to play with The Specials, called Paul Heskett, and by Mark Roberts and his wife Carol (Mark was in the Subterraneans). These people kept me sane. On New Year's Eve 2009, I sat alone in Mum's house watching the fireworks from the bathroom window, dreading the coming year. Mum came out of hospital with wonderful help from the community nursing staff headed by a pretty young and well-travelled matron called Angela and her beloved G.P. Dr Chohan. He also worked in homeopathy

Chapter Fifteen

and acupuncture. He and Mum had a long chat about her options and she chose not to have chemo as she didn't want her last months marred by sickness. Dr Chohan said the mind is strong and she shouldn't give up because she's been given a timescale. He said nobody can predict her lifespan with absolute certainty. This talk transformed our morose, death-and-dying mind-set to a life and 'live each day to the full' mind-set. I told Mum I would be with her every step of the way, and her journey would be my journey: no matter what. We began to live for as long as she had left and we would *live* it, not die from the sadness.

My brother came over from Canada to see her and it was so great to see him after five years' absence. With the looming possibility of Mum's death, I asked what her wishes and regrets were and if there was anything I could do... She wanted to be at home and retain her independence for as long as she could. She wished she could see her oldest granddaughter, Louise, whom she hadn't seen since Louise was a little girl and now she would be about twenty-five. I had written to Louise a few years before because I wanted to get to know her and she'd replied and slowly I think we would have got together. There was a rush on now to link Mum and Louise up. My friend Sal came up with an email address and made contact and I had her phone number within days. I phoned her. She sounded lovely and wanted to come meet her Gran as soon as possible. I met her at Coventry station a few days later. She came with her boyfriend Andrew and they were both beautiful people, full of kindness and compassion. Mum told me after their first meeting that she felt a pure rush of love when she saw her... Andrew and I went out for a walk to leave them to reclaim the years they had lost, it which was all very emotional but wonderful. From that day on they were in constant contact, emailing back and forth. They had found each other and they entirely clicked and continued their very close bond till the end.

I phoned my sax player friend Clare Hirst and asked if she was still into putting a jazzy type trio together. I'd asked her a year before, but hadn't done any more about it. With Mum's cancer it was a wake-up call not to put things you want to do on the back burner – get on and do them. I knew I'd be residing in

Coventry mostly for the duration and I knew I needed music in my life and a project that I loved to keep me sane. We had our first rehearsal in London that January with Sarah Fisher on piano. In the 80s Sarah had been a singer with the Eurythmics, and with Clare's pedigree of The Belle Stars, The Communards, and David Bowie, we were ready to give it a whirl. We gelled as a group and we had fun and the music we made sounded good. We called ourselves Bluja to cover the idea of our musical brief: 'blu' for the blues part and 'ja' for the jazz, and we covered material of mine that fit the remit. We did our first gig at the Cambria in Herne Hill, London, on the 25th of March and it went down a treat.

Meanwhile, Mum was holding her own and I thought I would irritate her being in her space too much, so I hopped off to France and worked some more on the house. I also did gigs with Clare on some of the 80s revival arena tour. It was great fun hanging out with Kim Wilde and Clare Grogan, along with meeting Kid Creole and his fabulous coconuts, and doing those huge arena concerts again. Best of all, there were caterers on the tour, so we ate gorgeous meals. The only bummer was I was only asked to do three songs and I had to start the show at 7.30p.m. Ten minutes later the gig was over for Clare and me.

During this tour I found out I was going to be added to Coventry's walk of fame, which means my name was going to join many other famous folk on a plaque on the pavement outside the BBC, along with The Specials and selected famous actors, writers, and sports people with Coventry roots. I had hoped Mum could come to the launch that May, next to the BBC, but she'd become quite ill and wasn't able to do so. But as soon as she recovered she went into town on the bus and took a photo of herself with my pavement stone.

Sometimes really scary things happened with Mum's health. One night a strange man was peering over my bed at 4a.m., saying, 'Hazel, we're the ambulance men and we're taking Joyce to hospital.' I ran down the stairs to see my tower of strength Mum half naked, flailing around, unable to breathe, and being carted off, looking so tiny so fragile. I threw my clothes on and followed the ambulance to the hospital. There were so many of these shocking episodes. Each time I was thinking, but not saying: Is this it? Is this her death? But no, she continued past her six month sentence. But now Geoff was also diagnosed with a terminal cancer. Oh God, never-ending sadness and all we can ever do is walk the road that's presented to us in this life, doing the best we can. Mum still saw many of her friends and her next door neighbours – the Tomes, as she called them – were so wonderful helping and caring, when I was and wasn't around. They were like her family as much as I was.

Autumn that year Cormac and I did a big tour of England as it was the tenth anniversary of our *Beyond Breaking Glass* show and physically the cracks were literally showing. I started to break out with eczema – first in the palms of my hands, then all over my arms, legs, and torso. The skin was cracking, bleeding, and peeling off my wounds. It was itchy at first, then painful, and then it all became swollen and infected. We were at a different place every night with no time for a visit to a doctor, just gig, gig, and more gig! I had a day off in Coventry and Mum forced me to the doctor's. I was given steroids, antibiotics, and cream. I did as I was told and it cleared up for the time being.

Later, I would discover the benefits of hemp oil drunk in copious amounts: six dessert spoonfuls a day can ward off a massive attack of eczema. My friend Viva saw the state I was in. I was terrified of Mum dying and kept it bottled up and she quoted the old saying, 'A coward dies a thousand deaths.' I gave up worrying about when her death might come and tried to be a good strong daughter and best friend to my wonderful Mum. She was a daily inspiration; always finding the humour in things, and always kind to people. By Christmas she was rushed into hospital and it looked like she was dying. Geoff came in and he looked worse, if that was possible; he had a yellow hue to his skin and Mum was worried sick about him. She asked me to contact Geoff's daughter to get help for him, as his doctor couldn't speak to me, with not being a blood relative. Mum was taken to Myton Hospice in Warwick and we wondered was this the final chapter? The idea of a hospice struck dread in me as a place to go and die...

How wrong I was. I found out that the hospice is a place to live, to rest up, to be able to go home again. And yes, it is a place to die eventually, but with compassion and dignity.

Once Mum was in her bed in the hospice and feeling safe she flourished and gathered strength. I spent my days at Myton rubbing her feet, watching our soaps. *Strictly Come Dancing* was a must on Saturday night, which we watched with the nurses and Betty, Mum's 'roommate', would join us. I'd run errands and sometimes just sit as she slept. At 8.30p.m. – kick-out time – I would go to Mark and Carol's for an hour or two. I was very lost at this time but they offered me sanctuary: they were goodness personified. A cup of tea and a chat about music and their kids Jake and Sam. I'd watch a bit of comedy on TV and stroke the cats as I was missing my dogs and my home. It was my bit of normality. It was obvious she would be in Myton over Christmas so I'd organised to bring Geoff over on Christmas Day to have our dinner together and open our gifts. On Christmas Eve I went to Mark and Carol's and wrote a little song that I wanted to sing to Mum and Geoff the next day as part of my Christmas gift, because in reality there's not much materially you can give to the dying. I marvelled that we were still here together a year on…

Another Christmas day has come
and we're still here to tell the tale,
Another year is moving on lets raise a glass lets raise a cheer,
We are here to celebrate together
we are here to make this moment last forever,
We are here we are here today

By 5a.m. I'd finished the song and crept back to Mum's house. I'd called it "Re-Joyce", as that was the nickname the nurses had given Mum as she always tried to be positive, gracious, and grateful to all the wonderful doctors, nurses, and staff. I took Geoff to Myton the next day for our Christmas Day together. It was to be our last…

I left Mum and Geoff alone for a while to have their own time and space. I helped serve the Christmas dinners to patients and their families for a while, then joined Mum and Geoff. After lunch we opened our pressies and then I sang my Christmas gift song to them. Geoff shed tears which I'd never seen before – he was always such a big strong handsome man – and Mum gleamed with love and pride: There we were trying to make our moment last forever.

The New Year came and I spent it with Carol and her kids. We lit those paper lanterns and watched them float off into the universe. I sent my prayers up into the sky: Let her passing be peaceful, let Geoff's be peaceful, and give me courage. This New Year's Eve was so much better than the year before when I'd watched the fireworks alone from Mum's bathroom window and thinking she would be gone before the year was out.

By mid-January she came home. The respite had really helped but within days we discovered that Geoff was to be put in a palliative care home. His daughter hadn't bothered to tell us. I took Mum to see him one last time in his own place and I put pictures of our happy Christmas into his suitcase so he might remember us, as he was quite confused at times, as his disease ravaged his mind and body. I went to his care home daily with hat and gloves so he could go outside for a cigarette, or I'd take him on little outings in the wheelchair, and one day I brought him to Mum's. On Valentine's Day I took her to him. Life was all about manoeuvring wheelchairs into my car now and trying to facilitate their last few meetings. They had been partners, lovers, and friends for 40 years. Oh God, it was sad and yet I knew I mustn't show it: Just carry on and do my best.

I had to go back to Ireland for a week as my house had flooded and bills needed paying. Geoff slept most of the time now. I went in to see him on the morning of my departure. He was very frail. I hugged him, told him how much I loved him, and he'd been like a dad to me, and said I would see him next week. Four days later he died. I took Mum to Geoff's funeral in her wheelchair. It was lovely to see his son Pete and family, as Pete was like a little brother to me, and Mum had always been close with Pete and his wife and kids. Geoff's daughter – whom I had spoken to once in my life when I'd phoned her to come up to Coventry to sort her dad's medical status – totally blanked us. For myself I didn't give a toss, but to be so cruel to Mum, when during Mum and Geoff's time together they had often visited and spent time with this woman. I guess she had long-standing issues which made her act like that. Pete invited us to the afters, but Mum's energy was shot, so we departed and stopped off at ASDA to do a little shopping and change our headspace. We were both very low from the loss of Geoff and because of his daughter's cruel treatment (behaviour) at the funeral. I wheeled her around in the ASDA wheelchair and when we finished I helped her out of the chair and her skirt got caught in the wheels. As she stood up, her skirt was entirely pulled down and we just had to laugh – We cried with laughter and wondered whether Geoff was looking on from some other place enjoying the scene. She still had her wicked sense of humour.

CHAPTER SIXTEEN

'Remember the laughter,
remember love, remember it all;
'cos you are my best friend – all you gotta do is call.'
"I Give You My Sunshine", 2011

The loss of Geoff knocked the stuffing out of Mum, but she soldiered on, filling her time with making handmade cards and doing a round robin email to all her friends and trying to keep in touch. Her joy was the gifts and beautiful cards and letters from Louise, her re-discovered granddaughter, and the two of them had the most beautiful friendship and love I have ever seen between a grandmother and granddaughter. Her eyesight was going and soon her greatest joys of reading and writing were not available to her anymore, so I bought her audio books and the blind society sent magnifying glasses and special light to help.

I had offered my services to Myton Hospice as a celebrity, because I was so profoundly grateful to them for bringing her back to life. I recorded a demo of the Christmas song with the aid of Mark and Kevin Lomas, then asked if Kevin's dad Roger Lomas – record producer and sound man with the Subs –if he would help to record the song and maybe I could get other musical friends to sing on it. The plan was to release it for the following Christmas and all money would go to Myton and help a hospice charity. Also the Subs and I were recording a commemorative album *Breaking Glass Now* as it was the 30th anniversary of the movie's release. Sadly, this got recorded and went a little pear-shaped, as a work partner of Roger Lomas offered me a deal on it, but wanted two more options on my next album and the one after that. There's not enough money in the whole world that could take my hard-won freedom away and there was no money offered. By now I had learned to live outside the mainstream record industry and did not want people with options over my life. I felt sad letting the Subs down as they are so talented and such good people, but Mum was adamant, and my lawyer was adamant, and I was sure it smelt like the mistake I made thirty-odd years ago: signing myself away for nothing to Albion records: No, no, no!

We did, however, do loads of gigs and festivals throughout the summer after Bluja and I had completed a spring tour. By the end of August I sang the vocal on "Re-Joyce", which Roger and the Subs had put together and started to make a list and record the artists I asked to sing on it also. First I'd asked Pauline Black of

Chapter Sixteen

Selecter who, besides being a friend of mine, had her own friendship with Mum. Dear Pauline said, 'Yes' straight away, during the one of the 80s' gigs. I knew I'd be seeing Toyah, so I asked her and she answered 'Yes' straight off the bat. Then in chirped Carol Decker who'd overheard me asking Toyah and said, 'Can I do it too - ? My ,mum lives in Coventry.' Thank you, thank you – Yes please! I asked Kid Creole that day too, who I also saw – Another blast from my past. There I was talking to Kid Creole and the Coconuts, when I feel a tap on my shoulder. I turn and say a cursory hello and turn away again only to realise that it was Midge: I hadn't recognised him. I went along to apologise later and asked after Bet, his mum. She had died the year before of cancer. He told me also Mick Karn from Japan (who we'd both been good friends with) had just been diagnosed with a brain tumour and was not long for this world. I phoned Coventry veteran crooner Vince Hill whom I'd met at the Walk of Fame do and we'd got along really well. Would he sing with us on the Myton Hospice single? 'Yes, of course,' was his answer, even though he had been fighting his own cancer battle for a couple of years. Mum was especially thrilled that Vince was helping as he was her heart throb in the 60s. Neville Staple from The Specials and Ranking Roger from The Beat said they were up for it too. The Bluja gals Clare and Sarah, and my brother Neil, sent their vocal and piece of film, as did Kid Creole. Cormac and his brother Eamonn De Barra added harp and low whistle, and Moya Brennan of Clannad added her beautiful voice by email. It was a very inspiring time to see Roger Lomas joyfully putting in all his expertise as the producer and The Subterraneans lending their talents and we filmed all the participants so we could put a video together to promote it. Pete Chambers and his wife Julie, who work tirelessly to bring Coventry's musical heritage to the fore, were documenting as we went along. The best laugh I had was watching Vince Hill's piece: When he's about to start singing, he says, 'Chocks away!' like he was in the air force and about to take flight, which as a singer I suppose he was.

We organised a launch concert in November at The Assembly in Leamington Spa, a stone's throw from my old art college where my travels had started all those years ago. Bob Brolly MBE did a wonderful job as MC. Everybody on the single did a small set each, except for our Neil who was in Canada, and Kid Creole who was away working, and Cormac, Eamonn, and Moya were all touring. The Subs, God love 'em, learned everybody's songs and was the band for the night. Other two-tone musicians joined to play in the second half which was to be the two-tone part of the evening with Pauline, Ranking Roger, and Neville doing outstanding sets. We filmed earlier in the day with Toyah and anybody who could get there early, as we were getting an exclusive piece to be shown on breakfast TV and Central on the day of release. At lunch break Toyah and us Bluja gals went for lunch where we met my PR lady Suzie Tullet (who had worked on the PR of *Breaking Glass* in 1980), and Kid Creole's assistant Harry the woman were coming up from London. We had such a fab time with Toyah telling us the inside gossip of her time on the TV show *I'm a Celebrity, Get Me out of Here*. Then we went to the venue to do this very special concert for Myton Hospice, for Mum and all the other unsung heroes fighting for their lives. Harry and my pals Malc and Richard were going to be stage-managing and we were to film the song once before the show opened. It was the biggest thrill in my life that night working alongside all the people involved: Stars and behind-the-scenes people, thank you forever.

    Mum had decided she would get to that gig, come hell or high water. A lovely carer of hers called Liz was to bring her and the night went off perfectly. There was the odd random hitch, like when poor old Carol Decker had forgotten all her clothes and makeup rushing from the studio to get to us in time, but we all shared and managed. After I'd done my bit with Bluja I went into the auditorium to sit with Mum and watch. She was glowing and humbled that night that all these people could make such an effort on behalf of the hospice. The grand finale was us all singing "Re-joyce" together. The mood was joyful and I felt this was the best, most achieved night of my life, and the little girl inside me who wanted to make my mum proud was glowing like her mum.

    We released the track on the 6th of December 2010 and I

Chapter Sixteen

appeared on breakfast TV. The same evening Central TV broadcast the extended film about the project which culminated in the pop video Andy Bevan had made for us along with the documentary on Central. My manager Maureen paid for the pressing and the accountant for the Subs. Loz gave his services as the projects accountant. I asked the managers of Coventry's two main shopping precincts if they would play it for the Christmas shoppers. The Coventry market stall holders gave some help to the project and the local HMV store manager agreed to sell it after we had a bit of a 'to do' initially. It is funny in retrospect as I walked through Coventry waxing lyrical to my musician friend Jimmy O'Neill about how weird it is that one can be far braver and more pushy when one's doing something for someone else. 'Let's go and ask the manager in HMV if he'll stock it,' I said. I asked to see the manager, whose name was Chris and didn't know me from Adam, and why should he – he was in his early twenties. I launched into my sales pitch which I was used to by now after having rung around all the big supermarkets to try to get the single on the shelves. Nobody came back to me with any help but I just kept trying: 'Hello, Chris, my name's Hazel O'Connor. I was quite a famous export of Coventry in the early 80s with a film and album called *Breaking Glass*. I realise that I was well before your time and you wouldn't have heard of me, but can you stock our single which includes lots of 80s' icons, and which is for the benefit of our local hospice?' He was a bit abrupt and said to email the request and he didn't know if it was possible. I started to raise my voice and say, 'We need help now,' and maybe one day his nan or his mum or dad may need the help of a hospice. Tears sprouted in my eyes. I was kind of angry that he didn't get it straight away, poor guy. Then the wonderful Jimmy gently broke the impasse. I apologised and Chris said 'Yes.'

Jimmy, Steve Dix, and I rehearsed the song to perform on some radio and local gigs. Just then, Mum got rushed into the Coventry Myton Hospice. This was her second hospice stay and this time the fight had nearly left her. I called Neil to come and spent my days in the hospice writing songs for our new Bluja album as Mum slept. Christmas was nearly come again. Neil arrived and we played some radio gigs together for the single and spent time with Mum. Neil and I joined Steve Dix at a local open mike gig just prior to Christmas Day. Neil met up with his ex-stepson, Richard who was now in his forties and a great blues singer-songwriter. It ran in his family. His older brother David Freeman had started The Flys with Neil all those years ago in the late 70s. After The Flys split up, David went on to greater things and a song he wrote called 'No More I Love Yous", which was a big hit for Annie Lennox. So on Christmas Day we had our dinner with Mum, and Neil sang his version of "Smile", which Mum loves, and then we found on the internet the song she was always talking about that she and her mum used to sing in harmony together when she was a kid. It's called "Smile Awhile". We laughed as we tried to learn it, as it wasn't really our type of music, but after Neil sang "Smile" we launched into "Smile Awhile", and Mum joined in and it was a special magic time. As Mum drifted off to sleep, Neil and I went to spend the evening with his ex-girlfriend from long ago – Esther – her son Richard, Neil's other stepdaughter Caroline, and her husband and two girls. We did Christmas stuff, the like of which Neil and I had not done in years: silly board games, stuffing our faces, and much love and laughter.

A week later Neil went home to Montreal and I spent a lot of time with Caroline, Esther, and Richard. Their friendship and that of Carol, Mark, Steve, and Jimmy got me through the final weeks. Mum came home from the hospice and was given twenty-four-hour care, but it was awful for her who was used to her own space, but she was weak as a kitten now. I asked her if she minded me going back to Ireland for a week, as I hadn't been home in two months and needed to pay bills, etc. I'd been home one day when her friend and neighbour Mandy rang me to say Mum had asked her to check out euthanasia websites and was very down – I rushed back. I sat with her on her sofa. Gone was her smile, her humour, her freedom, her independence. 'I don't want to smile any more, I don't want to be here anymore – I want to go,' she said very evenly. I knew time was upon us to let go. If I could have helped her go I would have, but she never asked it of

Chapter Sixteen

me, saying ages ago that she didn't want me to go to prison for helping her, so it was time to go back to the hospice for the final leg of the journey.

She went by ambulance back to the Myton Hospice. They made her comfortable and I asked Sarah – one of the amazing nurses there – to explain to me what to expect. Sarah told me that if there was anyone to see, now would be the best time, as she was expected to get worse from now on and the drugs would make her less and less coherent. Mum wanted nobody now, not even me, probably, but I called Louise and said, 'Come, please.' Louise and I arrived at the hospice and Mum got really mad at me 'Nobody,' she said, 'I told you nobody.' 'All right, Mum, Louise and I will go for tea and come back later,' I said, genuinely feeling really bad that I'd pissed her off, and poor Louise was standing there like a spare part. Louise gently said to both of us, 'It's okay, don't worry.' When we returned, Mum and Louise had a little hug, and Mum looked at me with such venom saying, 'I'm really angry with you.' I honestly thought she was joking, then I realised she was deadly serious: 'I told you I didn't want to see anyone.' 'But Mum, I needed to see Louise; I'm so sorry.' She tried to write a note to say sorry to Louise, and Sarah the nurse had to write it for her, as she was almost blind now. I told Louise the contents of the message over the phone.

Over the next few days she was rarely conscious and when I tried to hold her hand she swatted me away. She was having to walk the last mile on her own and her drugs were increased and I knew the time had arrived. I stayed in the hospice family room on the night of the 14th of February. I sat by her bedside sewing a stage dress all the next day. My manager of ten years Maureen had come to discuss the end of managing me, and making the change over, etc. Her own health was not good and she needed to retire to look after herself, not stressing out in the music industry. I'd only just left Mum's side and was having a cuppa with Maureen when the nurse came running in: 'She's leaving - Come quickly!'

Within thirty seconds her breathing had ceased. I held her hand and saw her colour drain away: She became cold so quickly.

Maureen came in for a second to say goodbye as she'd been a good pal to Mum, and then we left. Thank God Maureen was there. She came back to Mum's and sent out texts to all Mum's friends and to my friends as I wasn't capable for it. I went next door to the Tommos': Mandy and Mark and their children who had been like grandkids to Mum.

With the help of Mandy and many friends we organised the funeral. I went to put makeup on her as I didn't want some stranger doing that. Her funeral wishes were very clear and in our two-year journey to her departure we had talked all we needed to talk. Even so, my practical mum had written it down and filled in any gaps that needed filling. She wanted Cormac to play O'Carolan's "Farewell to Music" . We all sang "Amazing Grace". Neil played and sang and Louise spoke and we sang "Re-Joyce". Friends came from far and wide and after we had a great musical send-off party for her. Neil left for Canada and I went on tour a few days later. She was gone.

To be honest, I don't remember much of the next four or five months. I was touring with Clare and Sarah and the music was going very well. I was so lucky to have them around during those first months; sister musicians, sister friends, but I still couldn't really cry. I was numb when I went to France in May and built an extension on my house. And then a call came from Maureen to tell me my dear friend and record producer Martin Rushent had died. Here's the weird part: I could see him in my mind's eye and hear his voice and I cried and cried but I still couldn't bring Mum to mind. I suppose it all just hurt too much.

CHAPTER SEVENTEEN

'If I had another chance,
I would have the same romance,
With life and you – the lands we travelled through.
If I had my time again, I'd change it not, another way.
With you and life, the happiness and the knife.
That's Life'
"That's Life", (*Cover Plus*, 1981)

Sarah, Clare, and I released our second album, *I Give You My Sunshine*, in Autumn 2011 with a proper record label, and we had some marketing support and a bunch of great reviews. We toured it, people bought it, and we are continuing to be well received. As the first Christmas without Mum loomed, I did hospice gigs to keep promoting "Re-joyce", and then I left Coventry for my own home in Ireland to my dogs, my house, and my friends. I hadn't been in my own place for the last five Christmases. I spent a lot of time staring into space and didn't get out of my bedclothes, sometimes crying, sometimes staring for hours on end. One night I made a list of what I wanted to get done the next day, and then I made a list for the next day, and so on. I wanted to go back to my karate club and try to begin again. I wanted to learn a bit of ballroom dancing so I phoned an advert I saw in my local post office and discovered a great teacher and proper ballroom two hundred yards from my house. I slowly moved out of my depression by putting one foot in front of the other and giving life a go.

There is much to look forward to as I've been around as an outsider to the corporate record industry for so long now that I'm becoming a bit of a legend... I know how to survive without big cash injections of TV adverts and showbiz blah, blah reality TV shows, and I enjoy the music I make with Clare and Sarah and the fun we've had, and will continue to have as long as we have wind in our sails and breath in our lungs.

When Cormac and I get the chance to play some concerts, it is a great time we have together. How lucky we are to make the kind of music we like with the people we adore. And when I dance a waltz with my teacher Sean from down the road I think of my mum and dad's dancing days when all was hope and looking forward. When I throw a kick or a punch at karate I wonder at my body still being able to keep up. And when I sing I am happy to move people's hearts because that in turn keeps mine beating.

****

POSTSCRIPT
Languedoc, France, July 2012

I've just read through my life thus far... Some of it makes me sad, some makes me laugh, and I wonder, could it have been any different if I'd made other choices or are we all just paddling along on the river of life trying to survive the rapids? I remember a night in February this year when Ceri, the wife of record producer Martin Rushent, asked me to do a two-minute speech at the music producers guild in London. He was to receive a posthumous award. I didn't talk much about music, I talked about our friendship over the thirty years we have know each other, the laughter, the fun, and the creativity. After speaking, a guy with greying hair tapped me on the shoulder. 'Hello, Hazel, it's me; Brian Howard from Russells Solicitors.' Brian had taken me through all my court cases with Albion in the 80s. 'Were Albion as stubborn as I remember them to be? It was as if they were trying to ruin my career?' I said. 'Yes,' he replied. 'Your case has always pissed me off. They just wouldn't let you go!' After he'd said that, it was as if a huge weight was lifted off of my shoulders. I felt somehow vindicated. It wasn't me wrecking my own career, it was their intransigence bordering on destructiveness. And you know what? It's okay, all of it, 'cause I am what I am today because of all that has happened to me in the past, and long may if continue. I'm lucky; I survived, many of my peers didn't.

I'm sitting in the little kitchen that I built last year after Mum died. Building is my passion; building is a way of dealing with my grief. The fragrant honeysuckle that Mum planted waves at me through the windows. It's wrapped around the red rose bush Viva bought for the house. Vickie has been staying and I can smell the scent of the pink rose she planted last week in memory of her mum Peggy who passed away earlier this year. Today we watched my friend Kerry's twin three-year-olds, Mikayla and Khloé, romping about in the paddling pool. Earlier we all went swimming in the lake together. The twins hugged me today for the first time ever, and it melted my heart. So sweet. Claire and Sarah came over to play some concerts last weekend. The Lavender I picked from the garden sits on the old oak table that Adrian gave me fifty million years ago. I like being in France, it suits me well. My pretendy cousins Steph and Ju live three kilometres away. I gabble along in half-French, half-English to my new French pals, and old friends come to stay and mix with new.

I have no money, but I'm rich in friendship. I wish that I could phone my mum and tell her I built a porch today, that I am happy, that her seeds are flowering in my wild and crazy garden. I miss her, I miss Martin Rushent, Brain Gibson, Clive Parsons, Dodi Fayed, Rebbecca, Mich Karn, Claire Meeke, Dad, Geoff, and many more. And I wonder, will we meet again? I hope so.

I write my shopping list – I'm buying more blocks tomorrow to finish my porch. The woman in the 1940s' Parisian poster smiles at me from the wall in her blue overalls and red polka dot scarf. She flexes her muscles and I read the speech caption, which says, 'We can do it!' 'Yes we can do it!' I reply. With a lot of help from our friends.

ACKNOWLEDGEMENTS

Thank you to Gill Long my friend and neighbour who typed the first draft of this book, Evan Doyle and all the staff at Brookelodge Hotel, Macreddin, where I did most of the writing, Pat Lynch and Marianne Gunn O'Connor for trying to help me get it published and having belief in the book, Alison Walsh for doing the first edit, Peter Turner and Antonio Lafuente for helping me go through gazillions of photos and organise them, Malachy O'Loan for computer help and photos, Maureen Simpson for finding photos and Ruth Kennedy for doing the final edit with total commitment and enthusiasm, and her dog Wilson for letting me stroke his ears when the going got tough! Thank you David Shepherd my manager, and Jerry Bloom at Wymer Publishing for lovely chats and getting the book to its final destination - you the reader... and thank you to all the friends, the good, the bad and the ugly whose paths have crossed mine and become part of my story. And lastly thank you Joyce O'Connor, mum, for being such an inspiring influence in my life and doing the first proof read of this memoir.